The Cambridge Introduction to
Milton

John Milton is one of the most important and influential writers in English literary history. The goal of this book is to make Milton's works more accessible and enjoyable by providing a comprehensive overview of the author's life, times, and writings. It describes essential details from Milton's biography, explains some of the cultural and historical contexts in which he wrote, offers fresh analyses of his major pamphlets and poems – including *Lycidas*, *Areopagitica*, and *Paradise Lost* – and describes in depth traditional and recent responses to his reputation and writings. Separate sections focus on important concepts or key passages from his major works to illustrate how readers can interpret – and get excited about – Milton's writings. This detailed and engaging introduction to Milton will help readers not only to understand better the author's life and works but also to appreciate why Milton matters.

STEPHEN B. DOBRANSKI is Professor of early modern literature and textual studies at Georgia State University.

The Cambridge Introduction to
Milton

STEPHEN B. DOBRANSKI

CAMBRIDGE
UNIVERSITY PRESS

CAMBRIDGE UNIVERSITY PRESS
Cambridge, New York, Melbourne, Madrid, Cape Town,
Singapore, São Paulo, Delhi, Tokyo, Mexico City

Cambridge University Press
The Edinburgh Building, Cambridge CB2 8RU, UK

Published in the United States of America by Cambridge University Press, New York

www.cambridge.org
Information on this title: www.cambridge.org/9780521726450

© Stephen B. Dobranski 2012

First published 2012

Printed in the United Kingdom at the University Press, Cambridge

A catalog record for this publication is available from the British Library

ISBN 978-0-521-89818-8 Hardback
ISBN 978-0-521-72645-0 Paperback

for Shannon and Audrey

Contents

Chapter 4 Poetry

Chapter 5 Afterlife

Figures

Illustration acknowledgements

Wenceslaus Hollar's map of London on which I have plotted Milton's residences (Fig. 1) is reproduced by permission of The British Library Board (shelfmark maps C.6.d.8). The "Portrait of John Milton at the Age of Ten" (Fig. 2) is reproduced by permission of The Pierpont Morgan Library, New York, whose staff produced the transparency (shelfmark AZ163). The frontispiece and title page from *Poems of Mr. John Milton* (Fig. 3) are reproduced by permission of the Harry Ransom Humanities Research Center, The University of Texas at Austin (shelfmark Pforz. 722), whose staff produced the original photographs. The diagram of the cosmos in *Paradise Lost* (Fig. 4) is reproduced from Walter Clyde Curry, *Milton's Ontology, Cosmogony, and Physics* (Lexington: University of Kentucky Press, 1957). Special thanks are due to Lori Howard of Georgia State University for creating the digital images for this and the 1645 *Poems*'s illustration. "Milton and His Two Daughters" (Fig. 5) is reproduced by permission of the Folger Shakespeare Library, whose staff created the digital image.

Preface

John Milton often intimidates today's readers – and with good reason. He is one of the most important and imposing writers in British literary history. Introducing a selection of Milton's works, the editors of *The Norton Anthology of English Literature* coolly observe that "in his time" he "likely" "read just about everything of importance written in English, Latin, Greek, and Italian," adding parenthetically that "of course, he had the Bible by heart." The grand yet subtle style of Milton's individual works can seem especially daunting. Much of his poetry and prose addresses subjects that students find remote and explores or alludes to a historical period with which students are not conversant. Milton also wrote in unfamiliar genres – epic, ode, and pastoral, for example – and his works contain classical and biblical allusions that seem increasingly obscure to today's readers.

The goal of this book is to make Milton's works more accessible and enjoyable by providing an overview of the author's life, times, and writings. It describes essential details from Milton's biography, explains some of the cultural and historical contexts in which he wrote, offers suggestions for how to read his major pamphlets and poems – including *Lycidas, Areopagitica*, and *Paradise Lost* – and describes in clear language influential critical interpretations of Milton's works.

In each of these discussions, the book emphasizes Milton's social practices of writing. While Milton has traditionally been depicted as an isolated genius holding exclusive conversation with Homer, Virgil, and God, this introduction will demonstrate that, on the contrary, he was more engaged with his contemporaries than his classical forebears. Each of the first four chapters accordingly begins with one of Milton's literal conversations. These exchanges represent a crucial part of his process of writing, as Milton described it in *Areopagitica*, and also seem to have influenced the structure of his poetry and prose, both of which often depend on a dialogic form. The book's thesis is that Milton – from his interaction with early modern thinkers and writers, to the social genesis of his prose and occasional poetry, to his collaborations with members of the book trade – was not an isolated artist. This book will help readers better understand his works by illustrating how and why he wrote them and by explaining how various personal relationships affected his thinking. This inclusive approach to Milton's authorship should also help to make his individual works less daunting. As an instructor, I have found that students gain new confidence and take more risks with their own interpretations once they realize that Milton's texts are not the sudden inspiration of a solitary genius but instead consist of choices made by a human being who, like themselves, cooperated in a process of writing.

Another notable feature of this book is its practical focus on how to read Milton's prose and poetry. If the emphasis on Milton's writing practices helps to humanize him as an author, the book's close readings and detailed summaries should make the meanings of his individual pamphlets and poems more accessible. Sometimes set off from the rest of the text in shaded boxes with separate titles, these sections focus on important concepts or key passages from his major works to illustrate how readers can interpret – and get excited about – Milton's writings. Each of the separate analyses is supplemented by a discussion of the work's larger themes and structure so that readers can then apply the interpretive strategies used in these sections to an understanding of the work as a whole.

The book comprises five chapters: Life, Contexts, Prose, Poetry, and Afterlife. Following a list of Milton's significant dates, Chapter 1 presents an overview of the author's biography with an emphasis on how his experiences directly and indirectly shaped his writings. This first chapter also addresses Milton's engagement with specific historical events such as the controversy over church hierarchy during the 1640s and the creation of a new English government in 1649. Chapter 2 then provides a fuller treatment of some significant cultural and historical contexts. This chapter examines how Milton was influenced by – and how he influenced – the seventeenth century's literary, political, and theological climate.

Chapters 3 and 4, dealing respectively with Milton's prose and poetry, address his works' imagery, themes, and genres. These chapters also describe the genesis of his major works, Milton's revisions to his works after they were published, and the implications of his works' printed design and layout. In addition, both chapters incorporate separate sections of close readings to show students how to read Milton and to explain clearly what makes his writing so powerful.

Finally, Chapter 5 on Milton's critical reception should help readers understand the author's place within English literary history. This chapter describes both traditional and recent responses to Milton and illustrates how scholars have illuminated the meanings of Milton's works. Complementing this last chapter is a guide to additional readings for students who wish to pursue some of the subjects addressed in the preceding sections. Students should consult this list in combination with the works cited in the notes. The book's overarching goal is to provide a detailed and engaging introduction to John Milton so that readers not only will better understand his life and writings but also will be inspired to do further reading and research.

For their astute insights on individual chapters, I am indebted to John Rumrich, Dennis Danielson, Stephen Fallon, Laura Lunger Knoppers, and David Loewenstein. Their detailed suggestions and corrections helped me to improve matters, both large and small. For reading and commenting on the entire manuscript, I am especially grateful to my wife, Shannon. Her support during the researching and writing of this book was once again indefatigable. This book is also dedicated to our daughter Audrey, without whom it would have been written in half the time – and with half the joy. The mistakes that remain are my own.

Chronology

Moves to his own house in Aldersgate and begins teaching his first two pupils, his nephews John and Edward Phillips

Thomas Carew's *Poems* published

The assembly of the Long Parliament

Archbishop William Laud impeached

The civil wars begin

1641   *Of Reformation Touching Church-Discipline in England* published (May)

Of Prelatical Episcopacy published (June or July)

Animadversions upon the Remonstrants Defence published (July)

1642   *The Reason of Church-Government Urg'd against Prelaty* published (January or February)

An Apology against a Pamphlet Called A Modest Confutation published (April)

Thomas Browne's *Religio Medici* published

Parliament closes the theaters

Marries Mary Powell, who returns home to her family roughly one month later

1643   *The Doctrine and Discipline of Divorce* published (August)

1644   Revised second edition of *The Doctrine and Discipline of Divorce* published (February)

Of Education published (June)

The Judgement of Martin Bucer published (August)

Areopagitica published (November)

1645   *Colasterion* and *Tetrachordon* published (March)

Poems of Mr. John Milton, both English and Latin, Compos'd at Several Times registered (published January 1646)

Mary Powell Milton returns to her husband

1646   Daughter Anne born (July)

1647   Milton's father dies (March)

1648   Daughter Mary born (November)

Robert Herrick's *Hesperides* and *Noble Numbers* published

1649   King Charles I executed (January)

The Tenure of Kings and Magistrates published (February)

Appointed Secretary for Foreign Tongues (March)

Observations on the Articles of Peace published (May)

Eikonoklastes published (October)

1650   Revised second edition of *Eikonoklastes* published (after 19 June)

1651   *Pro Populo Anglicano Defensio* published (February)
       Son John born (March)

1652   Becomes completely blind
       Formally questioned regarding the licensing of *The Racovian Catechism* (also known as *Catechesis Ecclesiarum quae in Regno Poloniae*)
       Daughter Deborah born (May)
       Mary Powell Milton dies (May)
       Son John dies (June)
       Anglo-Dutch War begins (1652–54)

1653   Oliver Cromwell established as Lord Protector (December)

1654   *Pro Populo Anglicano Defensio Secunda* published (May)

1655   *Pro Se Defensio* published (August)

1656   Marries second wife, Katherine Woodcock (November)

1657   Daughter Katherine born (October)

1658   Katherine Woodcock Milton dies (February)
       Daughter Katherine dies (March)
       Oliver Cromwell dies; his son Richard is installed as successor (September)
       Revised second edition of *Pro Populo Anglicano Defensio* published (October)

1659   *A Treatise of Civil Power* published (February)
       Considerations Touching the Likeliest Means to Remove Hirelings published (August)
       Letter to a Friend Concerning the Ruptures of the Commonwealth written (October) (first published in 1698)
       Proposalls of Certaine Expedients written (November) (first published in 1938)

1660   *The Readie and Easie Way to Establish a Free Commonwealth* published (February) (the revised second edition published in April)
       The Present Means ... of a Free Commonwealth written (March) (first published 1698)
       Brief Notes upon a Late Sermon published (April)
       Charles II returns to London and monarchy restored in England (May)
       Briefly imprisoned and fined
       Royal Society founded

1663   Marries third wife, Elizabeth Minshull (February)

1665   Outbreak of the Great Plague

1666   Margaret Cavendish's *The Blazing World* published
        Great Fire (September)
1667   *Paradise Lost* published (October)
1669   *Accedence Commenc't Grammar* published (June)
1670   *The History of Britain* published (November)
1671   *Paradise Regained ... Samson Agonistes* published
1672   *Artis Logicae* published
1673   *Of True Religion, Heresie, Schism, Toleration* published (before May)
        Poems, &c. upon Several Occasions with *Of Education* published
            (before November)
1674   Revised second edition of *Paradise Lost* published
        Milton's translation of *A Declaration, or Letters Patent* published
            (July)
        Milton dies at age sixty-five (8 or 9 November) and is buried in
            St. Giles Church in Cripplegate (12 November)
        Epistolarum Familiarium published (May)
1676   *Literae Pseudo-Senatus Anglicani* (Letters of State) published
1681   *The Character of the Long Parliament* published
1682   *A Brief History of Moscovia* published
1694   *Letters of State* (English translation) published, including Milton's
            previously unpublished sonnets to Oliver Cromwell, Thomas
            Fairfax, and Cyriack Skinner
1823   Manuscript of *De Doctrina Christiana* discovered in the State Papers
            Office (published 1825)
1874   Milton's commonplace book is discovered at Netherby Hall,
            Cumberland (published 1876)

Abbreviations

CPEP   *The Complete Poetry and Essential Prose of John Milton*, ed. William Kerrigan, John Rumrich, and Stephen M. Fallon (New York: Modern Library, 2007).

CPMP   *Complete Poetry and Major Prose*, ed. Merritt Y. Hughes (New York: Macmillan, 1957).

CPW   *The Complete Prose Works of John Milton*, gen. ed. Don M. Wolfe, 8 vols. (New Haven: Yale University Press, 1953–82).

EL   *The Early Lives of Milton*, ed. Helen Darbishire (London: Constable, 1932).

LR   *The Life Records of John Milton*, ed. J. Milton French, 5 vols. (New Brunswick: Rutgers University Press, 1949–58).

OED   *The Oxford English Dictionary*, 2nd edn.

WJM   *The Works of John Milton*, ed. Frank Allen Patterson, 18 vols. (New York: Columbia University Press, 1931–38).

Citations and line numbers for Milton's poetry, unless otherwise noted, are taken from *CPEP*. Citations to classical works are to the Loeb editions published by Harvard University Press; citations to the Bible are taken from the King James Version.

Chapter 1

Life

We do not know what Milton and Galileo discussed when in 1638 they met outside Florence. Seventy-five and nearly blind, Galileo had been sentenced to prison five years earlier, but his punishment was commuted, and he was living under house arrest in his villa in Arcetri. As Milton would later recall in *Areopagitica*, "There it was that I found and visited the famous *Galileo* grown old, a pris[o]ner to the Inquisition, for thinking in Astronomy otherwise then the Franciscan and Dominican licencers thought" (*CPW* II: 538). Although Milton's interview with the famous physicist and astronomer might surprise readers who think of Galileo as a founder of modern science and instead associate Milton with his ancient poetic forebears, the meeting of these great men hints at Milton's social nature and, as we will see in Chapter 4, points to the inclusiveness of his epic's subject. Certainly the conversation made an impression on the young poet: Galileo is the only contemporary whom Milton mentions by name in *Paradise Lost* (V.262), and his stellar, lunar, and galactic discoveries underlie the epic's astronomy.[1]

The two men would also prove to have much in common. Milton would begin losing his sight within the next four years, and, perhaps more important, would later discover firsthand the consequences of espousing controversial opinions. Milton lived to witness the burning of his books, both in England and on the Continent, and, after the Restoration, he went into hiding, was briefly imprisoned, and narrowly escaped worse punishment. Whereas Galileo's published writings about the motion of the earth upset members of the Catholic Church, Milton's radical ideas about divorce alarmed Episcopal divines, and his support of regicide threatened the foundation of English monarchy. Milton's unfinished theological treatise – in which he argued that the Son was not eternal, insisted on the legality of polygamy, and defended the view that a person's soul dies with the body – he would not have dared publish during the seventeenth century for fear of being put to death.

This chapter provides an overview of Milton's life so as to illustrate the evolution of his career as a poet and polemicist and the development of his sometimes heterodox beliefs and ideas. The assumption is not that an author's biography should serve as an interpretive key for his works. However, knowing about crucial events from Milton's life and the tumultuous period in which he lived can help us interpret the effects of his circumstances on his various writings.

Too much information?

That we know the exact date and time of Milton's birth – Friday, 9 December 1608, at 6:30 a.m. – is itself revealing. This detail, recorded in Milton's own hand in his family Bible, not only suggests the author's orderly mind and acute self-concern but also indicates the wealth of information that survives about his life and writings.[2] Whereas biographies of Shakespeare occupy single books and require considerable guesswork, modern accounts of Milton's life are voluminous and copiously detailed. The best biographies remain David Masson's seven-volume *The Life of John Milton* (1859–80) and William Riley Parker's more than 1,500-page *Milton: A Biography* (1968; 1996). Admittedly, some significant gaps persist in our knowledge of the author's life – most notably, the obscure circumstances surrounding his first two marriages – but we have scores of personal, church-related, and governmental records as well as manuscript copies of several of his writings. The Trinity College Manuscript, for example, shows how Milton wrote and revised many of his early poems, and Milton's commonplace book records his reading and research from probably the late 1620s until about 1665. Also, because Milton revised and republished various of his poems and prose works, we can sometimes glimpse in print how his thinking developed. Some surviving copies of Milton's seventeenth-century publications even contain apparently authorial, hand-written corrections, reflecting either Milton's dissatisfaction with the printing process or his ideas for late revisions.

Yet, much of what we know about Milton, as with the date and time of his birth, comes from Milton himself, a not entirely reliable source. I do not mean to imply that Milton was especially dishonest, but the details that he preserved about his life often appear allusively within poetic works and thus require cautious interpretation, or he incorporated them rhetorically in polemical prose tracts to emphasize the integrity of his character and motives. When Milton in *An Apology against a Pamphlet* (1642) explains "that he who would not be frustrate of his hope to write well hereafter in laudable things, ought himselfe to bee a true Poem, that is, a composition, and patterne of the best and honourablest things" (*CPW* I: 890), he raises the possibility that he sometimes was writing his life like a poem, and imposing a self-aggrandizing pattern. Years later, for example, he would suggest in one of his tracts for the government, *Pro Populo Anglicano Defensio Secunda* (1654), that he had approached his prose works systematically. He identifies three types of liberty – ecclesiastical, civil, and personal – and then neatly divides the third category into three subjects, suggesting that he devoted a treatise to each one: "the nature of marriage …, the education of the children, and … the existence of freedom to express oneself" (*CPW* IV: 624).

Perhaps the most abiding misperception that Milton helped to foment concerns the mythos of the solitary creator. Again and again in his works, Milton depicts himself as an isolated genius, claiming to have composed *Paradise Lost* "In darkness … / And solitude" (VII.27–28) and even describing his treatises commissioned by the government as acts of individual heroism. He boasts that he defeated the French intellectual Claude Salmasius "in single combat" (*CPW* IV: 556), for example, and interrupts his defense of the English people to defend his own habits and character. Critics have accordingly tended to downplay Milton's early vision of mirthful sociability in *L'Allegro* and instead identify the author with the speaker in *Il Penseroso*, a person who finds inspiration in a solitary nighttime stroll and shuns companionship in favor of "some high lonely tow'r" or a "peaceful hermitage" (lines 86, 168).

The problem with this image of isolation is that it contradicts the other information we have about Milton's life and the provenance of his writings. If Milton's strong authorial voice encourages readers to approach his works in terms of his individual identity, knowledge of the changing cultural and historical circumstances in which he lived suggests that his experiences influenced what he wrote and how he wrote it. Throughout his life Milton was a social writer, engaging directly and indirectly with other people, whether participating in a printed debate about church hierarchy, writing on behalf of the Interregnum government, or composing occasional verses about people whom he met and admired. Even after his political hopes were crushed by the Restoration, Milton remained active, producing three of his greatest poetic works. As he explains in *The Reason of Church-Government* (1642), he valued poetry not as a mode of self-expression but as a means of civic improvement. Among its various functions, he lists first the power "to imbreed and cherish in a great people the seeds of vertu, and publick civility" (*CPW* I: 816). Certainly Milton wrote at times about himself – meditating, for example, on his poetic ability in several of his sonnets – but he understood writing first and foremost as a public act, repeatedly comparing it to preaching (*CPW* I: 816–17, II: 548). If, as he suggests in *Areopagitica*, writing is also a collaborative process, requiring that an author "consults and conferrs with his judicious friends" (*CPW* II: 532), then part of studying Milton's works should include an attempt to investigate the public context in which his works were written and printed.

Character and early years, 1608–1638

We can begin to appreciate the social nature of Milton's authorship by looking at his earliest days in London. He grew up not far from the madding crowd but in the midst of it; his family's home in Bread Street was in the heart of London, in the wealthy parish of All Hallows (see Figure 1). London was expanding rapidly during the early seventeenth century – its population more than doubled from 200,000 to 500,000 in Milton's lifetime[3] – and this bustling, metropolitan setting must have provided a wide array of experiences and opportunities for the young author. All Hallows was populated mostly by people we would today describe as middle class, prosperous merchants who for the first time were enrolling their sons at Cambridge or Oxford University. In addition to the bakeries on Bread Street and the lively produce market that filled nearby Cheapside, Milton would have grown up close to the center of the English book trade. In late 1620 when Milton began attending St. Paul's school, he would have walked daily past clusters of printers' and booksellers' shops as he made his way back and forth to the east end of the Old St. Paul's Cathedral. Among the other notable early influences on Milton were probably the parish's daily catechism for children (on alternating days for girls and boys) and the two services held on Sundays for the entire parish. Sitting in the congregation, Milton would have often heard Richard Stock, the rector of All Hallows church, vehemently denounce the popish threat and deliver unflinching reproofs of sinful behavior, even confronting the congregation's prestigious members when he thought it necessary.[4]

Milton's family home likely provided the young poet little opportunity for quiet and seclusion. He grew up in the Spread Eagle, a tenement comprising rooms on five floors of a larger house, the White Bear, in which at least seven other tenants had apartments or businesses. Milton lived with his parents, his younger brother Christopher, and his older sister Anne, along with the family's servants and his father's apprentices. Milton's father was a scrivener by trade, something akin today to a combination of public notary, copyist, and money-lender. About Milton's mother, we know comparatively little. Milton remembers her simply as "a woman of purest reputation, celebrated throughout the neighborhood for her acts of charity" (*CPW* IV: 612). A seventeenth-century portrait reveals a strong physical resemblance between mother and son, and the seventeenth-century biographer John Aubrey adds that Milton might have inherited his failing eyesight from her. Aubrey writes that Milton's "mother had very weake eies, & used spectacles p[re]sently after she was thiry yeares old" (*EL* 5).

By comparison, Milton has much to say in his writings about his father, who achieved some fame in his own right as a musician. Milton's father was invited to contribute to a collection of madrigals published as a tribute to Queen Elizabeth (1601), and he was awarded a gold medal and chain by a Polish prince for one of his longer compositions, probably written in 1611 in honor of the prince's visit to England. In *Ad Patrem*, Milton defends his own enthusiasm for writing poetry by appealing to his father's musical talent:

> Nunc tibi quid mirum, si me genuisse poetam
> Contigerit, charo si tam prope sanguine iuncti
> Cognatas artes, studiumque affine sequamur?   (lines 61–63)

> (Now, since it is my lot to have been born a poet, why does it seem strange to you that we, who are so closely united by dear blood, should pursue related arts and kindred interests?)

Although we cannot know how seriously Milton intended such defensive gestures or how strenuously his father ever objected to his son's literary ambitions, *Ad Patrem* mostly suggests that Milton senior supported his son's writing. Milton thanks his father for not forcing him to pursue a career in business or law and for helping with his education, specifically attributing to his father his knowledge of Latin, Greek, French, and Italian.[5]

One practical measure that Milton's parents took for their son was hiring private tutors before he began his formal schooling – a somewhat lavish provision more often associated with the sons of nobility than a businessman's child. Probably Milton's earliest tutor was Thomas Young, a staunch Presbyterian who instructed Milton for a period beginning around 1618. Young was one of five divines who later combined their initials into the pseudonym "Smectymnuus" and wrote a pair of treatises protesting the increased role granted bishops (also known as "prelates") within the Episcopal church hierarchy. Perhaps influenced by his friendship with Young, Milton would lend his pen to the Episcopal debate beginning in 1641 and ally himself with the Presbyterians in a series of anti-prelatical pamphlets (see Chapter 3). We might also detect Young's influence in Milton's earliest surviving portrait: it depicts a ten-year-old boy with closely cropped auburn hair, a fashion associated with those who supported Parliament and the Presbyterians (see Figure 2). According to Milton's widow, her late husband's schoolmaster, "a puritan in Essex," had "cutt his haire short."[6]

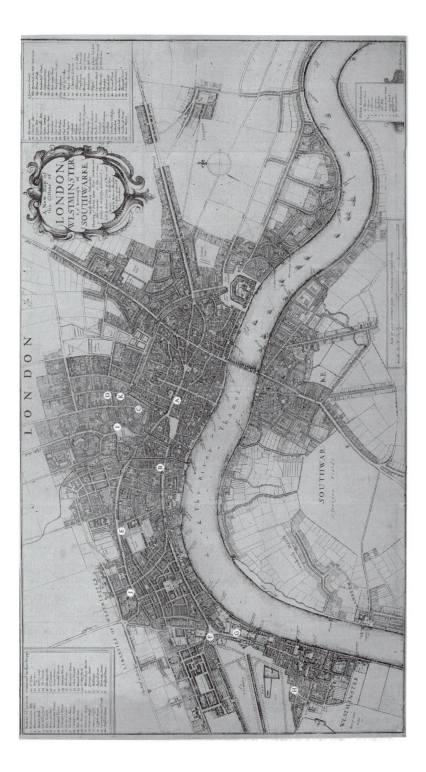

A	1608–32	On the east side of Bread Street
B	1640	St. Bride's Churchyard near Fleet Street
C	1640–45	Aldergate Street, in St. Botolph's parish
D	Fall 1645 – Fall 1647	Barbican
E	Fall 1647 – 1649	High Holborn, near Lincoln's Inn Fields
F	March–November 1649	Charing Cross, next to the Bull Head tavern
G	1649–51	Scotland Yard, Whitehall
H	December 1651–1660	Petty France in Westminster
I	May–August 1660	Bartholomew Close near West Smithfield
J	1660–61	Holborn, near Red Lion Fields
K	1661–63	Jewin Street (near Red Crosse Street)

Figure 1 Milton's London residences. Wenceslaus Hollar, *A New Map of the Citties of London, Westminster & ye Borough of Southwarke* (1675)

Figure 2 "Portrait of John Milton at the Age of Ten," by Cornelius Janssen van Ceulen

We do not know exactly how long Young continued as Milton's tutor, but their student–teacher relationship must have ended by 1620 when Young traveled to Germany as chaplain for a group of English businessmen. In that same year, Milton most likely enrolled at St. Paul's School where he would have continued to study classical languages and literature. The school's humanist curriculum focused on the linguistic arts – grammar, rhetoric, and logic – along with history, poetry, and moral philosophy. The goal was to produce boys who could write elegant Latin in verse and prose: students were expected to memorize their Latin and Greek grammars as well as their rhetoric textbooks and to gain proficiency through declamations and imitative exercises. While Milton's widow reported that her late husband had already begun writing verses at age ten (*EL* 2), it was the time he spent analyzing, translating, and paraphrasing classical literary works at St. Paul's that provided him with the indispensable technical preparation he needed to become a great poet.

We cannot pinpoint when Milton graduated from St. Paul's – the Great Fire of 1666 destroyed the school and its records, along with Milton's boyhood home and much of the surrounding parish – but two months after he turned sixteen, on 12 February 1625, he entered Christ's College, Cambridge. He would earn his BA in 1629 and three years later graduate *cum laude* with an MA. With 265 members, Christ's was the third-largest college at Cambridge at that time, while the university as a whole comprised roughly 3,050 students, fellows, and other members.[7] Comparing Milton's experience at Christ's with modern university life is difficult. The university's statutes, though not consistently enforced, contained a set of rigid restrictions, including a nightly curfew at nine or ten, depending on the season; prohibitions against playing cards or dice, except at Christmas; and the expectation that students would speak only Latin, Greek, or Hebrew, except during free time.[8]

At Christ's, Milton would have probably studied Greek and Hebrew along with ethics, logic, and rhetoric as well as some metaphysics and mathematics. Almost certainly he also studied theology and likely became familiar with Reformist works by such recent fellows as William Perkins and William Ames. In particular, Ames's *Marrow of Sacred Divinity* (London, 1642) later served as one of the base texts for Milton's own theological treatise, *De Doctrina Christiana*, and the Ramist logic that Milton studied at Christ's shaped both *De Doctrina* and his *Artis Logicae*. Also studying at Cambridge during Milton's seven years there were the dramatist Thomas Randolph, the poet John Cleveland, and the Neoplatonic philosopher Henry More – none of whom Milton mentions by name in his works but with whom he probably became familiar. Milton also must have known Joseph Mede, the most renowned tutor at Christ's, best known as the author of a millenarian scholarly book, *Clavis Apocalyptica* (1627).

Milton apparently became popular among his peers and instructors at Cambridge. He was invited to write and deliver orations at university events, and his nickname, "The Lady of Christ's" – perhaps attributable to his fair features or long hair – rather than a term of derision, seems to have been given him in good humor. Milton pokes fun at it in one of his surviving college speeches and devises a bawdy list of possible explanations: "because my hand has never hardened with gripping the shaft of a plough-handle, or because I have never lain down with someone, supine in the midday sun" ("*quia manus tenendâ stivâ non occaluit, aut quia nunquam ad meridianum Solem supinus jacui septennis bubulcus*").[9] Milton would later recollect that he received at Cambridge "more then ordinary favour and respect … above any of my equals" (*CPW* I: 884), and his nephew Edward Phillips would similarly recall that Milton "was lov'd and admir'd by the whole University, particularly by the Fellows and most Ingenious Persons of his House" (*EL* 54).

Nevertheless, Milton experienced some difficulty during his first year at Christ's and may have been temporarily suspended for misconduct. The seventeenth-century biographer Aubrey learned from Milton's brother that the poet received "some unkindnesse" from his tutor, William Chappell; Aubrey adds in the margin that Chappell, who had a reputation for both considerable learning and strict discipline, "whip't" Milton (*EL* 10). The evidence for Milton's subsequent suspension derives chiefly from one of his early poems, *Elegia prima*, in which he refers cryptically to his "rough tutor," "forbidden quarters," and "banishment" or "exile" in London (lines 11–20) – all of which could have been his playful way of describing a standard university vacation or could allude to a punishment doled out by Chappell. Whatever the nature of Chappell's "unkindnesse," we know that in 1626 by the start of the Easter term Milton was assigned a new tutor, Nathaniel Tovey. Tovey continued in that role during Milton's remaining time at Cambridge, and five years later he went on to tutor Milton's brother Christopher.

Milton's *Elegia prima* remains perhaps more notable for what it reveals about the young author's habits and character. Addressed to his closest boyhood friend, Charles Diodati, the poem offers a provocative glimpse into Milton's interests: he writes that he enjoys reading, going to the theater, taking walks, and watching girls (he brags that English girls are the most beautiful). We can also begin to appreciate the strong bond that Milton and Diodati forged. The two attended St. Paul's together before Diodati went off to Oxford and Milton enrolled at Cambridge. In addition to this poem and two surviving letters, Milton wrote *Elegia sexta* to Diodati along with Sonnet IV and a Latin pastoral elegy on his friend's early death. Hearing on one occasion that Diodati was visiting London, Milton writes that he rushed "straightway and as if by storm" to meet his boyhood friend ("*confestim & quasi* αὐτοβοεὶ *proripui me ad cellam tuam*," *WJM* XII: 20–21). And in another letter to Diodati, Milton describes his affection for his friend in Neoplatonic terms: Milton tells Diodati, "I cannot help loving people like you. For though I do not know what else God may have decreed for me, this certainly is true: He has instilled into me, if into anyone, a vehement love of the beautiful" (*CPW* I: 326).

Although not all of Milton's friendships were as close as his relationship with Diodati, Milton's enthusiasm for his former schoolfellow contributes to our sense of the author's sociable disposition. The early biographers depict Milton as a good-natured man who, even when he later suffered from painful bouts of gout, "would be chearfull … & sing" (*EL* 5). The German scholar

Christopher Arnold observed in 1651 that Milton "enters readily into talk";[10] Milton's daughter Deborah remembered her father as "Delightful Company, the Life of the Conversation, … [of] an Unaffected Chearfulness and Civility" (*EL* 229); and the diplomat Henry Wotton fondly recalled that, after the "first taste" of Milton's acquaintance, he was "left with an extreme thirst" and would have liked Milton's "conversation again … at a poor meal or two, that we might have banded together som good Authors of the ancient time."[11] Perhaps the most striking account of Milton's amicability comes from his nephew Edward Phillips. Although he compliments his uncle's "hard Study, and spare Diet," he also writes that "once in three Weeks or a Month, he would drop into the Society of some Young Sparks of his Acquaintance, the chief whereof were Mr. *Alphry*, and Mr. *Miller*, two Gentlemen of *Gray's-Inn*," with whom "he would so far make bold with his Body, as now and then to keep a Gawdy-day" (*EL* 62).[12]

Finishing at Cambridge in 1632, Milton seems to have had no firm career plans. Initially, he moved back with his parents, living first in Hammersmith, a suburban town about six or seven miles west of St. Paul's Cathedral, and from about 1635 to May 1638 in Horton, a town even further west, approximately seventeen miles outside of London. Many university graduates enjoyed a similar respite before taking their final orders and entering the priesthood, but most likely Milton chose to live with his family for the sake of convenience. Just out of college, he had no ostensible means of supporting himself while settling on a vocation.

Living outside London, away from the city's distractions – "*Londini inter urbana diverticula*," as he put it in a letter to one of his friends from St. Paul's, Alexander Gil, Jr. (*WJM* XII: 6) – also allowed Milton to continue concentrating on his studies. The entries in Milton's commonplace book suggest that he read a great deal after graduating from Cambridge. In a letter to Charles Diodati from London in 1637, Milton describes the intensity of his reading habits: "my temperament allows no delay, no rest, no anxiety – or at least thought – about scarcely anything to distract me, until I attain my object and complete some great period, as it were, of my studies" (*CPW* I: 323). We should not mistake Milton's avidity for reclusiveness, however. On the contrary, in another of Milton's letters, this one penned to an unknown friend shortly after graduating from Cambridge, Milton denies that he has chosen a secluded life and defends himself against the charge that he has not yet entered "credible employment" (*CPW* I: 319). Although he admits that "I am something suspicio[us] of my selfe, & doe take notice of a certaine belatednesse in me" (*CPW* I: 320), he insists that he is not indulging in "the endlesse delight of speculation"; instead, he is preparing himself for a career, "not taking thought of beeing late so it give advantage to be more fit" (*CPW* I: 320).

Two of Milton's early poetical works suggest that he was considering the possibility of seeking an aristocratic patron. While still living in Hammersmith, he composed *A Mask Presented at Ludlow Castle* in 1634, and a few years earlier, probably in late summer 1632, he received an invitation from the Countess Dowager of Derby to contribute *Arcades* to an entertainment which "some Noble persons of her Family" had planned in her honor (*CPMP* 77). Most likely, both of these opportunities arose through Milton's friendship with Henry Lawes, the music tutor to the children of the countess's stepson, John Egerton, Earl of Bridgewater. But we don't know why such a prestigious family would have specifically called on the unknown Milton. A recent university graduate in his early twenties, Milton had only two published poems to his credit: the printed Latin verses, now lost, that he enclosed in a letter in 1628 or 1631 to Alexander Gil, Jr. (*CPW* I: 314); and the English poem "An Epitaph on the Dramatic Poet William Shakespeare," which – perhaps through his father's assistance – appeared anonymously in 1632 in the second folio of Shakespeare's collected plays.

The Egertons were arguably taking a great chance by commissioning the relatively untested Milton to compose *A Mask*. On the evening of 29 September 1634, the family was celebrating not just Michaelmas but, more important, the Earl's recent installation as Lord President of the Council of Wales and Lord Lieutenant of the Welsh and border countries. Certainly the Earl, whose children were performing in the masque, would have wished to guide Milton and supervise the production; the more established Lawes, who wrote the music for the songs and performed in the role of Thyrsis, also likely helped his younger friend by lending a hand to the work's composition. Although some critics have been tempted by the text's rich allegory to read *A Mask* as an expression of Milton's own psychological development, it may represent the poetic work over which he exercised the least practical authority.

Collectively, many of Milton's other early writings – such as "At a Solemn Music," "At a Vacation Exercise," and his two affectionately humorous poems to the University Carrier, Thomas Hobson – also indicate that he was not a shy, bookish young man but an active, sociable, and involved author. Even his three early poems about the life of Christ – "On the Morning of Christ's Nativity," "Upon the Circumcision," and "The Passion" – suggest that his poetry was inspired by a looking outward more than a turning inward. While Milton was clearly self-concerned and often addressed his own career in his writings, most of his shorter poetry focuses on day-to-day events, friendships, and public ceremonies. These occasional verses express the temperament and experience of an outgoing author who especially valued, as Milton put it in one of his prolusions, "the society of one's fellows and the formation of friendships" ("*humana societate & contrahendis amicitiis,*" *CPW* I: 295; *WJM* XII: 262).

The year after *A Mask* was printed, Milton wrote another of his early masterpieces, the pastoral elegy *Lycidas*. It was first published with only Milton's initials in *Justa Eduardo King Naufrago* (1638), a collection of English and Latin poems commemorating Edward King, a student with Milton at Christ's College who had drowned the previous year. Here we see Milton within his university community – surely his initials were easily identifiable by the book's readers and other contributors – but we also get the sense that Milton "with his garland and singing robes about him" towered over his peers (*CPW* I: 808). The collection seems to culminate in Milton's contribution: *Lycidas* is the last poem, the only pastoral elegy, and the only poem with a title independent of King's death. As with many of Milton's other early works – "On the Death of a Fair Infant," "An Epitaph on the Marchioness of Winchester," *Epitaphium Damonis*, and the Hobson poems – Milton was again inspired to write about a deceased person's life and virtues. As he attempts to understand why King died so young and why he himself should continue to "strictly meditate the thankless muse" (line 66), the poem anticipates both the theodicy and the introspection of *Paradise Lost*. It would not be the last time that Milton would write so eloquently about death.

Italy, 1638–1639

Part of the headnote that Milton added to *Lycidas* when it was reprinted in 1645 and 1673 points to the earliest controversy in which he became embroiled. The note explains that *Lycidas* focuses on the death of a friend, "And by occasion foretells the ruin of our corrupted Clergy then in their height" (*CPMP* 120). Within the poem Milton then rebukes the self-serving Episcopal clergy as "Blind mouths!" (line 119) for failing to lead and feed their congregations. These corrupted clergy, Milton writes, have entered the church "for their bellies' sake" while their congregations "Rot inwardly, and foul contagion spread" (lines 114, 127).

Milton would go on to develop his critique of the Episcopal hierarchy in his prose works – in one tract, he condemns bishops as "*Vassals of Perdition*" (*CPW* I: 617) and, in another, he refers to the "impertinent yoke of prelaty" as an "inquisitorius and tyrannical duncery" (*CPW* I: 820). But less often noted is that Milton distinguished between the institution and its individual members.[13] He wrote, for example, two Latin poems praising specific bishops, "On the Death of the Bishop of Winchester" (*Elegia tertia*) and "On the Death of the Bishop of Ely." In the former poem, he eulogizes Lancelot Andrewes as a "most worthy bishop" and the "great ornament of your Winchester" (lines 13–14), and, in the latter, he calls Nicholas Felton the "glory of humankind" and "the prince of the saints in the island named of Ely" (lines 12–13).

Milton's ability to discriminate between people and principles must have also served him well in Italy, where he refused to recant his objections to Catholicism but nevertheless formed lasting friendships with Italian writers and thinkers. Milton, in fact, faced some danger as an outspoken Protestant traveling in a Catholic country; he writes that he "was warned by merchants that they had learned through letters of plots laid against me by the English Jesuits … because of the freedom with which I had spoken about religion" (*CPW* IV: 619), and the Dutch poet and philologist Nicholas Heinsius confirms that Milton was in danger when he returned to Rome for two months after visiting parts of southern Italy (*LR* III: 322).

Probably Milton began his Continental journey in early May 1638 and returned in late July 1639. Accompanied by a gentleman servant and bearing letters of introduction from, among others, the diplomat Henry Wotton, Milton visited Venice, Florence, Rome, Naples, and various cities along the way. While Galileo is the most prominent figure whom Milton met during his fifteen-month Continental journey, he is by no means the only significant acquaintance the young author made. As Milton would later write, "Time will never destroy my recollection – ever welcome and delightful – of you, Jacopo Gaddi, Carlo Dati, [Pietro] Frescobaldi, [Agostino] Coltellini, [Benedetto] Buonmattei, [Valerio] Chimentelli, [Antonio] Francini, and many others" (*CPW* IV: 616–17). To this list of Italian intellectuals and writers, we can add the poets Giovanni Salzilli and Antonio Malatesti; the patron Cardinal Francesco Barberini; and the statesman and author Giovanni Battista Manso, Marquis of Villa, who had been the patron of both Giambattista Marino and Torquato Tasso. In addition, traveling through Paris on his way to Italy, Milton spent time with Hugo Grotius, a Dutch jurist and philosopher who supported religious toleration for Protestants and held political opinions that Milton, too, would later reach concerning republicanism and free will.[14] And on Milton's return to England, traveling through Geneva, he stayed with John Diodati, a theologian, translator, and the uncle of Milton's boyhood friend Charles.

Interestingly, when in *Defensio Secunda* Milton recollects his Continental journey, he describes exclusively the people whom he befriended, not the places or things he saw. Trying to establish his credibility within a polemical tract, he would naturally have emphasized his distinguished foreign acquaintances so as to illustrate that "I have always led a pure and honorable life" (*CPW* IV: 611). But Milton's enthusiasm for Italian academies seems to exceed the requirements of his tract's rhetorical context. He celebrates the academies "not only for promoting humane studies but also for encouraging friendly inter-course" (*CPW* IV: 615–16), and in another pamphlet he urges his English read-ers to set up their own "learned and affable meeting of frequent Academies" (*CPW* I: 819).

Milton also suggests that the success he enjoyed sharing his works in Italy confirmed his poetic aspirations. In part because the poems he recited from memory "met with acceptance above what was lookt for" and "were receiv'd with written Encomiums, which the Italian is not forward to bestow on men of this side the *Alps*," he decided to pursue writing seriously: "I began thus farre to assent both to them and divers of my friends here at home, and not lesse to an inward prompting which now grew daily upon me, that by labour and intent study (which I take to be my portion in this life) joyn'd with the strong propensity of nature, I might perhaps leave something so written to aftertimes, as they should not willingly let it die" (*CPW* I: 809–10).

Simultaneously, Milton's Continental trip seems to have confirmed his sense of national identity: he began signing his name "John Milton, Englishman" and, while visiting the home of Camillo Cerdogni, a Protestant nobleman in Naples, Milton boldly jotted in Cerdogni's autograph book an epigraph from Horace, "I change my sky but not my mind when I cross the sea" ("*Coelum non animam muto dum trans mare curro*").[15] We should not be surprised, then, that Milton soon after his return to England resolved to write in English instead of Latin. In *The Reason of Church-Government*, he announces his intention "to be an interpreter & relater of the best and sagest things among mine own Citizens throughout this Iland in the mother dialect" (*CPW* I: 811–12). More specifically, he explains that he hoped to write a great, national poem "a work not to be rays'd from the heat of youth, or the vapours of wine … but by devout prayer to that eternall Spirit who can enrich with all utterance and knowledge" (*CPW* I: 820–21). In 1640, eight years after graduating from Cambridge, hav-ing supplemented his education and seen a bit of the world, Milton was now poised to pursue an ambitious poetic career – only to discover, as we will see, that civil war and personal problems would delay his plans.

Poet and pamphleteer, 1639–1648

In *Defensio Secunda*, Milton explains that he had originally intended to take a longer Continental journey. He had wanted to travel from Naples to Sicily and then to Greece, but "the sad tidings of civil war from England" prompted him to cut his grand tour short: "For I thought it base that I should travel abroad at my ease for the cultivation of my mind, while my fellow-citizens at home were fighting for liberty" (*CPW* IV: 618–19). The specific conflict that summoned Milton back to England was the First Bishops' War, which began when Charles I led an army north to Scotland. As I discuss more fully in Chapter 2, aristocrats and clergy in that country had challenged the king's authority by rejecting various religious innovations, in particular a new prayer book and the promotion of prelates within the Scottish church hierarchy.

Milton appears to have taken a personal interest in this conflict. He recalls in *The Reason of Church-Government Urg'd against Prelaty* that he himself had been "destin'd of a child" to become a minister both by the "intentions of my parents and friends" and "my own resolutions" (*CPW* I: 822). But, he writes in this same work, he was "Church-outed by the Prelats" (*CPW* I: 823), that is, he was forced out of the church by the same Episcopal hierarchy to which the Scottish nobility objected. He refused to accept the Church's canons and to pledge his allegiance to the king, the Book of Common Prayer, and, as he called it, the prelates' "tyranny" (*CPW* I: 823).

Returning to London in 1639, Milton sought out an alternative career and set up a school for his sister's two children, his nephews John and Edward Phillips, then aged eight and nine (see Figure 1). Milton was an apparently strict teacher – according to Aubrey, Milton's wife found it "irksome" that she "often-times heard his Nephews cry, and beaten" (*EL* 14) – but both boys eventually came to live with their uncle, and ultimately they proved to be important collaborators. We can likely detect Milton's hand in John Phillips's *Responsio* (1651 or 1652), a satirical defense of his uncle's *Pro Populo Anglicano Defensio* (1651), and Edward Phillips not only helped Milton as an amanuensis in writing his Latin thesaurus, now lost, but also translated and edited Milton's letters of state for publication in 1694. Edward recalled that he and his brother sometimes assisted their uncle even before he went blind. Edward notes, for example, that Milton would ask him to write "from his own dictation, some part, from time to time, of a Tractate which he thought fit to collect from the ablest of Divines" (*EL* 61).

Eventually, as he took on more students, Milton published a brief essay on his pedagogical approach. In *Of Education* (1645), he argues for reforming England's educational system based on an extensive, interdisciplinary reading program of mostly classical texts covering a wide variety of subjects. As he explains near the start, he believed that "The end … of learning is to repair the ruins of our first parents by regaining to know God aright, and out of that knowledge to love him, to imitate him, to be like him" (*CPW* II: 366–67). It was also during this time that Milton likely began to research and write *The History of Britain* (not published until 1671), and we know that around 1640 he composed *Epitaphium Damonis*, a Latin pastoral elegy for his friend Charles Diodati, who had died while Milton was still abroad. As with *Of Education*, Milton had *Epitaphium* printed in a single quarto sheet of eight pages, and presumably he shared copies with close friends both in England and on the Continent. Although most of the poem praises Milton's boyhood friend, who, he writes in the poem's headnote, "was outstanding for genius, learning, and every other splendid virtue" (*CPMP* 132), Milton also used this occasion to foretell his aspirations to write an English epic about King Arthur: "I, for my part, am resolved to tell … of Igraine pregnant with Arthur by fatal deception, the counterfeiting of Gorlois' features and arms by Merlin's trechery" (lines 162–63, 166–68). Milton's surviving notes in the Trinity College Manuscript include a long list of other possible biblical subjects, including a tragedy about John the Baptist, as well as plans for an epic about King Alfred. The manuscript also contains his initial ideas for a tragedy about the fall of humankind, *Adam Unparadised*, and we know from Milton's nephew that around this time Milton composed a short speech that ultimately became the first ten lines of Satan's soliloquy in *Paradise Lost*, Book IV (*EL* 72–73).

More immediately, though, Milton on his return from the Continent was devoting his time to the Episcopal controversy. He wrote five anti-prelatical tracts in what must have been a flurry of agitation and activity. In 1641, his first three pamphlets were published anonymously within the space of a few months – *Of Reformation Touching Church-Discipline in England* (May), *Of Prelatical Episcopacy* (June or July), and *Animadversions upon the Remonstrants Defence* (July). With his fourth tract, Milton openly stepped into the fray: not only does *The Reason of Church-Government* (late January 1642) announce "By Mr. *John Milton*" on the title page, but, in the middle of the pamphlet, Milton digresses from his argument about the bishops to talk briefly about himself. He describes his motives for writing, summarizes his education, and reveals his poetic goals. Reading this part of his tract, we might forget that Milton was already thirty-three: he disingenuously implies that he is much younger, presumably to make himself appear precocious. He writes that readers will "thinke I undertake a taske too difficult for my yeares" and claims to have entered the debate "out of mine own season" while "green yeers are upon my head" (*CPW* I: 749, 807, 806).[16]

In his fifth and final anti-prelatical tract, Milton continues to construct this authorial persona as he refutes an ad hominem attack on his character that had been published in January 1642.[17] In *An Apology against a Pamphlet* (April 1642), Milton again emphasizes his learning and virtue, and continues to depict himself as a reluctant prose writer. He claims that he is magnanimously sacrificing "a calme and pleasing solitarynes" to "imbark in a troubl'd sea of noises and hoars disputes" and endure the "unlearned drudgery" of his Episcopal opponents (*CPW* I: 821–22).

Today, readers are probably most interested in Milton's anti-prelatical tracts for these autobiographical digressions. However, contrary to his suggestion that such works distracted him from his literary ambitions, his prose-writing often complemented his poetry. The experience that he gained as a pamphleteer – first during the anti-prelatical debate, and later, as we will see, during the divorce controversy and as a defender of regicide – helped Milton to mature as an author and to fulfill the role he casts for himself in his prose digressions and poetic asides. Poets ought not to isolate themselves, Milton writes in *Reason*, but instead should fulfill, as he did, their social responsibilities. By presenting the truth "elegantly drest," a good writer can open "paths of honesty and good life" so that they appear "to all men both easy and pleasant" (*CPW* I: 818).

One of the primary impediments to such a pursuit, as Milton saw it, was governmental interference. Milton specifically opposed pre-publication licensing, a system of regulating the press by which Parliament required authors and printers to obtain official approval (or license) for their works before they could be entered in the Stationers' *Register* and published. In November 1644 Milton fervently argued his case in *Areopagitica*, named after a fair-minded Athenian court that met on a hill called the Areopagus; as we will see in Chapter 3, Milton was trying to encourage England's Parliament to follow this classical precedent and allow for a freer exchange of ideas.

But if Milton's *Areopagitica* ultimately became a landmark argument against censorship, he also had personal reasons for opposing licensing. His defense of divorce, published without a license two years earlier, had proven highly controversial. An anonymous critic in 1644 found fault with Milton's "intolerable abuse of Scripture," which, the writer asserted, "smels very strongly of … blaphemie against Christ himself," and on 13 August 1644 the Presbyterian divine Herbert Palmer, speaking before both houses of Parliament, cited the "impudent" author of a "wicked booke" about divorce that was "deserving to be burnt."[18] Later that same month the Stationers' Company submitted a petition to the House of Commons complaining about recent unlicensed and unregistered books, including Milton's divorce pamphlets.[19]

While Milton's detractors unfairly tried to paint him as a libertine advocating divorce at pleasure, his specific position in *The Doctrine and Discipline of Divorce* (1643) was much narrower and hardly seems scandalous by today's standards. He argues that, if the chief purpose of marriage as defined in Scripture is to cure loneliness, then divorce should be allowed for couples who prove incompatible. Milton describes marriage as an "apt and cheerfull conversation of man with woman" (*CPW* II: 235) and insists that both Hebraic and

Christian scripture allowed for divorce in cases other than adultery. Rather than heedlessly accept custom, Parliament should follow a principle of charity, he argues, since even "the soberest and best govern'd men" can make mistakes in marriage (*CPW* II: 249).

That Milton dared to tackle such a difficult subject and challenge contemporary beliefs about marriage is remarkable – and years later he publicly acknowledged that he probably should not have written about divorce in English but instead should have pursued an elite audience in Latin (*CPW* IV: 610). Between 1643 and 1645, he published a total of four tracts defending divorce; as with his anti-prelatical pamphlets, he immersed himself in the controversy. He quickly followed the publication of *The Doctrine and Discipline of Divorce* in August 1643 with a much-expanded, second edition in early 1644. He then composed *The Judgement of Martin Bucer* (August 1644), a translation of a sixteenth-century Latin work by a Protestant reformer who mostly agreed with Milton's argument; *Tetrachordon* (1645), named after a scale of four notes to signify the four primary scriptural passages that address marriage and divorce, which, Milton believed, were in harmony with each other; and *Colasterion* (1645), whose title is a Greek word that literally means a place or instrument of punishment, so named because Milton wrote it as a virulent response to one of his detractors. Milton also composed two sonnets about the poor reception of his divorce pamphlets (sonnets 11 and 12), playfully adapting a poetic form traditionally devoted to romantic love to defend his position about loveless marriages.

As with *Areopagitica* and his anti-prelatical pamphlets, Milton had a personal stake in writing about divorce. We know from his commonplace book that he had supported divorce as a young man (*CPW* I: 414), but the number and sometimes vehement tone of his divorce tracts suggest that his own marital difficulties influenced his argument. The surviving details about Milton's first marriage are provocatively sketchy. In June 1642 he traveled to Oxfordshire, apparently to visit family and/or collect the interest due on a loan of £300 that his father had made in 1627 to Richard Powell. When shortly afterwards Milton returned to London, he was not alone: he brought back with him a seventeen-year-old bride, Mary, Powell's eldest daughter. In August, Mary traveled back to Oxfordshire for what was supposed to be a one- or two-month visit. She did not return to London for almost four years. Milton's letters to his wife went unanswered, and, according to Milton's nephew, the messenger whom Milton sent to the Powells requesting that Mary come back to London was "dismissed with some sort of Contempt" (*EL* 65).

We don't know why Mary left her husband. Perhaps she felt lonely in the city and missed the company of her nine brothers and sisters; perhaps she discovered too late that she had rushed into an ill-advised marriage.[20] Certainly the outbreak of civil war complicated the couple's reconciliation: when in 1642 the king fled London and set up an alternative government in Oxford, travel between the two cities became dangerous. Did the Powells, who sided with the Royalists, also discourage their daughter from returning to her new husband because he sympathized with Parliament? Whatever the reasons for the couple's estrangement, Milton must have felt hurt and embarrassed, and he may have taken some satisfaction arguing publicly for his right to seek a divorce. Yet, for a writer who so often writes about himself in his works, he never refers to his own marriage in any of his divorce tracts, and he says almost nothing about the more general subject of desertion.

And Milton never was divorced. Mary returned to her husband in 1645, and, whatever the nature of her and Milton's difficulty, he appears not to have held a grudge: the next year, a few days after the surrender of Charles I's headquarters in Oxford, Mary's parents and at least five of her siblings moved in with the couple. Within a month of the family's arrival, on 29 July 1646, Mary gave birth to their first child, Anne, and their second child, Mary, was born two years later on 25 October 1648. Milton would never be paid the £1,000 dowry he had been promised from Mary's father, but the couple evidently lived as husband and wife until Mary's death six years later. Milton may have even been moved by his abiding affection for his first wife to write one of his most beautiful poems, Sonnet 23, "Methought I saw my late espoused saint."

The year that Mary returned to her husband in London also marked one of Milton's most significant poetic achievements: his shorter poems were published in a lavish octavo volume by Humphrey Moseley, one of England's leading literary booksellers. Divided into two parts, the English (and Italian) poems and the Latin (and Greek) verses, *Poems, of Mr. John Milton* (1645) provides a mostly conservative portrait of the artist as a young man: perhaps designed as a response to attacks on Milton's character prompted by his divorce pamphlets, the book contains fifty-four poetic works, many of which emphasize the author's erudition and prestigious connections. The Milton whom readers encounter in *Poems* has written for aristocrats such as the Countess Dowager of Derby, the Earl of Bridgewater, and the marquis Manso; he has also received, as Moseley announces in his preface, "*the highest Commendations and Applause of the learnedst* Academicks, *both domestick and forrein.*"[21]

Remarkably, the collection encourages readers to experience the individual works in terms of the unknown Milton's poetic development. At a time when more than half of the items published were still printed anonymously, *Poems* foregrounds Milton's identity.[22] Following his portrait on the frontispiece, the title page bears his full name and highlights that the collection has been "*Printed by his true Copies.*"[23] In addition to containing laudatory poems and letters from various of Milton's acquaintances, the volume most strikingly frames seventeen of the texts with biographical tags, noting Milton's age when he wrote a specific poem or the circumstances surrounding the composition.[24] The book even includes Milton's incomplete "The Passion." As the note at the end of this poem explains, "*This Subject the Author finding to be above the yeers he had, when he wrote it, and nothing satisfi'd with what was begun, left it unfinisht*" (B2r). The implication – audacious, but ultimately prescient – was that Milton in time could complete such an ambitious work and that readers should therefore take interest in even his less successful efforts. He had only begun to prove what he would achieve.

Government employee, 1649–1660

But, instead of now undertaking the great national poem he had forecasted in both *Epitaphium Damonis* and *The Reason of Church-Government*, Milton once again took up his pen with his "left hand," as he put it (*CPW* I: 808), and devoted his energies to writing prose.[25] In *The Tenure of Kings and Magistrates*, published on 13 February 1649, a few weeks after Charles I's execution, Milton provides a radical theoretical justification for regicide. Although he avoids mentioning the late monarch by name, he challenges the Stuart theory of divine right and argues instead that a contract exists between a monarch and his subjects. The people can thus depose a ruler who does not pursue the public good – even if he is not a tyrant – "meerly by the liberty and right of free born Men, to be govern'd as seems to them best" (*CPW* III: 206). In *Tenure*, Milton also criticizes Presbyterians for "fall[ing] off from thir first principles" and advocating a negotiated settlement with Charles I (*CPW* III: 238). Milton, as we have seen, had allied himself with the Presbyterian cause during the early years of the civil wars, but he was bitterly disappointed that many Presbyterians did not support the king's trial and execution. They were now, in Milton's words, siding with the "worst of men, the obdurat enemies of God and his Church" (*CPW* III: 238).

The force of Milton's argument in *Tenure* probably led to his appointment as Secretary for Foreign Tongues under the new government. One month after *Tenure*'s publication the Council of State offered Milton the position, "without any seeking of his," according to Milton's nephew, "by the means of a private Acquaintance" (*EL* 26). As secretary, Milton's duties mostly involved translating into Latin the Council's correspondence with foreign countries and translating into English diplomatic letters and documents received from other states. We learn from the Council's order books that Milton was also asked to supervise the publication of official documents and to investigate the papers of suspicious people. On 8 January 1650, for example, the Council ordered "Mr. Milton to confer with some printers or stationers about the speedy printing" of a book "containing examinations of the bloody massacre in Ireland," while on 11 June of the previous year, the government required Milton and the Sergeant-at-Arms Edward Dendy to inspect "the papers of Mr. Small" and confiscate any that dealt with public matters.[26]

The new government also began to employ Milton as a censor. He regularly licensed one of the government's newsbooks, *Mercurius Politicus*, and two other entries appear in the Stationers' *Register* "under the hand of Master Milton," one on 16 December 1649 for a French book about Charles I's trial and execution, and another on 6 October 1651 for a copy of the newsbook *The Perfect Diurnall*.[27] Readers might reasonably wonder how the author of such a passionate argument against licensing in *Areopagitica* could have agreed to work as a licenser within just five years. Clearly Milton was inconsistent: in *Areopagitica* he had bluntly criticized pre-publication licensing as "the greatest displeasure and indignity to a free and knowing spirit that can be put upon him," and he predicted "that no man of worth, none that is not a plain unthrift of his own hours is ever likely to succeed" the current group of licensers (*CPW* II: 531, 530). Part of the explanation for Milton's inconsistency probably lies in the period's tumultuous politics. When Milton wrote *Areopagitica*, he could not have imagined that in 1649 a newly formed government would want to control the book trade as a means of bolstering its public image. And, when Milton advocated less regulation of the press in 1644, he probably also was influenced by practical considerations: he may have wanted to aid opponents of Presbyterianism so that they could freely publish their counterarguments to Presbyterian calls for negotiation of a treaty with Charles I.

Yet Milton as licenser appears not to have entirely abandoned his tolerationist ideals. While we ought not to soft-pedal his inconsistency, other evidence suggests that he still respected the free exchange of ideas. When, on 27 January 1652, the Council of State seized a heretical, Socinian manifesto known as *The Racovian Catechism*, it may have been Milton who originally had approved the book's publication.[28] Among the documents examined by the House of Commons's special committee was "a Note under the Hand of Mr. *John Milton*" dated 10 August 1650, and the committee later questioned Milton as part of its investigation.[29] Although details of the proceedings have been lost, and the official resolutions that the committee presented to the House make no mention of Milton, Liewe van Aitzema, a Dutch ambassador newly arrived in England, recorded in his journal that Milton had approved ("*hadde gelicentieert*") the catechism's printing. According to van Aitzema, Milton openly admitted that he had licensed the book: "Milton, when asked, said Yes, and that he had published a tract on that subject, that men should refrain from forbidding books; that in approving of that book he had done no more than what his opinion was."[30]

If, however, we can begin to understand why Milton nevertheless modified his position on licensing while working for the government, his authorship in 1649 of *Observations on the Articles of Peace* more forcefully challenges his modern reputation as a champion of civil liberty and religious freedom. As secretary, Milton was never a voting member of the 41-member Council of State and thus had limited opportunity to shape official policy; in fact, according to one of Milton's early biographers, "hee was a Stranger to thir private Counsels" (*EL* 30). Yet, Milton did write five tracts in defense of the new government and, at least for a while, became the Council's de facto spokesman. Collectively, these tracts attempted to shore up the Council's legitimacy at home while advancing its standing within Europe.

Milton's first tract, *Observations*, specifically responded to the terms of a treaty by which James Butler, the Earl of Ormond, offered Ireland political independence and Irish Catholics religious freedom in exchange for their support of the Royalist cause. In *Observations*, Milton repeats part of his argument from *Tenure*: he insists that a sovereign is accountable to the people and is never above the law. He also argues for the separation of church and state, and, in the tract's final and longest section, he once again emphasizes what he deemed to be Presbyterian hypocrisy, condemning the Scottish Presbyterians in Ulster for both supporting Butler's Royalist articles and challenging England's new commonwealth government. The troubling part of Milton's tract concerns his unwillingness or inability to see the Irish rebellion as a war of national liberation. Exploiting anti-Catholic anxiety, he vilifies the Irish rebels as "Barbarians" and "Malignants" (*CPW* III: 308, 334), and lays the groundwork for Cromwell's vengeful military campaign later that same year.

Milton's second authorial assignment as secretary was more difficult and more important: the Council of State asked him to respond to *Eikon Basilike* (literally, "the king's image"), an immensely popular volume published in 1649 that purported to contain Charles I's prayers and private meditations while in prison awaiting trial. Beginning with an elaborate frontispiece portrait, *Eikon Basilike* depicts the king as a benevolent, misunderstood martyr, tirelessly devoted to God and the good of his people. It was arguably Charles I's most successful political act, although he likely did not write these prayers; years later, the Episcopal divine John Gauden revealed that he was the author. In the meantime, the unenviable task fell to Milton to quell the ardent sympathy for a wronged king that *Eikon Basilike* was inspiring. He approached the assignment by appealing primarily to logic, attempting, as his tract's title suggests, to break apart the king's image by methodically breaking the *Eikon Basilike* into a series of short passages that he could then refute, one by one. Milton's argument in *Eikonoklastes* not only dovetails with his theoretical justification of regicide in *Tenure* but also anticipates the emphasis on free will in *Paradise Lost*. He asserts, for example, that,

> The happiness of a Nation consists in true Religion, Piety, Justice, Prudence, Temperance, Fortitude, and the contempt of Avarice and Ambition. They in whomsoever these vertues dwell eminently, need not Kings to make them happy, but are the architects of thir own happiness; and whether to themselves or others are not less then Kings.   (*CPW* III: 542)

But whereas *Eikon Basilike*'s sentimental appeal resonated with seventeenth-century readers – the book ran through some sixty editions within a year of its initial appearance – Milton's *Eikonoklastes* had no discernible political effect and was republished only once in his lifetime in English, in an expanded, second edition in late 1650 or early 1651.[31]

Much more successful was Milton's Latin treatise justifying regicide that the government asked him to write in response to the classical scholar Claudius Salmasius. In November 1649, Charles I's son, the future Charles II, commissioned Salmasius to write *Defensio Regia*, an attempt both to vindicate the late king and to undermine the regicides' authority. The Council of State's official response, Milton's *Pro Populo Anglicano Defensio*, appeared on 24 February 1651. Freed from the constraint he may have felt in *Eikonoklastes* as he tried to challenge the recently deceased and still-beloved monarch, Milton in this third tract could write more zealously on behalf of the new government. With *Defensio*, he trounced his famous opponent. Before the end of the year, Milton's treatise had already appeared in at least ten editions,[32] and its combative approach found appreciative readers across Europe, in France, Germany, Portugal, Spain, Sweden, and the Netherlands. More than any of Milton's other publications, the *Defensio* helped to established his contemporary reputation. Visitors to London began asking to meet the talented Mr. Milton, some requesting his autograph or inviting him to their homes for dinner.

Milton went on to write two more Latin tracts, *Pro Populo Anglicano Defensio Secunda* (1654), a defense of Cromwell's Protectorate, and *Pro Se Defensio* (1655), a defense of himself as a polemical writer. But even as Milton was enjoying his greatest public success, he suffered from poor health; as he explains in the preface to his *Defensio*, he could only "work at intervals and hardly for an hour at a time" (*CPW* IV: 307). In 1652, Milton also experienced a series of personal losses. His wife Mary died three days after giving birth to their third daughter, Deborah, who was born on 2 May. Six weeks later, Milton buried his only son, John, at fifteen months.

In the same year, as the controversy over *The Racovian Catechism* was cresting, Milton lost his remaining sight. In a letter dated 28 September 1654 to the scholar and diplomat Leonard Philaras, Milton recalls how his vision had been gradually worsening over ten years; he writes that "colors proportionately darker would burst forth with violence and a sort of crash from within" (*CPW* IV: 869). Doctors warned Milton that he would go completely blind if he continued to work so hard on behalf of the new government. But in *Defensio Secunda* Milton insists that he "was not in the least deterred" and resolved to sacrifice his sight "while yet I could for the greatest possible benefit to the state" (*CPW* IV: 588). We can only imagine just how great a sacrifice this was for the 44-year-old poet, statesman, and father of three, but his letter to Philaras finds him dealing philosophically with the loss: "if, as it is written, man shall not live by bread alone, but by every word that proceedeth out of the mouth of God, why should one not likewise find comfort in believing that he cannot see by the eyes alone, but by the guidance and wisdom of God" (*CPW* IV: 870).

In the 1650s, Milton returned to writing poetry, translating Psalms 1–8 between 8 and 14 August 1653 and composing two sonnets to members of the Council of State, Oliver Cromwell and Henry Vane, in which Milton urges them to preserve religious liberty. Milton also resumed work on *The History of Britain*, which had been interrupted by his initial appointment as secretary, and around this time he seems to have accomplished most of his work on his theological treatise, *De Doctrina Christiana*, published posthumously for the first time in 1825. On 12 November 1656, Milton once again married a much younger woman, Katherine Woodcock, then aged twenty-eight. As with his first marriage, we know little of the circumstances that brought the couple together, and whatever happiness the two shared did not last long. The second Mrs. Milton died on 3 February 1658, after only two years of marriage. Also tragically, her and Milton's five-month-old daughter, also named Katherine, died the next month on 17 March.

Life after the Restoration, 1660–1674

In this same year, Milton's political fortunes began to decline precipitously. Amid the political turmoil that followed Oliver Cromwell's death on

3 September 1658, the military leader George Monck became commander-in-chief of the army, and in 1660 he forced the dissolution of the Rump Parliament, setting the stage for a new, Royalist government and the Restoration of Charles II. Milton argued courageously but ultimately in vain in *The Readie and Easie Way to Establish a Free Commonwealth* (February 1660) for the need to preserve the current government and to make the restored Rump permanent. Above all, he stressed his desire to avoid the restoration of monarchy: "people must needs be madd or strangely infatuated, that build the chief hope of thir common happiness or safetie on a single person; who, if he happen to be good, can do no more then another man, if to be bad, he hath in his hands to do more evil without check, then millions of other men. The happiness of a nation must needs be firmest and certainest in a full and free Councel of their own electing, where no single person, but reason only swayes" (*CPW* VII: 361–62). Less than two months later, Milton tried again to appeal to his fellow Englishmen and published an extensively revised version of this tract in which he more fully attempted to justify a government by an informed minority against the "madness" of the people who were taking the country back to the "bondage" of kingship (*CPW* VII: 463, 407). That Milton had difficulty getting this version printed points to the unpopularity of his ideas and the ultimate futility of his argument. Livewell Chapman, the publisher of the first edition, was already in hiding, and Milton, too, would be forced to leave his home and go into hiding shortly after the second edition's printing.

On 8 May 1660, Charles II was proclaimed king (he assumed the throne on 29 May, his thirtieth birthday), and a week later on 15 May Cromwell and the regicides John Bradshaw, Henry Ireton, and Thomas Pride were posthumously found guilty of high treason by the House of Commons. As an outspoken defender of the king's trial and execution, Milton must have feared for his life. We know that on 16 June 1660 the House of Commons denounced Milton and his first *Defensio*, along with the works of the theologian John Goodwin, who had also opposed the divine right of kings and advocated Charles's execution. But, for whatever reason, Milton's and Goodwin's names were not added to the list of non-regicides who were to be punished.[33]

Milton's *Eikonoklastes* and *Defensio* were nevertheless deemed traitorous. In September 1660, copies of both tracts were confiscated and publicly burnt, and in November Milton was fined and imprisoned.[34] Surprisingly, though, Milton was released and pardoned after only a month. According to Edward Phillips, his uncle was saved "through the intercession of some that stood his Friends both in Council and Parliament; particularly in the House of Commons, Mr. *Andrew Marvel*, a member for *Hull*, acted vigorously in his behalf, and made a considerable party for him" (*EL* 74).

All these events and experiences must have influenced Milton's late poetic works. Surely we can detect an allusion to these turbulent times in *Paradise Lost* when, for example, the epic narrator complains that he is "fall'n on evil days" and composes his epic "with dangers compassed round" (VII.25, 27). Or, in *Samson Agonistes*, when the Chorus laments how God suddenly turns his back on his chosen, Milton could have been describing what had happened to the regicides and their supporters after the Restoration:

> Oft leav'st them to the hostile sword
> Of heathen and profane, thir carcasses
> To dogs and fowls a prey, or else captíved:
> Or to th' unjust tribunals, under change of times,
> And condemnation of the ingrateful multitude.   (lines 692–96)

Apart from such direct, topical allusions, the experience of defeat seems more generally to have added emotional weight to Milton's three great long poems. Having witnessed the end of the revolution and the brutal punishment exacted on his friends and colleagues, he could now write about the Son's temptation, Samson's degradation, and Adam and Eve's expulsion from Paradise with a gravity and sympathy that had escaped him in, say, his unfinished "The Passion."

But if Milton after the Restoration was disillusioned with politics and hampered by blindness and ill health, he did not retreat from public life. In addition to *Paradise Lost*, *Paradise Regained*, and *Samson Agonistes*, he published a great deal of prose. As Samuel Johnson derisively noted, Milton in later life "did not disdain the meanest services to literature."[35] While the diversity of Milton's publications after 1660 has prompted some biographers to imagine the elderly author ridding himself of half-forgotten manuscripts as a way of tidying his desk, Milton may have had a more specific purpose in bringing out so many works: his final books encapsulate his career as both a prose writer and poet. *Of True Religion* (1673) reiterates the principles of toleration that inform *Areopagitica* and his early anti-prelatical pamphlets; *Artis Logicae* (1672), *Accedence Commenc't Grammar* (1669), and *Of Education* (1673) demonstrate his enduring interest in pedagogy; *The History of Britain* (1670) alludes to the recent civil wars within his narrative of early Britain; and *A Declaration, or Letters Patents of the Election of this Present King of Poland* (1674) implicitly supports Milton's theory from his regicide tracts that a contract exists between a king and his people. Even one of Milton's divorce tracts, *Tetrachordon*, was republished in 1674, and Milton may have felt somewhat vindicated about his writings on this subject: according to his former student Cyriack Skinner, a member of the House of Lords consulted Milton regarding the case of John

Manners, Lord Roos, who wished to remarry after having divorced his wife for infidelity (*EL* 33).

In 1673, Milton also published a second, expanded edition of his collected *Poems*. The collection contains a total of 87 shorter poems, including all those works that had appeared in 1645. Although the second edition lacks the elaborate presentation of the earlier volume, Milton still seems to have participated in its publication.[36] The 1673 *Poems* reflects the author's experience of defeat in the theme of loss that dominates the newly added works, whether it be a loss of understanding and liberty (sonnets 11 and 12), the poet's lost or diminishing sight (Sonnet 19), a lost book (*Ad Joannem Rousium*), a lost gift (*Apologus de Rustico & Hero*), lost innocence and spent passion ("The Fifth Ode of Horace"), England's lost faith ("On the New Forcers of Conscience under the Long Parliament"), or the ultimate loss, death ("On the Death of a Fair Infant," and sonnets 14, 18, and 23). Even the psalms that Milton chose to translate are primarily laments (for example, 3, 4, 6, 80, 83, 85, 88), and Sonnet 13, "To Mr. H. Lawes, on his Airs," first composed in 1645 and first published in 1648, sounds elegiac within the 1673 *Poems*, eleven years after Lawes's death.[37]

This sense of loss is enhanced by the poems that Milton must have deliberately left out of the 1673 volume. Missing from the collection are his sonnets to the regicides Cromwell, Vane, and Thomas Fairfax. In the context of post-Restoration England, Milton and the book's publisher Thomas Dring could not have safely published these verses praising Cromwell's "faith and matchless fortitude" (line 3), Vane's "sage counsel" (line 1), and Fairfax's "firm unshaken virtue" (line 5); presumably a licenser would not have allowed it. Also missing is Milton's sonnet to his former student Skinner, which emphasizes Milton's earlier political achievements by referring to his regicide pamphlets as "liberty's defense, my noble task, / Of which all Europe talks from side to side" (lines 11–12). The collection lacks as well the Latin poem *Carmina Elegiaca*, a minor, youthful work without any obvious political overtones. It begins exuberantly, "Get up, let's go, get up; now it is fit to shake off sleep / The light rises; leave the frame of your passionless bed" ("*Surge, age, surge, leves, iam convenit, excute somnos, / Lux oritus, tepidi fulcra relinque tori*," lines 1–2). In 1673, following the loss of a revolution and, more personally, the deaths of two wives and two children, Milton apparently had little interest in a poem recalling the country pleasures of *L'Allegro*. Lacking the hope of twenty-eight years earlier, he instead felt inclined to keep company with Melancholy more than Mirth.

In November of the next year, John Milton died, probably on Monday, 9 November, most likely from kidney failure associated with his gout.[38] Milton had been suffering from painful bouts of gout for several years; the pain was so bad that even walking had become difficult. "Hee dy'd in a fitt of the Gout," according to one early biographer, "but with so little pain or Emotion, that the time of his expiring was not perceiv'd by those in the room" (*EL* 33). Milton was survived by his three daughters and his third wife, Elizabeth Minshull, whom the biographer Aubrey described as "a gent. person" having "a peacefull & agreable humour" (*EL* 3). Milton's friend Dr. Nathan Paget had introduced the blind author to the 24-year-old Minshull, Paget's first cousin once removed, and she and Milton had been married three years after the Restoration, on 24 February 1663. That Milton in his will left her almost all of his estate suggests that he felt some deep affection for her, and it is pleasing to speculate whether we can find evidence of the poet's own late marriage in the portrayal of Adam and Eve's blissful relationship in *Paradise Lost*.

As Milton's health worsened in his later years, he must have also leaned on his third wife to manage the household. According to Milton's former student Skinner, the blind author would awaken at four or five in the morning, have someone read to him from the Hebrew bible, and devote some time to quiet contemplation. He was then ready to compose: "leaning Backward Obliquely in an Easy Chair, with his Leg flung over the Elbow of it," Milton asked (as he sometimes called it) "to bee milkd" – that is, he would dictate to an amanuensis the "good Stock of Verses" that he had formulated during the previous night (*EL* 291, 33). Eighteenth- and nineteenth-century portraits of Milton depict a sullen author reciting his works to his submissive daughters, but contemporary accounts suggest a much more agreeable experience and a wider group of collaborators. The biographer Jonathan Richardson reports that Milton was "perpetually Asking One Friend or Another who Visited him to Write a Quantity of Verses he had ready in his Mind, or what should Then occur" (*EL* 289), and Skinner adds that "some elderly persons were glad for the benefit of his learned Conversation, to perform that Office" (*EL* 33). Edward Phillips also recalled that he helped his blind uncle to compose *Paradise Lost*:

> I had the perusal of it from the very beginning; for some years, as I went
> from time to time, to Visit him, in a Parcel of Ten, Twenty, or Thirty
> Verses at a Time, which being Written by whatever hand came next, might
> possibly want Correction as to the Orthography and Pointing.   (*EL* 73)

Phillips' firsthand account is especially valuable; it suggests both Milton's exacting nature and his dependence on other people to compose his works. Despite blindness and ill health, he still took pains to repair even his epic's minor details.

Paradise Lost was first published in 1667 and seems to have sold fairly well. Although the printer Samuel Simmons did not publish a second edition until 1674, the first edition sold at least 1,300 copies within 17 months, certainly a respectable success, and during this same period Milton himself may have given away an additional 200 complimentary copies to friends and acquaintances. The discovery of a copy of *Paradise Lost* owned by Charles II suggests that the poet's reputation would not have prevented even the king's most loyal supporters from reading Milton's epic.[39] On the contrary, the notoriety of a defender of regicide and divorce would more likely have helped attract customers: on five of the seven title pages associated with *Paradise Lost*'s first edition, Milton's name is featured in upper-case letters and constitutes almost the only reason offered for readers to purchase the poem.

It seems fitting to conclude a biography of Milton by noting that the second edition of *Paradise Lost* appeared the year he died. In 1674, the blind author remained undaunted, continuing to fine-tune his greatest work. For the second edition, he reorganized the epic from ten to twelve books by dividing the original Book VII into VII and VIII, and the original Book X into books XI and XII. Milton also made some more subtle adjustments: he added eight lines (VIII.1–3; XII.1–5), revised one line (VIII.4), and appears to have made at least four other substantive revisions (I.504–5, V.636–41, XI.485, XI.551).[40]

Perhaps most striking to modern readers, Milton also was willing to revise *Paradise Lost* according to early readers' reactions. In a reissue of the first edition he added a defense of the verse and the arguments that summarize each book. As the printer/publisher Samuel Simmons explains,

> *Courteous Reader*, There was no Argument at first intended to the Book, but for the satisfaction of many that have desired it, I have procur'd it, and withal a reason of that which stumbled many others, why the Poem Rimes not. *S. Simmons.*   (A2r)

This note provides a provocative, final glimpse of the author John Milton, rigorous but not rigid, collaborating with members of the book trade, and striving tirelessly both to accommodate and to instruct his book's fit readers. Through this process, he created some of the greatest works in English literary history.

Chapter 2

Contexts

Sometime in the early 1670s John Dryden, probably accompanied by the poet Edmund Waller, visited Milton at his final London residence in Bunhill (see Figure 1). Dryden, twenty-three years Milton's junior and newly appointed Poet Laureate, wished to adapt *Paradise Lost* into rhyme for the stage. According to seventeenth- and eighteenth-century accounts, Milton received Dryden "civilly" (*EL* 7) and agreed graciously to the dramatist's plan:

> Well, Mr. *Dryden*, says *Milton*, it seems you have a Mind to *Tagg* my Points, and you have my Leave to *Tagg 'em*, but some of 'em are so Awkward and Old Fashion'd, that I think you had as good leave 'em as you found 'em.[1]

Here Milton might sound surprisingly self-deprecating – in particular, that he is said to have called his verse "Awkward" and "Old Fashion'd" – but his sartorial metaphor undercuts this apparent humility. Given that "Tagging" referred to the then current style of wearing ribbons ornamented at the tips with metal tags, Milton seems to suggest that Dryden's request reflects merely a whim of fashion. After all, as Dryden must have known, just a few years earlier in a prefatory note to *Paradise Lost* Milton had dismissed the "troublesome and modern bondage of Riming" as "the Invention of a barbarous Age, to set off wretched matter and lame Meter" (*CPMP* 210). We can probably also detect some mild contempt in Milton's widow's recollection that her late husband considered Dryden "no poet, but a good rimist" – although, she hastily added, "this was before Dryden had composed his best poems."[2]

Dryden's *The State of Innocence, and Fall of Man* (1677) would not, however, prove to be one of his best poems. In trying to rewrite *Paradise Lost* in heroic couplets, Dryden robbed the verse of its vitality, simplified Milton's characters, and weakened the epic's broader themes. And yet Milton evidently endorsed Dryden's plan, perhaps because he wished to attract new readers to *Paradise Lost*, or perhaps, as Milton was preparing to publish his own drama, *Samson Agonistes*, he harbored some lingering enthusiasm for the English stage.

While this anecdote about the meeting of the two poets corresponds to the other information we have about Milton's attitude toward collaboration – as we saw in the previous chapter, he worked closely with his nephews, for example – the culture of authorship in early modern England also encouraged the type of cooperative project that Dryden proposed. Writers during the early modern period freely borrowed from one another's works, not just ideas or plots (as in the case of many of Shakespeare's plays) but sometimes specific phrases or words. To appropriate another writer's works was not considered unethical but instead was deemed enterprising and admirable.[3] Thus Ben Jonson attacks plagiarism in his *Epigrams*, but praises the true poet's ability

> to convert the substance, or Riches of an other *Poet*, to his owne use. To make choise of one excellent man above the rest, and so to follow him, till he grow very *Hee*: or, so like him, as the Copie may be mistaken for the Principall. Not, as a Creature, that swallowes, what it takes in, crude, raw, or indigested; but, that feedes with an Appetite, and hath a Stomacke to concoct, divide, and turne all into nourishment.[4]

In this passage from *Discoveries*, Jonson distinguishes between careless borrowing and careful imitation: good poets were expected not to steal from other writers but to appropriate thoughtfully, selecting useful ideas and phrases and effectively assimilating them into their own works. Jonson's digestive metaphor emphasizes and naturalizes this process of adaptation; writers first had to "make choice," as he puts it, then "concoct, divide, and turne."

This chapter introduces some of Milton's choices and addresses how he concocted and turned both his predecessors' and his contemporaries' works to his own purpose. Whom did Milton read and know, and how did he respond to these other authors and their works? The chapter also shows how Milton may have been influenced, consciously or unconsciously, by his own practical circumstances as well as by larger intellectual trends and the period's tumultuous politics.

The chapter comprises five sections, each one addressing a historical or cultural context that sheds light on Milton's life and works. A discussion of Milton's relationship with both classical and early modern writers leads to a more general consideration of the seventeenth-century book trade and the effects of Milton's collaboration with printers and booksellers (in particular, Humphrey Moseley and the Simmons family). The government's changing policies for regulating the book trade then serve as a transition to a discussion of the civil war period. This section presents a concise narrative of the causes of the civil wars and Milton's direct involvement in these controversies. The final part of the chapter turns to a key intellectual context for Milton's writings: seventeenth-century religious beliefs.

Literary traditions and predecessors

Like many other English schoolboys, Milton at an early age became deeply engaged with the works of Greek and Roman writers, most notably the poetry of Homer, Ovid, and Virgil. Humanist education, as we saw in Chapter 1, was founded on the study of classical authors. After mastering Latin grammar in their first year of school, students began reading works by Terence, Ovid, and Justinus, gradually advancing to Virgil, Sallust, Horace, and Cicero. In the fifth grade (or, as it is called in Britain, the "fifth form"), students also began studying Greek literature, again beginning with grammar, then turning their attention to the New Testament and progressing from Hesiod and Theocritus to Euripides, Isocrates, and Homer. Because students learned by copying and imitating these writers' works, classical ideas and conventions seeped into early modern literature in various ways. The genres, subjects, meters – and, in some cases, even the syntax – of Greek and Roman poetry were the starting points for English writers during the Renaissance as they strived to establish their own literary traditions and forms.

But if Milton's profound classicism had its roots in early modern pedagogy, he also demonstrated an extraordinary personal affinity for classical languages and literature. Even after graduating from Cambridge, he continued to immerse himself in Latin and Greek works, both the authors' original writings and the wealth of Renaissance commentaries that grew up around them. Clearly we can hear echoes and borrowings from Ovid's elegies, for example, in the meter, style, and tone of Milton's Latin poems, written before he turned twenty-one.[5] In *An Apology against a Pamphlet* (1642), Milton recalls that as a young man he especially enjoyed reading the "smooth Elegiack Poets … both for the pleasing sound of their numerous writing, which in imitation I found most easie; and most agreeable to natures part in me, and for their matter which what it is, there be few who know not, I was so allur'd to read, that no recreation came to me better welcome" (*CPW* I: 889). Shortly after Milton's death, his daughter Deborah reported that she so often read Ovid, Homer, and Euripides to her father that she herself had memorized and could recite long passages from each. Homer was most likely Milton's favorite poet. He extols Homer in one of his university exercises as "the rising sun or morning star of cultured literature, at whose birth all learning was born also, as his twin" (*CPW* I: 272), and a seventeenth-century biographer confirms that Milton admired Homer in particular, "whose two Poems he could almost repeat without book."[6]

Part of the challenge for modern readers of Milton stems from his avid classicism. Milton frequently weaves into his works a dense network of allusions to classical figures and myths that no longer have the cultural currency that they enjoyed in seventeenth-century England. Even when aided by an editor's commentary, we thus may remain deaf to his works' subtle intonations and echoes. But, for Milton and his early modern audience, a reference to, say, Bellerophon or Zephyrus would quickly convey meaningful ideas and associations, the way a passing reference today to Dumbledore or Wolverine evokes a specific literary or cultural context that most modern readers would readily comprehend. Milton's allusions function as a poetic shorthand. In the proem to Book IX of *Paradise Lost*, for example, he need only refer to "the wrath / Of stern Achilles on his foe pursued / Thrice fugitive about Troy wall" (IX.14–16), and his seventeenth-century readers could recollect the climactic, one-on-one battle between Achilles and Hector in Book XXII of the *Iliad* as the gods aggressively intervene to ensure that Achilles defeats his Trojan foe. Or, in the Attendant Spirit's final speech in *A Mask Presented at Ludlow Castle*, Milton's contemporary readers could have immediately identified the sad "Assyrian Queen" (line 1002) sitting with the young Adonis as Venus or Aphrodite, and would likely have recalled the story of the couple's tragic love, if not specifically the version in Ovid's *Metamorphoses* (Book X, lines 500–739), perhaps Edmund Spenser's treatment of the myth in Book III of *The Faerie Queene.*

The quantity and density of such allusions can make Milton's poetry more difficult to understand than other early modern literary works (see box, pages 35–36). Often he embeds his references to his literary predecessors, so that in the midst of one, potentially obscure classical allusion, he inserts a second and a third, a series of nested Russian dolls that readers must unpack while trying to determine how they relate to one another and how they contribute to the work's larger narrative or themes. Part of the pleasure of reading Milton thus derives from the way his works gradually reveal themselves. The full significance of one of his metaphors or images must be earned through slow, deliberate analysis, and even relatively simple formulations are potentially steeped in classical analogues. Thus, when Samson rejects Dalila's "enchanted cup" and "warbling charms" in *Samson Agonistes* (line 934), the passage's meaning might initially seem straightforward, but Milton's specific diction recalls Horace's *Epistles* as the author warns against the threat that Circe poses for Odysseus (1.2.23), and it also evokes the description of Circe in the *Odyssey* as Eurylochus and his companions approach her palace and hear her sweet song (X.220–23). Or, Milton could have been thinking of the Sirens' similarly misleading "charms" from later in the *Odyssey* (XII.166–200). Or, as other critics have suggested, the reference to cup and charms could allude to the images of debauchery in Jeremiah 51:7 or Revelation 17:3–7. Readers, of course, need not choose just one possible analogue for Milton's language. All these allusions and associations simultaneously lie behind Milton's account of Samson's

Milton's allusions: the example of Eve's departure

Paradise Lost contains various passages with embedded allusions as Milton strives to capture the magnitude and majesty of the epic's events and characters. When, for example, Eve separates from Adam to garden alone, Milton introduces a string of classical comparisons that both emphasize her stature and foretell her ruin:

> ... from her husband's hand her hand
> Soft she withdrew, and like a wood-nymph light
> Oread or Dryad, or of Delia's train,
> Betook her to the groves, but Delia's self
> In gait surpassed and goddesslike deport,
> Though not as she with bow and quiver armed,
> But with such gard'ning tools as art yet rude,
> Guiltless of fire had formed, or angels brought.
> To Pales, or Pomona thus adorned,
> Likeliest she seemed, Pomona when she fled
> Vertumnus, or to Ceres in her prime,
> Yet virgin of Proserpina from Jove.   (IX.385–96)

In this passage, Milton compares Eve to eight figures from mythology, beginning with a mountain nymph (Oread) or wood nymph (Dryad), two types of beautiful maiden deities. The subsequent detail, "of Delia's train," is more specific and slightly more complimentary: Eve in her departure might resemble one of the nymphs who followed Diana, the goddess of the hunt and a symbol of chastity (sometimes, as here, called Delia because she was born on the island of Delos). The poet then elevates Eve further, suggesting that she actually exceeds Delia herself in gait and demeanor. But the comparison to Delia also highlights Eve's defenselessness: her innocence and lack of weaponry point up the threat that Satan poses.

The passage's subsequent allusions similarly ennoble Eve while hinting at her vulnerability. She resembles Pales, the Roman goddess of flocks and shepherds; Pomona, the Roman goddess of fruit trees; and Ceres, the Roman goddess of agriculture. We might detect in this group of nature goddesses a sequence of increasing domestication, which could foreshadow the hard labor that will be one of the consequences of the disobedience of Adam and Eve. Milton also incorporates details that recall Eve's flight when she first met Adam and look forward to the serpent's seduction. That she specifically resembles "Pomona when she fled / Vertumnus" could suggest that in separating from Adam, Eve is regressing to the time when she preferred her own image over his company.[7] But the same simile also anticipates Eve's fall: Pomona was tricked into marrying Vertumnus when, like Satan, he disguised himself. And while the brief account of "Ceres ... / Yet virgin of Proserpina from Jove" clearly foreshadows Eve's lost purity, it may more subtly suggest her postlapsarian role as the first mother.

The introduction of Ceres's daughter Proserpina provides yet a final, embedded allusion to Eve's fall while glancing at her ultimate redemption. Proserpina was abducted by Pluto, the god of the underworld; through her father Jupiter's intervention, she was allowed to return to the world of the living for six months each year, thus symbolizing the change of seasons and the annual return of spring. Although Milton does not directly compare Eve with Proserpina, Eve will also be tempted by the leader of Hell and, through divine intervention, will also in a sense return to the living. Simultaneously, Milton's allusion is contrastive, for Eve differs from Proserpina in two significant ways: Eve falls through her own free will and is not abducted by Satan, and the Son's intervention will allow Eve and her children to live eternally, not just for six months each year.

Perhaps most notable about Milton's allusive technique is that, as with the description of Eve's departure, he often connects his references to mythology with "or" (instead of "and"). In doing so, he creates the effect of thinking aloud and revising his comparisons extemporaneously; instead of each new allusion canceling out the previous one, they seem to complement each other. In such passages in *Paradise Lost*, Milton suggests the epic's scope through an accumulation of detail. He is not content to settle on a single allusion or comparison to describe something as grand as the first woman and mother of humankind.

antipathy for Dalila, and, at least for well-informed readers, provide valuable points of reference for understanding Samson's distrust and rage.

One strategy for coping with the erudition that undergirds Milton's prose and poetry is simply to ignore it. On first reading one of Milton's shorter poems or a section of a longer work, readers don't need to bother with the editor's commentary or attempt to comprehend all of a work's allusions – unless the references are distracting or they impede even a basic understanding of the work as a whole. Instead, an effective strategy is to try to grasp only the work's or passage's general meaning. Then, returning to the text, readers can more closely consult an editor's annotations and gradually build up their classical acumen, by taking into account more and more details, classical and otherwise. By comparison, a reader who dips often into an editor's commentary on first reading one of Milton's works can drown out the grace and power of his rhythmic lines and reduce the act of reading Milton's poetry and prose into a merely academic exercise.

Of course, studying Homer's, Ovid's, and Virgil's major works will greatly improve an appreciation of Milton; readers of his three great long poems would ideally have at least a working knowledge of the *Iliad*, the *Odyssey*, and the *Aeneid* (as well as Hebrew scriptures and the New Testament). But even without a thorough background in classical literature and Christian theology, readers can improve their understanding of Milton simply by working with a well-annotated edition. The best way then to supplement an editor's notes is to use Ovid's *Metamorphoses* or Hesiod's *Theogony* as a reference work and consult its index to research individual figures or myths. Also valuable in this regard are reliable, modern handbooks on classical culture, such as *The Meridian Handbook to Classical Mythology* by Edward Tripp, *The Dictionary of Classical Mythology* by John Edward Zimmerman, or *The Oxford Companion to Classical Literature* by M. C. Howatson.

Readers of Milton also need to understand the poetic traditions that he inherited. Although it sounds contradictory, his works are both highly derivative and strikingly original. In other words, Milton was a conscientious student of classical language and literature, but he simultaneously found new and creative ways to transform the conventions of his classical forebears to suit his own circumstances and purposes. Sometimes he has been accused of what we might call "genre busting": he did not just use classical traditions, he used them up. His exploration and reinterpretation of ancient models were so innovative and thorough that his poetic successors could do little new with the old forms, and much of what they did achieve was inevitably indebted to him. On the one hand, as Milton explains in *Of Education*, literary genres follow a set of fixed "laws" that are so important that they should be included in an ideal grammar school curriculum (*CPW* II: 404–5); on the other hand, Milton seems to have believed, following the sixteenth-century Italian poet Torquato Tasso, that writers can deviate from poetic laws according to both natural reason and scriptural revelation.

The three primary classical traditions that Milton inherited and adapted were pastoral, dramatic, and epic. While Aristotle in his *Poetics* had elevated tragedy over epic, Renaissance writers tended to agree with Philip Sidney that epic was "the best and most accomplished kind of Poetry," a belief that grew largely from medieval and humanist commentaries surrounding the *Aeneid*.[8] Most editions of Virgil's heroic poem published during the Renaissance thus began with a proem, allegedly by Virgil, announcing a progression from pastoral to epic:

> Ille ego, qui quondam gracili modulatus avena
> carmen, et egressus silvis vicina coegi
> ut quamvis avido parerent arva colono,
> gratum opus agricolis; at nunc horrentia Martis.

> (I am he who once tuned my song on a slender reed, then, leaving the woodland, constrained the neighbouring fields to serve the husbandmen, however grasping – a work welcome to farmers: but now of Mars' bristling.)[9]

Although the authenticity of these opening lines is doubtful, both Spenser and Milton seemed to have taken them to heart. Both pursued the same poetic trajectory, beginning their careers with pastoral and aspiring in their later years to write epic poems. Neither Spenser nor Milton, however, completely abandoned the pastoral or dramatic mode, even when they began writing epic poetry. Instead, as we will see, the grandeur of epic was large enough to encompass various literary styles and subjects – Aristotle, for example, refers to epic's "special scope for substantial extension"[10] – further justifying its status during the Renaissance as the ultimate type of poetry.

Pastoral

Originating with the Greek poet Theocritus in the third century BCE, the pastoral mode idealizes the simple, peaceful charms of life in the coun- try, usually from the perspective of a nostalgic, urban poet. Pastoral scenes and characters can occur in a wide variety of works but the two principal pastoral genres are *songs* – lyric poems of various types, often presented within a dialogue as a contest between two herdsmen – and *eclogues* (liter- ally, "selections"), dialogues between herdsmen typically about love, their muse, or a fellow herdsman. In both genres, the pastoral poet emphasizes art and nature while depicting idyllic landscapes and celebrating the theme of *otium*, meaning ease and peace, in contrast to *negotium*, the pains and business associated with the city and court. Broadly defined, the pastoral mode also includes georgic, a type of poetry which shares the same values but, instead of shepherding, focuses on farming and other agricultural labors, and sylvan poetry, which alternatively takes as its subject forests and wooded landscapes.

During the sixteenth century, the pastoral mode was associated with pol- itical allegory both in England and on the Continent. In France, for example, Clément Marot veiled his critique of the Catholic Church in the pastoral imagery of *Eglogue au Roy* (1538), while in England pastoral conventions allowed Spenser in *The Shepheardes Calender* (1579) to comment satirically on, among other subjects, the queen's treatment of Puritan clergy. As Philip Sidney explained in his *Apology for Poetry* (1595), "sometimes under the pretty tales of wolves and sheep, can include the whole considerations of wrong-doing"[11] – a concept that another theorist, George Puttenham, traced back to antiquity. In *The Art of English Poesy* (1589), Puttenham argues that ancient writers origin- ally wrote "under the veil of homely persons and in rude speeches to insinuate and glance at greater matters, … such as perchance had not been safe to have been disclosed in any other sort."[12]

In this context, Milton's decision to use the occasion of *Lycidas* to foretell, as he puts it, "the ruin of our corrupted Clergy then in their height" is not as surprising as it might initially seem (*CPMP* 120). In the guise of bemoaning poorly trained herdsmen who fail to feed their sheep, the poem's speaker criticizes England's self-serving clergy: "Blind mouths! that scarce themselves know how to hold / A sheep-hook, or have learned aught else the least / That to the faithful herdman's art belongs" (lines 119–21). Here Milton draws on the parable of corrupt preachers as wolves (John 10:1–28) and the image of "sheep in the midst of wolves" (Matthew 10:16) to revive and give a new, Christian meaning to the pre-Christian conventions of pastoral poetry.

Milton would return to the settings and imagery of pastoral in various works throughout his career. While the mode's popularity had begun to wane by the time he began experimenting with it in the early 1620s, pastoral conventions and subjects continued to influence some dramatic performances at the court of Charles I, and many of the funeral elegies written in 1612 on the untimely death of Charles's older brother, Prince Henry, contain pastoral elements. In addition to *Lycidas*, Milton incorporated the pastoral mode in *L'Allegro*, "On the Morning of Christ's Nativity," *Arcades*, *A Mask*, and *Epitaphium Damonis*. Pastoral also plays a crucial role in *Paradise Lost*, most obviously in the idealized settings of Heaven and Eden, but it is nevertheless surprising that a few years later Milton would refer to *Paradise Lost* as a pastoral. In the opening lines of *Paradise Regained*, he alludes to the *Aeneid's* four-line proem and casts *Paradise Lost* as a pastoral that by implication pales in comparison to the superior heroism of Jesus in *Paradise Regained*: "I who erewhile the happy garden sung, / By one man's disobedience lost, now sing / Recovered Paradise to all mankind, / By one man's firm obedience fully tried" (I.1–4).

The questions readers should ask when trying to interpret Milton's use of pastoral are, one, how exactly does he include it? and, two, how does this mode then affect the poem's or passage's broader meaning? In the Nativity Ode, for example, Milton's pastoral references seem both to dramatize the consequences of the Son's birth and to suggest the continuity between the classical and the Christian worlds:

> The shepherds on the lawn,
> Or ere the point of dawn,
>   Sat simply chatting in a rustic row;
> Full little thought they then,
> That the mighty Pan
>   Was kindly come to live with them below;
> Perhaps their loves, or else their sheep,
> Was all that did their silly thoughts so busy keep.   (lines 85–92)

In this stanza, the traditional subjects of pastoral poetry seem "silly" after the Son's arrival. The references to "simply chatting" and "Full little thought" convey the relative triviality of the shepherds' conversation, which Milton undermines again through the bathos of allying "loves" and "sheep." These lines also hint at the way Christianity builds on and reforms the classical world. Here "mighty Pan" from the shepherds' point of view represents the classical god of flocks. But, from the perspective inaugurated by the birth of the Son, it also literally means the mighty "all" or "all mighty," that is, the omniscient and omnipotent Christian God. With this one word, Milton thus connects classical and Christian beliefs, and subtly suggests that the latter encompasses the former.

Or, to take another example, Milton turned to pastoral elegy to commemorate two of his friends who tragically died young: he wrote *Lycidas* on the death of his university friend Edward King, and *Epitaphium Damonis* on the death of his closest friend Charles Diodati. Once again, readers should ask how specifically Milton includes pastoral in these works, and how this mode affects the poems' broader meanings. In both cases, Milton builds on the pastoral works of his predecessors – namely, Petrarch, Mantuan, Theocritus, and Virgil – but he also adds new potency to the pastoral mode and widens its traditional focus. In both *Epitaphium Damonis* and *Lycidas*, for example, pastoral allows Milton to meditate on his own poetic career, and in *Lycidas*, as we have already seen, the pastoral mode also enables him to attack his country's corrupt clergy.

Still, readers might reasonably wonder why in both of these poems Milton even bothered with pastoral. Instead of openly expressing his grief and honoring his friends' lives and accomplishments, he encodes his sorrow in allusive poems about herdsmen and pastures – a potentially strange choice that seems comparable to, say, a modern poet mourning the death of two college friends in poems about aliens and space travel. But we need to remember that in choosing to write a pastoral elegy Milton was embracing a specific type of poem with its own long history. A pastoral elegy depicts a shepherd or goatherd who not only nostalgically recalls the pleasures of the country, but also mourns the loss of a fellow herdsman. The genre itself seems to reassure Milton in his time of grief; whereas King and Diodati died young, antiquity's forms and conventions represent something long-lasting from which Milton can take comfort. Thus *Lycidas*'s opening phrase, "Yet once more" (line 1), alludes specifically to Hebrews 12:26–27 and the idea of an unshakeable divine presence that will remove "those things that are shaken." But the phrase more generally includes the broad, classical tradition in which Milton was participating. Milton signals at the start an awareness that he is not alone in his suffering and is instead reiterating something much older than himself – a theme that finds further expression in, for example, his use of a refrain in *Epitaphium Damonis* and the frequent use of repetition in *Lycidas*.

Drama

Drama is probably the most familiar of the three modes that Milton explored but the one with which he is today least often identified. Yet, in various ways Milton embraced drama and dramatic conventions throughout his career – a somewhat surprising position for him to have taken, given his strong religious convictions. During the seventeenth century, playgoing was often attacked as frivolous and immoral, and in 1642, with the outbreak of civil war, the government shut down the theaters altogether (they reopened in 1660 after the Restoration). The primary opponents to plays were Puritans, who claimed, among other things, that going to the theater distracted spectators from attending church, that the impersonation of evil characters corrupted actors, and that plays depicting treachery encouraged spectators to commit sin.[13]

But if Milton agreed with Puritans' zealous pursuit of devout worship and sympathized with their objections to Catholicism, he evidently did not share their disdain for playgoing. Milton's father had been one of the trustees of Blackfriars Playhouse, and Milton himself while at Cambridge played the role of the Aristotelian principle Ens or Absolute Being in a theatrical production performed at the end of the term.[14] Writing from London in *Elegia prima*, Milton tells Charles Diodati, "When I am tired, the magnificence of the arched theater diverts me, and the talkative actors invite my applause" ("*Excipit hinc fessum sinuosi pompa theatri, / Et vocat ad plausus garrula scena suos*," lines 27–28). And in his commonplace book, Milton challenges Lactantius' objections to the "moral error" of drama as "absurd beyond measure" and responds with the rhetorical question, "What in all philosophy is more important or more sacred or more exalted than a tragedy rightly produced?" (*CPW* I: 490–91).

Theatergoing accordingly plays a prominent part in Milton's companion poems *L'Allegro* and *Il Penseroso*. In *L'Allegro*, the poet imagines the happy man turning to "the well-trod stage anon, / If Jonson's learned sock be on, / Or sweetest Shakespeare, Fancy's child, / Warble his native wood-notes wild" (lines 131–34). And in *Il Penseroso*, Milton suggests that the theater can also suit the opposite disposition: his pensive speaker wishes to "Sometime let gorgeous Tragedy / In sceptered pall come sweeping by, / Presenting Thebes, or Pelops' line, / Or the tale of Troy divine. / Or what (though rare) of later age, / Ennobled hath the buskined stage" (lines 97–102).

Dramatic conventions also inform many of Milton's other writings, sometimes in surprising or subtle ways. Often he conceives his polemical prose works as dialogues, so that, for example, he structures *Animadversions upon the Remonstrants Defence* as a debate about prelacy between the Remonstrant, meant to represent Bishop Joseph Hall, and the righteous Answerer, who expresses Milton's own anti-prelatical views. A few typical exchanges read thus:

> REMON. Those verbal exceptions are but light froth, and will sink alone.
> ANSW. O rare suttlety! … [W]hen, I beseech you, will light things sink? …
>
> REMON. And if the Lords Praier be an ordinary, and stinted form, why not others?
> ANSW. Because there bee not other Lords that can stint with like authority.
>
> REMON. No one Clergie in the whole Christian world yeelds so many eminent schollers, learned preachers, grave, holy and accomplish'd Divines as this Church of *England* doth at this day.
> ANSW. Ha, ha, ha.
> REMON. And long, and ever may it thus flourish.
> ANSW. O pestilent imprecation! flourish as it does at this day in the Prelates?
> REMON. But oh forbid to have it told in *Gath!*
> ANSW. Forbid him rather, Sacred Parliament, to violate the sense of Scripture, and turne that which is spoken of the afflictions of the Church under her pagan enemies to a pargetted concealment of those prelatical crying sins …. (*CPW* I: 671, 683, 726)

Milton used a similar technique in his other anti-prelatical tracts, in *Eikonoklastes*, and in his three Latin defenses: he quotes from the tracts that he is answering so extensively that in places his prose works resemble dramatic scripts. Even *Paradise Lost* and *Paradise Regained* echo this dramatic style as their action frequently evolves into oratorical contests – between, for example, Adam and Eve, or the Son and the Tempter – and both poems comprise a series of vivid, dramatic scenes. We know from Milton's surviving notes in the Trinity College Manuscript that he originally conceived *Paradise Lost* as a drama and that probably between 1640 and 1642 he sketched plans for various other biblical and historical plays.

The prominent use of dramatic techniques in non-dramatic works was not, however, unique to Milton. This style characterizes the social nature of much seventeenth-century discourse, probably reflecting in part the polemical experience of university culture with its emphasis on argument and competitive disputations and perhaps finding its origin in the ongoing influence of English medieval drama in the popular consciousness (the so-called mystery plays). We can also probably attribute the dialogic style of so many prose tracts from this period to the closing of the theaters, which seems to have prompted an outpouring of sublimated dramas, in particular political play-pamphlets with allegorical or stock characters engaging in dialogues about contemporary events and issues.[15]

Although Milton himself never wrote for the public theater, he composed three outright dramatic works: *Arcades, A Mask Presented at Ludlow Castle,* and *Samson Agonistes*. The first, *Arcades*, is a brief pastoral piece, comprising three songs and a speech by the Genius of the Wood. As we saw in Chapter 1, Milton wrote it for the Countess Dowager of Derby, whom he praises in the refrain as a "rural queen" (line 94) and to whom Spenser dedicated *Tears of the Muses* (1591). By labeling *Arcades* "Part of an entertainment" in his 1645 *Poems* (D2r), Milton underscored the work's dramatic qualities: entertainment during the Renaissance referred not just to any pleasurable diversion but to a specific type of drama usually performed to honor royalty when they visited a noble person's house.

Milton's next dramatic work, *A Mask*, is much more ambitious than *Arcades* – and more sophisticated than most other surviving courtly entertainments from this period. Although James Thomson and David Mallet composed a masque about Alfred the Great as late as 1740, the genre flourished much earlier, during the reigns of Elizabeth I, James I, and Charles I. Typically centered around slight, allegorical plots, masques were the original multimedia genre; these costly, one-off performances combined music, song, and poetry with lavish costumes, dances, and theatrical special effects. The performers, who wore masks (thus lending the genre its name), were usually amateurs from the court, so that some of the pleasure of attending a masque must have derived from the intertextual relationship between the character in the piece and a performer's real-life reputation and personality. And if any doubt remained about who played whom, the performers at the conclusion of the piece doffed their masks, as players and audience members joined in a parting dance.

In *A Mask*, Milton develops the genre of courtly entertainment by drawing on various contemporary sources, most notably Shakespeare's *A Midsummer Night's Dream* (c. 1595) and such pastoral dramas as John Fletcher's *Faithful Shepherdess* (c. 1609) and Torquato Tasso's *Aminta* (1573). Milton also adapts Ben Jonson's concept of the antimasque, a performance presented separately from the masque proper that attempted to dramatize the opposite values from the ones on display in the masque. Whereas a masque typically celebrated order and ceremony, the antimasque focused on ludicrous action and unruly characters. The antimasque allowed these subversive forces to run amok – until they were reformed and restrained by the ruling authority, usually the king, in the masque itself.

Milton's innovation in *A Mask* is to combine the masque and antimasque so that he presents Comus and his motley crew as part of the primary narrative. The resulting dramatic work resembles a play because more is at stake than in other court performances from the period. Comus is no mere clown figure, but a truly threatening force, difficult to defeat and ultimately able to escape punishment. Order might be restored and royal power honored at the end of *A Mask*, but the ruinous impulses embodied by Comus remain unchecked.

Milton modeled his final drama, *Samson Agonistes*, not on the conventions of Renaissance courtly performances – or even contemporary English plays – but on the style and structure of classical tragedy, what he lauds in the preface as "the gravest, moralest, and most profitable of all other poems" (*CPEP* 707). *Samson* resembles a classical tragedy in, among other things, the simplicity of its diction, the ordering of the incidents, and the use of ancient dramatic conventions (such as the arrival of a messenger). As Samuel Taylor Coleridge reportedly remarked in conversation, "it was the finest imitation of the ancient Greek drama that ever had been, or ever would be written."[16]

In the play's Preface, Milton explains that he conceived *Samson* as a closet drama, that is, he wrote it in the form of a play but intended that it would be read, not performed. Here Milton also takes pains to distinguish his work from that of his immediate predecessors: his specific objection to the "error of intermixing comic stuff with tragic sadness and gravity; or introducing trivial and vulgar persons" (*CPEP* 708) seems directed at recent Restoration tragedies, although it could also refer to the practices of Shakespeare and other Elizabethan dramatists. Similarly, Milton's homeopathic concept of catharsis seems based on his classical forebears more than on Renaissance dramatic conventions: he explains that he will attempt to raise "pity and fear, or terror, to purge the mind of those and such-like passions, that is to temper and reduce them to just measure with a kind of delight, stirred up by reading or seeing those passions well imitated" (*CPEP* 707). Critics have traced this medical theory of catharsis to both the Dutch scholar Daniel Heinsius and sixteenth-century Italian criticism, in particular the work of Giovanni Battista Guarini, Antonio Minturno, and Lorenzo Giacomini.

In the Preface to *Samson*, Milton also identifies his chief classical influences, announcing that the readers best suited to evaluate his drama "are not unacquainted with Aeschylus, Sophocles, and Euripides, the three tragic poets unequaled yet by any, and the best rule to all who endeavor to write tragedy" (*CPEP* 708). That Milton lists three dramatists suggests he drew on several ancient sources in composing the poem and had no one model in mind. Yet, of the three authors whom he names, Euripides was probably the most influential. Milton has one other direct reference in his extant writings to Aeschylus (in *Pro Populo Anglicano Defensio*, *CPW* IV: 439), and he refers to Sophocles only eight times in five separate works. But Milton refers to Euripides eighteen times in twelve separate works, and two of his publications, *Areopagitica* and *Tetrachordon*, were printed with quotations from Euripides on their title pages.[17]

Euripides's influence probably finds its strongest expression in *Samson*'s final lines. That the Chorus speaks the poem's conclusion is another common convention that Milton borrowed from Greek tragedy, but the specific sentiment at the end of *Samson* comes directly from the final lines in five of Euripides's plays, *Alcestis, Andromache, Bacchae, Helen*, and *Medea*. In *Medea*, for example, the Chorus ultimately pronounces thus:

> In many forms the gods appear,
> And many things unhoped they do;
> Forecasts of men they bring not to pass;
> What is unforecast they bestow.
> So happens this marvel now.   (*CPMP* 593)

Similarly, in *Samson Agonistes*, the Chorus's final speech emphasizes that God's ways remain beyond human comprehension. But once again Milton does not merely imitate one of his classical forebears; instead, he modifies Euripides's idea by also stressing consolation and peace:

> All is best, though we oft doubt,
> What th' unsearchable dispose
> Of highest wisdom brings about,
> And ever best found in the close.
> Oft he seems to hide his face,
> But unexpectedly returns
> And to his faithful champion hath in place
> Bore witness gloriously; whence Gaza mourns
> And all that band them to resist
> His uncontrollable intent;
> His servants he with new acquist
> Of true experience from this great event
> With peace and consolation hath dismissed,
> And calm of mind, all passion spent.   (lines 1745–58)

Here Milton seems to be saying that God's ways may remain beyond our understanding, but they are always good. The Chorus's concluding speech conveys a cathartic calmness and a summarizing reaffirmation of faith. Yet these exquisite final lines also suggest a sense of loss, another element missing in Milton's classical sources. If the present tense of "returns" points to the consolation that the Chorus emphasizes, the past tense of "bore" indicates the cost at which such peace can be achieved: Samson, God's "faithful champion," has suffered and died.

Epic

As with Milton's concept of tragedy, his ideas about epic grew primarily out of classical traditions but were also shaped by the works of his contemporaries. Most simply, an epic is a narrative poem about a heroic subject written in an elevated style. Everything about an epic is big: it tells a grand story that affects the fate of a tribe or nation; it encompasses vast amounts of diverse information; and it traditionally has "big feet," that is, early epics were written in dactylic hexameters or lines with six feet of three syllables each (stress-unstressed-unstressed). Epic poets also generally follow various formal conventions – beginning in the middle of the narrative (*in medias res*), depicting supernatural events and characters, and incorporating specific stylistic features such as an invocation of a muse, long lists (known as epic catalogues), and extended comparisons (known as epic similes). Some critics, following C. S. Lewis, also distinguish chronologically between "primary" epics – historical, oral, heroic poems such as Homer's *Iliad* and *Odyssey* – and "secondary" epics – literary, stylized, and more personal poems such as Virgil's *Aeneid*.[18] That so few successful epics of either type have been written indicates the genre's demanding nature. Writers of epic must sustain a lofty tone in telling long, sweeping narratives that incorporate virtually everything then known.

During the early modern period, humanist scholars used the principles set out in Aristotle's rediscovered *Poetics* to devise rules for epic poets to follow, but mostly Homer's *Iliad* and *Odyssey* and Virgil's *Aeneid* remained the foundation for all subsequent heroic poems. The *Aeneid* was especially influential: beginning in the Middle Ages, it inspired centuries of moralizing commentary, whereas Homer's poetry was not rediscovered in the West until the fourteenth century. Some early Renaissance poets, striving to emulate Virgil's model, focused on religious warfare as a way of infusing the scope and style of classical epic with Christian values and beliefs. Long before Milton, for example, Francesco Petrarch composed an unfinished neoclassical epic, *Africa* (*c.* 1343), about Scipio's invasion of north Africa in the Second Punic War. And Torquato Tasso, whose patron Milton would later visit in Italy, followed the same narrative strategy in *Gerusalemme Liberata* (1581), a hugely successful neoclassical epic about the First Crusade.

In the late sixteenth century, poets began to undertake other types of epic writing – creation poems such as Guillaume du Bartas's *La Semaine* (1578,

1584) and epyllia (Greek for "little epics") such as Shakespeare's *Venus and Adonis* (1593) and Christopher Marlowe's *Hero and Leander* (1598). Around the same time, French epics about the Carolingian empire merged with legends about the court of King Arthur to produce the chivalric romance, a widely popular medieval and Renaissance genre. The most successful chivalric romance was Ludovico Ariosto's *Orlando Furioso* (1516, 1532), which embeds the story of "mad" Orlando's unrequited passion for the princess Angelica within a series of fantastical episodes. Ariosto's epic appeared in numerous editions throughout the early modern period, inspiring hundreds of imitations and influencing countless other poems and prose romances, including Sidney's *Arcadia* (1590) and the first epic masterpiece in English, Spenser's *The Faerie Queene* (1590, 1596). Part of Spenser's genius was to combine the entertaining apparatus of a chivalric romance with a historical allegory of Queen Elizabeth and a moral allegory of the Protestant faith.

But in the middle of the seventeenth century when Milton at last turned to epic, some Renaissance theorists worried that the genre was no longer relevant, a concern that Milton seems to have shared. In the proem to Book IX of *Paradise Lost*, Milton acknowledges that he might live in "an age too late" to write a successful epic (IX.44). The spread of gunpowder and the immediate experience of the English civil wars undermined the heroic conventions of neoclassical epics, while advances in natural philosophy, combined with the experiment-based methodology of the New Science, challenged the credibility of epic poetry's supernatural figures and stories. Perhaps because of these changing cultural circumstances, some seventeenth-century writers struggled to complete their works. William Davenant published a preface (1650), then only the first three books (1651) of his epic *Gondibert*, and Abraham Cowley also left unfinished the two heroic poems he undertook, *Civil War* (c. 1643) and *Davideis* (1656).

Milton had long entertained the possibility of writing an epic. Already at age nineteen he was using the occasion of speaking to his university class to state publicly his ambition to write about "some graver subject" ("At a Vacation Exercise," line 30). Comparing himself with Demodocus, the bard who entertains Odysseus in Book VIII of the *Odyssey*, Milton announces his specific hope of composing a poem on the "last of kings and queens and heroes old" (line 47). Ten years later in an encomiastic poem addressed to *John Baptista Manso*, the patron of the epic poet Tasso, Milton says he plans to "summon back our native kings into our songs, and Arthur, waging his wars even under the earth" (*Mansus*, lines 80–81); the next year in *Epitaphium Damonis* he more fully describes the possible subjects of his heroic poem: "I … am resolved to tell the story of the Trojan ships in the Rutupian sea and of the ancient kingdom of Inogene, the daughter of Pandrasus, and of the chiefs, Brennus and Arviragus, and of old Belinus, and of the Armorican settlers who came at last under British law. Then I shall tell of Igraine pregnant with Arthur by fatal deception, the counterfeiting of Gorlois' features and arms by Merlin's treachery" (*CPMP*, lines 162–68).

Milton, however, never wrote an epic about any of these figures or subjects. As late as 1642 in *The Reason of Church-Government Urg'd against Prelaty* he was still musing aloud about possible epic topics and wondering "what K[ing] or Knight before the conquest might be chosen in whom to lay the pattern of a Christian *Heroe*" (*CPW* I: 813–14), but ultimately he abandoned what he called "the British Mars" (*Mansus*, line 84) in favor of a biblical subject. Instead of finding a single "Christian *Heroe*," he would begin with the opening chapters from Genesis and pursue the origin of all Christian heroism. This subject naturally upped the genre's already exorbitant ante: Milton was choosing to write about no mere tribe or nation, but the whole of humanity, and he was aspiring to describe not merely the world's present knowledge but events that preceded the creation of the world.

The capaciousness of *Paradise Lost*'s subject also finds expression in Milton's densely inclusive approach to the poem's genre. Following Renaissance theories of epic as a compendium of styles and subjects – the early Renaissance scholar Julius Caesar Scaliger, for example, asserted that epic provides "the universal controlling rules for the composition of each other kind [of poetry]"[19] – Milton in *Paradise Lost* not only incorporates pastoral and dramatic elements but also assimilates almost all of these modes' subgenres. As John Dennis observed in 1704, Milton's poem, "by vertue of its extraordinary Subject, cannot so properly be said to be against the Rules, as it may be affirmed to be above them all."[20]

In pushing the boundaries of epic, Milton once again re-evaluated his literary predecessors. As with Milton's pastoral and dramatic poems, *Paradise Lost* allusively engages with the works of many of Milton's forebears – not just the epics of Homer, Virgil, Ariosto, and Spenser but also lesser-known heroic poems by Apollonius Rhodius, Boiardo, Claudian, Marino, Pulci, and Statius. Yet Milton once again critiqued and made his own the elements that he borrowed from these writers' works. He thus incorporates various epic conventions in *Paradise Lost*, but he crowds them into the first two books to depict Hell and the fallen angels, as if to suggest that these devices have little value if not put within a Christian hierarchy.

The poem's opening lines hint at the ambition of Milton's critically inclusive approach: whereas Virgil aspired to surpass Homer, Milton announces his desire to surpass both Homer and Virgil, a strikingly bold proposition given the status of these poets during the seventeenth century. We might compare

Milton's gesture to a writer today beginning a play with the announcement that she intends to surpass Shakespeare. As Milton puts it, his "advent'rous song … / … with no middle flight intends to soar / Above th' Aonian mount" (I.13–15), meaning that he wants his song to reach higher than Mount Helicon, where the classical muses dwelled. By comparison, Virgil famously begins the *Aeneid* with the promise that he will out-Homer Homer: "I sing of arms and the man," Virgil boasts. Whereas Homer had written the *Odyssey* about a man and the *Iliad* about a battle, Virgil gives notice, in other words, that he will improve on Homer's two epics by including both their subjects in his one long poem. When Milton then writes at the beginning of *Paradise Lost* that he sings of "one greater man" (I.4), he clearly refers to the Son of God, who, according to Christian belief, is "greater" than humankind. But Milton also signals at the start that he wishes to outdo his poetic forebears; he seems to proclaim that his "one greater man" will surpass both Homer's Odysseus and Virgil's Aeneas.

Later in *Paradise Lost*, Milton argues for the superiority of his epic's subject by providing a fuller literary context:

> Wars, hitherto the only argument
> Heroic deem'd, chief mast'ry to dissect
> With long and tedious havoc fabled knights
> In battles feigned; the better fortitude
> Of patience and heroic martyrdom
> Unsung.   (IX.28–33)

Here Milton suggests not only that "patience" and "martyrdom" are "better" than the "tedious havoc" depicted in other heroic poems, but also that his story supersedes his predecessors' poems because his story is true and their plots and characters were merely "feigned." Interestingly, Milton goes on to claim that he is not, in fact, "skilled nor studious" enough to write a chivalric romance or neoclassical epic (IX.42); instead, he says, he will pursue a "higher argument / … / … unless an age too late, or cold / Climate, or years damp my intended wing / Depressed" (IX.42–46). These lines express an important paradox that surfaces when Milton tries to talk about himself in *Paradise Lost*: he repeatedly expresses a combination of audacity and humility. Here, in the proem to Book IX, he simultaneously proclaims his vaunting ambition and acknowledges the possibility that he might not succeed for reasons beyond his control.[21] But even with this gesture Milton is reimagining the epic and personalizing the convention of invoking a muse; he does not just beseech the muse's aid but incorporates his own process of writing as one of the poem's subjects.

Literary contemporaries

Perhaps because of the audacity of *Paradise Lost*'s scope and its engagement with so many ancient works and traditions, Milton can seem a relatively isolated figure in English literary history. We imagine him composing his poetry alone, silently invoking his muse and holding exclusive conversation with his classical literary predecessors.

But if Milton never belonged to a contemporary literary group – such as Samuel Hartlib's circle of thinkers and writers, or the society of poets and dramatists who in the early 1600s gathered at the Mermaid Tavern – he nevertheless interacted, directly and indirectly, with many of his now-famous peers. He not only was acquainted with Dryden, as we saw at the beginning of this chapter, but also befriended Andrew Marvell, collaborated with and wrote a sonnet to the musician Henry Lawes, and worked closely with the pioneering journalist and propagandist Marchamont Nedham. Milton also celebrates Shakespeare in one of his poems, refers favorably to Chaucer and Ben Jonson in various works, compliments "our sage and serious Poet *Spencer*" in *Areopagitica* (*CPW* II: 516), and evidently knew Sidney's vast *Arcadia* well enough to detect an unattributed passage from that work when it was presented as one of Charles I's private meditations in *Eikon Basilike* (*CPW* III: 362). Although we find both explicit and subtle references to various writers in Milton's poetry and prose, in this chapter I will discuss his relationship with Marvell, one of his closest and most highly regarded friends, as well as Milton's association with three contemporaries mentioned by his third wife. When she was asked whom her husband "approved most of English poets," she reportedly singled out Shakespeare, Spenser, and Abraham Cowley.[22]

Abraham Cowley (1618–1667)

Milton may have never met Cowley, but the two had much in common. Like Milton, Cowley was learned and precocious – he, too, reportedly began writing poetry at age ten – and both writers attended Cambridge University (Cowley graduated from Trinity College with a BA in 1639, ten years after Milton). Both writers were also self-concerned. Just as Milton meditates on his own poetic aspirations in some of his prose works and occasional verses, Cowley in his publications sometimes seems preoccupied by his possible fame. Cowley's collection *Poetical Blossoms*, for example, begins with a preface in which he discusses his evolving poetic career, and in "On the Death of Mr William Hervey" Cowley focuses as much on his own emotional response as the late physician's merits: "Had I a wreath of bays about my brow, / I should contemn that flourishing honour now, / Condemn it to the fire, and joy to hear / It rage and crackle there" (lines 65–68).[23] Milton and the publisher Humphrey Moseley may even have modeled Milton's 1645 *Poems* on Cowley's *Poetical Blossoms*, published in 1633. Like Milton's *Poems*, the layout of Cowley's collection encourages readers to experience his works in terms of his poetic development. The first part is a miscellany with some of his youthful works; the second part contains his love poetry; the third part contains his Pindaric odes; and, in keeping with Renaissance theories of genre, the fourth part contains his most ambitious and mature work, his incomplete epic about the life of King David, *Davideis*.

Milton may also have Cowley in mind when he complains in Sonnet 7 that his "inward ripeness doth much less appear, / That some more timely-happy spirits endu'th" (lines 7–8). Here Milton is comparing himself disparagingly with poets such as Cowley whom he would have considered more "seasonable" for having published a volume of poetry while still a student at Westminster School. Milton's related concern that "my late spring no bud or blossom shew'th" (line 4) might also subtly allude to a manuscript copy of Cowley's *Poetical Blossoms*.[24] Milton implies that he is a late bloomer; he has not yet produced a significant poem (*blossom*), or even the promising start of such a poem (*bud*).[25] But *blossom* could also refer specifically to the title of Cowley's collection: Milton might be saying that he has not produced even one poem comparable to the blooms in Cowley's volume.

Among the works included in *Poetical Blossoms*, Milton would presumably have most admired Cowley's lyric poems and odes, the latter modeled on the odes of Pindar. In *The Reason of Church-Government*, Milton refers to "those magnifick Odes and Hymns wherein *Pindarus* and *Callimachus* [another Greek poet and scholar] are in most things worthy" (*CPW* I: 815–16). In particular, Cowley's "Ode. Of Wit" posits a theory of matter that tentatively resembles the animist materialism that Raphael espouses in Book V of *Paradise Lost* (see Chapter 4). Cowley refers to "the first matter" (line 3) that comprises all creation, which he then more fully explains as "the primitive forms of all / (If we compare great things with small) / Which without discord or confusion lie / In that strange mirror of the Deity" (lines 61–64). A version of Cowley's parenthetical allusion to Virgil, the idea of comparing great things with small, occurs three times in *Paradise Lost* (II.917–24, VI.306–15, X.301–10). But, more important, Milton develops an articulate version of this philosophy in *Paradise Lost* as Raphael teaches Adam and Eve that body and soul are different degrees of the same substance, "one first matter all, / Endued with various forms, various degrees / Of substance, and in things that live, of life" (V.472–74).

While Cowley and Milton also shared an interest in epic, Cowley believed that the best subject for such a poem was God, and he rejected what he perceived to be the folly of writing an epic about classical mythology. Cowley dismisses "the obsolete threadbare tales of *Thebes* and *Troy*," adding that "those mad stories of the *Gods* and *Heroes* … seem in themselves so ridiculous" and "ought to appear no better arguments for *Verse*, then those of their worthy *Successors*, the *Knights Errant*."[26] Milton of course shared Cowley's deep religiosity, but in *Paradise Lost* he still found ways to incorporate and subordinate classical myth, which suggests that he held such "tales" in higher esteem than Cowley did. Most notably, Milton uses the fallen angels to explain the origin of ancient Greek and Roman deities. He claims that the names of the angels who rebelled with Satan have been "blotted out and razed / By their rebellion, from the Books of Life" (I.362–63), but later, "among the sons of Eve," the fallen angels corrupted "the greatest part / Of mankind … to forsake / God their Creator" and became "known to men by various names, / And various idols through the heathen world" (I.364, 367–69, 374–75). Milton, as the saying goes, thus gets to have his cake and eat it: writing a Christian epic, he ingeniously preserves but repudiates ancient myth by associating it with Satan and his followers.

And whereas Cowley followed "the *Pattern* of our Master *Virgil*" (b1v) in structuring *Davideis* into twelve books (of which Cowley only completed four), Milton conceived *Paradise Lost* as a ten-book epic in 1667 and did not revise it into twelve until the second edition in 1674. We don't know what motivated Milton's specific structural choices. Because Royalist writers at the Restoration frequently cited Virgil to mark the new Golden Age that they felt a return to monarchy would bring the nation, Milton may have wished during the 1660s to distance himself from the political implications of publishing a heroic poem that cleaved too closely to Virgil's model. In writing *Paradise Lost* in ten books Milton was instead allying himself with Luís de Camões's epic *Os Lusíadas* and perhaps more specifically Lucan's *Pharsalia*, an epic whose tragic tone appealed to supporters of republicanism during the civil war period.[27]

This is one of the significant differences between Milton and Cowley: they were on opposite sides during the civil wars. Whereas Milton defended the execution of Charles I and vehemently opposed the king's party, Cowley sided with Charles and the Royalists. Cowley thus joined the king in Oxford in 1642 when the court set up an alternative government there, and he went on to work at the court of Queen Henrietta Maria when she went into exile in Paris. We can glimpse Cowley's conservative political sympathies as he justifies why he chose to write an epic about King David: "For what worthier *subject* could have been chosen among all the *Treasuries* of past times … the greatest *Monarch* that ever sat upon the most *famous* Throne of the whole Earth? whom should a *Poet* more justly seek to *honor*, then the highest person who ever *honored* his Profession?" (b2r). Milton in *Paradise Lost*, by comparison, most closely associates the trappings of regal authority with the building of Pandemonium in Hell. The "greatest *Monarch*" whom Milton "seek[s] to *honour*" in his epic is God, not King Charles. And while God in *Paradise Lost* sits on a throne, Milton takes pains to depict the singularity of divine rule and to describe the rest of Heaven as a thoroughgoing meritocracy in which even God's Son is "By merit more than birthright ... / Found worthiest" (III.309–10).

Milton and Cowley nevertheless appear to have agreed on some of the fundamental stylistic features of epic writing. Just as Milton dismisses rhyme as the "jingling sound of like endings" in the note that he added to a reprint of *Paradise Lost* (*CPEP* 291), so Cowley asserts, "For if any man design to compose a *Sacred Poem*, by onely turning a story of the *Scripture* ... into *Rhyme*; He is so far from elevating *Poesie*, that he onely *abases Divinity*" (b3r). Both Milton's and Cowley's epics also conclude with a sense of anticipation. *Paradise Lost* ends with the expulsion of Adam and Eve from the Garden of Eden and foreshadows the redemptive sacrifice that the Son will make; in like manner, Cowley intended to conclude *Davideis* with Saul's and Jonathan's deaths and planned only to point to David's arrival and anointment in Hebron. As Cowley explains, "it is the custom of *Heroick Poets* ... never to come to the full end of their *Story*; but onely so near, that every one may see it; as men commonly play not out the game, when it is evident that they can win it, but lay down their Cards, and take up what they have won" (b1v).

Although Cowley was perhaps writing with false modesty, he came to refer to his unfinished epic as a "weak and imperfect attempt." *Davideis*, he claimed, was "ambitious of no other fruit" than "opening of a way to the courage and industry of some other persons, who may be better able to perform it throughly and successfully" (b3v). With Milton, Cowley found that other person. But if in *Paradise Lost* and later in *Paradise Regained* Milton "perform[ed]" more "thoroughly and successfully" than Cowley and other contemporary English writers, Cowley's incomplete *Davideis* also reminds us that Milton's decision to write a biblical epic was not without precedent. When Milton in *Paradise Lost* claims to undertake "Things unattempted yet in prose or rhyme" (I.16), we need to question what similar things had been attempted in Milton's time. That he borrows this boastful phrase from another near contemporary, Ariosto, reminds us to examine Milton's works not just in relation to antiquity but also within his immediate literary context.

Andrew Marvell (1621–1678)

In contrast to Cowley, Andrew Marvell formed a close relationship with Milton. While many of the details about Marvell's life remain sketchy, Milton's nephew Edward Phillips includes Marvell among those "particular Friends" who "had a high esteem" for his uncle (*EL* 74), and, according to another early biographer, John Toland, when Milton lived near St. James's Park, Marvell "us'd to frequent him the oftenest of any body" (*EL* 175).[28]

As we saw in Chapter 1, Marvell was probably one of the friends who worked to get Milton released from custody after the Restoration. We at least know that Marvell complained to the Sergeant at Arms and argued that the fee of £150 stipulated by the House of Commons was too high to pay for Milton's release.[29] We also know that almost ten years earlier when Milton served as Secretary for Foreign Tongues under the Commonwealth, he enthusiastically recommended Marvell as his assistant. In a letter from 21 February 1653, Milton describes Marvell as "a man whom both by report, & the converse I have had with him, of singular desert for the state to make use of … [I]t would be hard … to find a Man soe fit every way for the purpose as this Gentleman" (*CPW* IV: 859–60).

The second part of one of Marvell's treatises, *The Rehearsal Transpos'd* (1673), provides additional insight into the two authors' relationship. In this tract, Marvell insists on the right of individuals to follow their conscience in religious matters, a position that Milton before and after the Restoration strongly endorsed. Marvell, though, defends himself against the charge that Milton had actually written most of the tract's first part, published the previous year:

> I take it … very ill that you should have so mean an opinion of me, as not to think me competent to write such a simple book as that without any assistance … *J. M.* was, and is, a man of great Learning and Sharpness of wit as any man. It was his misfortune, living in a tumultuous time, to be toss'd on the wrong side, and he writ *Flagrante bello* [i.e., while the war was waging] certain dangerous Treatises … But he never having in the least provoked you, for you to insult thus over his old age, to traduce him by your *Scaramuccios*, and in your own person, as a School-Master, who was born and hath lived much more ingenuously and Liberally then your self; to have done all this, and lay at last my simple book to his charge, without ever taking care to inform your self better … is inhumanely and inhospitably done.[30]

While this defense demonstrates Marvell's respect and admiration for Milton – in particular, Marvell refers to the elder poet's "great Learning and Sharpness" – the passage also hints at the two men's different political perspectives. Milton probably would not have described his Commonwealth writings as "dangerous" – perhaps preferring "misunderstood but righteous" – and certainly Milton would not have said that he had been "toss'd on the wrong side" of the war: Milton believed that he had freely chosen to oppose Charles I, and, given his vehement warnings against the country's return to monarchy in 1659 and 1660, he continued to see his choice as the right one.

The distinction between Marvell's and Milton's political positions may seem relatively subtle when compared to Milton's differences with Cowley, but Milton and Marvell did not agree entirely on major political events. Although both supported the republican cause and were probably assigned to walk together at Cromwell's funeral,[31] Marvell originally sided with the Royalists during the 1640s, and his support for Cromwell grew during the subsequent decade. Milton, by comparison, consistently opposed the Royalist cause, and his enthusiasm for Cromwell as Lord Protector waned over the 1650s.[32] Later, serving as a member of Parliament from 1659 until his death in 1678, Marvell worked on behalf of the protectoral regime under Richard Cromwell. Milton's relationship with Richard Cromwell must have been comparatively strained. Although Milton stayed on as a secretary under the new regime and initially prepared letters for the new Protector, by 1659 in *A Treatise of Civil Power* Milton appealed to Parliament to challenge the protectorate's policies and broaden religious toleration.

Yet, even with these political differences, Milton and Marvell clearly respected and admired each other. In a letter from 2 June 1654 addressed to "my most Honoured Freind [sic] John Milton," Marvell compliments a tract that Milton had sent him (most likely, *Pro Populo Anglicano Defensio Secunda*) and promises to "[s]tudie it even to the getting of it by Heart" (*CPW* IV: 863–64). Marvell was also evidently familiar with Milton's poetry; in *The First Anniversary*, for example, Marvell refers to "the Dragon's tail" that "[s]winges the volumes of its horrid flail" (lines 151–52), an apparent allusion to Milton's image in the Nativity Ode of the "old Dragon under ground" that "[s]winges the scaly horror of his folded tail" (lines 168–72). And in *A Poem upon the Death of His Late Highness the Lord Protector*, Marvell gently reconfigures Milton's description in *Lycidas* of "Fame" as "That last infirmity of noble mind" (line 71); instead, Marvell writes, both "Love and Grief" are "nobler weaknesses of human mind" (line 22).[33] Marvell's personification of Excise in "The Last Instructions to a Painter" also resembles Milton's depiction of Sin and Death in *Paradise Lost*.[34] In particular, Death's rape of his mother in Milton's epic (II.747–802) informs Marvell's description of Excise's birth by the government auditor John Birch: "Her, of a female harpy, in dog-days, / Black Birch, of all the earth-born race most hot, / And most rapacious, like himself, begot, / And of his brat enamoured, as 't increased, / Buggered in incest with the mongrel beast" (lines 142–46).[35]

Aside from such echoes and allusions, the most significant poetic connection between Marvell and Milton is undoubtedly "On Mr. Milton's *Paradise Lost*," the encomiastic poem that Marvell, perhaps at Milton's or his printer's request, contributed to the epic's second edition.[36] In this poem, Marvell cleverly anticipates and deflects possible objections to Milton's biblical epic by charting his own evolving response. Initially, Marvell says, he feared that Milton "would ruin … / The sacred truths to fable and old song" (lines 7–8); then he worried that Milton might "[perplex] the things he would explain, / And what was easy he should render vain" (lines 15–16); but ultimately, Marvell writes, he became convinced of the epic's greatness: "Thou hast not missed one thought that could be fit, / And all that was improper dost omit" (lines 27–28). Marvell's poem is valuable in part because he keenly identifies so many of *Paradise Lost*'s extraordinary features – its reigning "majesty" (line 31), Milton's apt phrasing and "vast expense of mind" (line 42), and the verse's combination of "gravity and ease" (line 36).

Most important for Milton's seventeenth-century readers, though, may have been Marvell's defense of the epic's lack of rhyme. Even as Marvell himself chose to write in couplets – a characteristically coy gesture of abasement – he calls attention to the superiority of Milton's blank verse (that is, unrhymed iambic pentameter):

> Well might'st thou scorn thy readers to allure
> With tinkling rhyme, of thine own sense secure;
> While the *Town-Bays* writes all the while and spells,
> And like a pack horse tires without his bells.
> Their fancies like our bushy points appear:
> The poets tag them; we for fashion wear.
> I too transported by the mode offend,
> And while I meant to *praise* thee must *commend*.
> Thy verse created like thy theme sublime,
> In number, weight, and measure, needs not rhyme.   (lines 45–54)

Here again Marvell recognizes one of *Paradise Lost*'s most distinctive features. Reading Milton today, we might forget that after the Restoration, blank verse was most closely associated with drama and even then was contested for serious plays. While Henry Howard, the Earl of Surrey, had introduced unrhymed iambic pentameter in English in the 1540s, the heroic couplet continued to dominate poetic compositions for the next two hundred and fifty years. Thus Dryden in his *Essay of Dramatick Poesie* (1668) advocates the "quick and poignant brevity" that rhyme contributes to dialogue over the wordiness caused by blank verse.[37] Another of Milton's friends, Robert Howard, attempted to refute Dryden by arguing that rhyme was unnatural in performance, but Howard also conceded that blank verse was "much too low" for non-dramatic verse.[38] Milton's Preface to *Samson Agonistes* may represent his own reply to such critical beliefs. Although he does not directly refer to the debate about the relative merits of using rhymed verse as a vehicle for tragedy, his critique of tragedy "at this day" and his dislike of "intermixing" tragedy with "comic stuff" could allude to tragicomedies by Dryden and other post-Restoration playwrights (*CPEP* 708).

It is in this context that we should read Marvell's defiant celebration of *Paradise Lost*'s lack of rhyme. Marvell insists that both the epic's theme and its verse are "sublime," and he casts rhyme as a mere "fashion," comparing it to "spells," "bells," and "fancies," and dismissing the purveyors of "tinkling rhyme" as tired "pack horse[s]." Marvell then completes his defense of Milton's style by presciently anticipating how a poet such as Dryden might try to tame *Paradise Lost* by adapting it into a rhymed play: "some less skilful hand / (Such as disquiet always what is well, / And by ill imitating would excel) / Might hence presume the whole Creation's day / To change in scenes and show it in a play" (lines 18–22). If Marvell's language sounds too forceful here – he is suggesting in effect that a drama would be an inappropriate genre for Milton's subject and that writers of heroic tragedy are unskilled – we should consider that Marvell's stridency reveals not just his disdain for the period's dominant style but also the depth of his affection and admiration for his friend John Milton.

William Shakespeare (1564–1616)

It is pleasing to speculate that Milton and Shakespeare may have met. The young poet could have encountered the famous dramatist and actor at the Blackfriars Playhouse, where Milton's father served as a trustee, or the two authors could have come into contact through a mutual acquaintance, such as Thomas Morley, one of Shakespeare's closest neighbors and a patron of Milton's father.[39] Or perhaps the two writers simply passed each other in the streets of London. Growing up in the heart of the city, the seven-year-old Milton could have chanced upon Shakespeare making his way to or from one of his favorite haunts, the Mermaid Tavern, located on the corner of Bread Street, not far from Milton's boyhood home (see Figure 1).

Regardless of such a possible encounter, Milton was clearly familiar with Shakespeare's plays, in print or on the stage or both. In *L'Allegro*, the mirthful speaker anticipates going "to the well-trod stage" where he will enjoy comedies by Ben Jonson or hear "sweetest Shakespeare, Fancy's child, / Warble his native wood-notes wild" (lines 131, 133–34). And in *Eikonoklastes* Milton quotes one of Richard III's speeches from Shakespeare's play (II.1.70–73) to describe Charles I's dissembling, "not of his affections only, but of Religion" (*CPW* III: 362). Milton seems to know *Richard III* fairly well, adding that in the play's opening soliloquy Richard speaks "in as high a strain of pietie, and mortification, as is utterd in any passage" in Charles's *Eikon Basilike*, "sometimes to the same sense and purpose" (*CPW* III: 361).

Among the characters that Milton himself created, Satan and Samson are probably the most Shakespearean. Their psychological complexity and tortured soliloquies call to mind such similarly conflicted tragic figures as Hamlet, Lear, and Macbeth. Writing in the early twentieth century the critic Alwin Thaler helped to solidify the case for Shakespeare's influence on Milton by compiling hundreds of verbal echoes from Shakespeare's plays in Milton's works. Some of the resemblances that Thaler found are fairly persuasive, such as "pillars of the state" in *2 Henry VI* (I.1.72) and "pillar of state" in *Paradise Lost* (II.302) or "past hope" in both *Romeo and Juliet* (IV.1.45) and *Samson* (line 120).[40] But other similarities that Thaler detects are more subtle, such as Samson's reference to his "counterfeit" friends (lines 189–90), a term which reminds Thaler of Shakespeare's Timon, who also becomes disillusioned in his friendships (*Timon of Athens* II.2.193; III.2.79–80; III.6.34, 99, 106).

Probably Milton's *A Mask* most fully reflects Shakespeare's influence. The character of the Attendant Spirit seems modeled on Ariel from *The Tempest*, while those who succumb to Comus's charms and choose to drink from his enchanted cup undergo a more pernicious version of Bottom's transformation in *A Midsummer Night's Dream*. The fairy Puck gives an unwitting Bottom the head of an ass, but Comus changes his victims' countenances

> Into some brutish form of wolf, or bear,
> Or ounce, or tiger, hog, or bearded goat,
> All other parts remaining as they were;
> And they, so perfect is their misery,
> Not once perceive their foul disfigurement,
> But boast themselves more comely than before,
> And all their friends and native home forget,
> To roll with pleasure in a sensual sty.   (lines 70–77)

In particular, the idea of not perceiving one's "foul disfigurement" and thinking oneself "more comely" recalls Bottom's ignorance about his heady change and Titania's magically induced infatuation with what she mistakes for Bottom's beauty and wisdom (III.1).

Individual phrases and images in Milton's masque also contribute to the drama's pervasive Shakespearean tone; most striking is the wide variety of Shakespeare's works to which Milton appears to allude, as if he had recently been perusing the second folio of Shakespeare's plays, published two years earlier. The Lady's anxiety about "airy tongues" (line 208), for example, recalls a passage in *Romeo and Juliet* (II.1.163), and her subsequent defense of moderation over excess (lines 756–79) echoes the language in *King Lear* (IV.1.70–74). Even the sylvan setting of Milton's court drama seems indebted to Shakespeare's depiction of magical woods in not just *A Midsummer Night's Dream* but also *As You Like It* and *The Merry Wives of Windsor*.

When Milton in his later years wrote his own play, *Samson Agonistes*, he adhered to the classical model of tragedy, as we have already seen, more than the conventions of Shakespearean drama. But this choice of form does not necessarily indicate Milton's dissatisfaction with Shakespeare. In the note on "The Verse" that Milton added to *Paradise Lost*, he praises "our best English tragedies" for rejecting rhyme (*CPEP* 291), a quality certainly true of most of Shakespeare's plays. And, as we saw in the discussion of Marvell, Milton's comment in *Samson*'s Preface about "the small esteem, or rather infamy [of tragedy], which in the account of many it undergoes at this day" (*CPEP* 708) might have been directed at post-Restoration writers, not Shakespeare.

But even if Milton in his later years disagreed with some aspects of Shakespeare's dramaturgy, he wrote enthusiastically about the playwright in one of his earliest poems. It seems fitting that Milton's first published poem in English was "On Shakespeare," as if Milton were consciously allying himself with England's other great poet. The poem's value stems in part from what it reveals about Milton's sense of the relation between writer and readers. Milton suggests that Shakespeare will achieve immortality through his verse because his writing makes such a "deep impression" on his audience's imagination (line 12). He tells Shakespeare directly that a traditional memorial built of "pilèd stones" (line 2) is not needed because Shakespeare has "built thyself a livelong monument" (line 8). This latter phrase emphasizes both the author's agency and his monument's liveliness: while "thyself" indicates that Shakespeare has personally ensured he will be remembered, "livelong" fits with other details in the poem that suggest his monument will long endure because his readers keep it alive. Milton seems to take consolation in the possibility that the "heart" of each reader can actively "conceive" Shakespeare's writings (lines 10, 14). The specific choice of *conceive* points to both readers' imaginative faculties and their generative function; Shakespeare depends on readers to preserve his memory imaginatively and to create his poetic authority.

Interestingly, Milton in "On Shakespeare" never refers to the theater. Instead, he addresses Shakespeare's accomplishments exclusively in terms of his poetry and publishing – the poet's "easy numbers" (line 10), "Delphic lines" (line 12), and "unvalued book" (line 11). This more narrow focus may be attributed to Puritan anxieties about the licentiousness of theatergoing and/or the poem's original bibliographical context: "On Shakespeare" first appeared in 1632 as one of seven encomiastic poems at the start of Shakespeare's second folio, *Mr. William Shakespeare's Comedies, Histories, and Tragedies.*[41] In this context, Milton's poem commemorated not only Shakespeare's artistry but also, it seems, the publication of such a prestigious volume. Milton may also have been anticipating his own volume of collected poetry, first published in 1645 and containing his encomium to Shakespeare. Milton suggests as much in the poem's final lines which may convey a twinge of envy: "so sepulchered in such pomp dost lie, / That kings for such a tomb would wish to die" (lines 15–16). Here Milton hints that, despite the "shame" of his own "slow-endeavoring art" (line 9), he hopes one day to build his own poetic monument.

Edmund Spenser (1552–1599)

Passages in various works by Milton clearly demonstrate his familiarity with Spenser's poetry. The pastoral critique of the clergy in *Lycidas* echoes Spenser's depiction of false shepherds in the May eclogue of *The Shepheardes Calendar* (which Milton also quotes directly in *Animadversions, CPW* I: 723); the description of Sin in *Paradise Lost* derives in part from Spenser's allegory of Error (*The Faerie Queene* I.1.14–15); and in *Il Penseroso*, when Milton alludes to Chaucer's unfinished *The Squire's Tale*, he specifically recalls Spenser's attempt to complete the story of Cambuskan (*FQ* IV.3.52). A few lines later in *Il Penseroso*, Milton still seems to have in mind Spenser's chivalric poem:

> ... great bards beside,
> In sage and solemn tunes have sung,
> Of tourneys and of trophies hung;
> Of forests, and enchantments drear,
> Where more is meant than meets the ear.   (lines 116–20)

Not only does this list correspond to some of the most prominent subjects of *The Faerie Queene* but the final line seems to allude to Spenser's use of allegory. As we have already seen, Milton early on considered writing his own epic about tourneys and trophies. His plans for an epic, as described in his early poems and the Trinity Manuscript, suggest that he was thinking seriously about a classical epic based on the same subjects that interested Spenser.

But while Milton ultimately decided not to write a chivalric romance like Spenser's, the central image in *The Faerie Queene* – a Christian hero triumphing over temptation and choosing good – finds parallels in the plots of not only *Paradise Lost* but also *A Mask, Paradise Regained*, and *Samson Agonistes*. As E. M. W. Tillyard first suggested, Milton was "profoundly influenced all through his life by Spenser's version of the medieval theme of the soul's pilgrimage.

It must have been permanently present in his mind."[42] This theme helps to explain Dryden's provocative claim that "Milton has acknowledged to me, that Spencer was his original."[43] The keyword is *original*, which could mean "beginning, commencement" or someone who "serves as a model or basis for later imitations."[44] That Milton in *Areopagitica* praises the "sage and serious" Spenser as "a better teacher" than the medieval theologians Thomas Aquinas and Duns Scotus (*CPW* II: 516) indicates how Milton understood the nature of his relationship to Spenser: Milton implies that he turned to Spenser more for the meaning of his poetry than its style, specifically for Spenser's moral teachings.

One significant connection between Spenser and Milton that often goes unnoticed concerns the two authors' depictions of erotic love. In contrast to the endless pursuit of an unrequited passion that dominates sixteenth-century Petrarchan love poetry, Spenser in his sonnet sequence *Amoretti* idealized a reciprocal love relationship. His speaker and beloved achieve a mature, selfless love by giving up the chase and willingly choosing each other. Thus in *Amoretti* 67, Spenser describes how the speaker "had the chace forsooke" when the beloved suddenly "beholding me with milder looke, / Sought not to fly," and "I in hand her yet halfe trembling tooke."[45] Milton in *Paradise Lost* similarly explores an ideal wedded love between Adam and Eve, founded, as we will see in Chapter 4, on a profound mutuality. Milton's narrator denounces both a "loveless, joyless, unendeared, / Casual fruition" and the "court amours / Mixed dance, or wanton masque, or midnight ball, / Or serenade, which the starved lover sings / To his proud fair, best quitted with disdain" (IV.766–70). Instead, Eve's recollection of first meeting Adam echoes Spenser's description in *Amoretti* of the speaker's and his beloved's mutual surrender of their selves. Adam appeals to her as "My other half," and she chooses to yield as he reaches out with his "gentle hand" (IV.488).

We ought not to overstate Spenser's influence on *Paradise Lost*, however. Although Milton contemplated writing a classical epic based on England's mythic past, the heroic poem that Milton ultimately wrote differs in significant ways from *The Faerie Queene*. Most notably, Milton uses allegory sparingly in *Paradise Lost*, reserving it for such figures as Sin, Death, and Chaos. And the two poets wrote for different purposes: whereas Spenser in his "Letter to Raleigh" defined the "generall end" of his epic as "to fashion a gentleman or noble person in vertuous and gentle discipline," Milton in *Paradise Lost* is less concerned with social refinement than devotion to God.[46]

Milton and Spenser also had sharply different views about politics and religion. Spenser dedicated his epic to Elizabeth I and incorporates various references to her virtue and nobility within the narrative's allegory; Milton, in contrast, did not dedicate *Paradise Lost* to anyone and had contempt for both

Charles I and Charles II. Also, in Book I of *The Faerie Queene*, Spenser – perhaps in an attempt to appeal to Queen Elizabeth's values – depicts Catholicism through the character of Duessa as a threat to Protestantism, and he defines holiness through Una explicitly in Protestant terms. Milton, by comparison, believed that Catholicism had already contaminated Charles I's court with its renewed emphasis on churchly ceremonialism, and in place of a devout Protestantism in *Paradise Lost*, Milton, as we will see, espouses his own heterodox theology.

The work by Milton that most fully reflects Spenser's influence is probably not *Paradise Lost* but A *Mask*. Just that the Lady in A *Mask* refers to her "doctrine of Virginity" as "sage / And serious" (lines 786–87) suggests the connection in Milton's mind between his own court drama and Spenser's works: Milton later, in *Areopagitica*, uses the same phrase to describe Spenser (*CPW* II: 516). Clearly Spenserian is the masque's broad narrative of three noble children overcoming threats to their virtue as they make their way through an allegorical wood. In particular, Milton appears to have been thinking about the narrative structure of Book III of *The Faerie Queene*. Like A *Mask*, Book III dramatizes the virtue of chastity, and it portrays an evil enchanter capturing a beautiful maiden who is rescued by another strong, beautiful maiden. The Attendant Spirit in his final speech then develops the relation between A *Mask* and Book III of *The Faerie Queene* as he describes the Elysian plain:

> Beds of hyacinth, and roses
> Where young Adonis oft reposes,
> Waxing well of his deep wound
> In slumber soft, and on the ground
> Sadly sits th' Assyrian queen;
> But far above in spangled sheen
> Celestial Cupid, her famed son, advanced,
> Holds his dear Psyche sweet entranced
> After her wand'ring labors long,
> Till free consent the gods among
> Make her his eternal bride,
> And from her fair unspotted side
> Two blissful twins are to be born,
> Youth and Joy; so Jove hath sworn.   (lines 998–1011)

In this passage, Milton engages with Spenser's Garden of Adonis (*FQ* III.6), but with significant differences: Milton puts Adonis in the sky, for example, whereas the garden in which Adonis lies in Spenser's poem grows on earth (*FQ* III.6.29). Also, Spenser casts Pleasure as the daughter of Cupid and Psyche

(*FQ* III.6.50), whereas Milton makes them the parents of twins, completing the passage's emphasis on couples.

The other significant Spenserian element in *A Mask* is the character of Sabrina, whom "Meliboeus old" mentions to the Attendant Spirit (line 821). Sabrina's character comes largely from *The Faerie Queene*, although Milton could also have borrowed elements of her story from works by Geoffrey of Monmouth or Michael Drayton. That the Lady in Milton's court drama depends on Meliboeus's wise advice to escape from Comus – the Attendant Spirit describes Spenser/Meliboeus as the "soothest shepherd that e'er piped on plains" (line 823) – further suggests Milton's high regard for his poetic forebear. As we will see in Chapter 4, Milton appears to use Spenser/Meliboeus within the allegory of *A Mask* to stand for the crucial role that poets must play in the education of the aristocracy.

Milton again emphasizes the educational value of *The Faerie Queene* in perhaps his best-known allusion to Spenser. The passage occurs not in *A Mask* but in *Areopagitica* as Milton criticizes "a fugitive and cloister'd vertue, unexercis'd & unbreath'd, that never sallies out and sees her adversary" (*CPW* II: 515). Instead, Milton argues, the truly virtuous person – the "true warfaring Christian" (*CPW* II: 515) – must confront the powerful temptation of vice and still choose good. To illustrate his point, Milton alludes to the episode of Mammon's Cave from Book II of *The Faerie Queene*. But whereas Spenser depicts Guyon, the Knight of Temperance, entering alone into this cave of vice, Milton in *Areopagitica* revises Spenser's text by having the Palmer accompany Guyon "that he might see and know, and yet abstain" (*CPW* II: 516). This alteration provides a fitting conclusion to a discussion of Milton's relation to his literary peers and predecessors; Milton's appropriation of the episode of Mammon's Cave illustrates how he consistently uses but rewrites ideas and images that he borrows from both contemporary and classical works. Just as Milton alters Spenser's text so that Guyon can benefit from the wisdom that the Palmer embodies, so the Palmer can be seen as a symbol for Milton's own textual intervention. Instead of venturing forth alone into the literary traditions that Milton's works explore, readers can rely on Milton's presence so that they, too, can see, know, and gain a new perspective.

The book trade

Whereas some of Milton's contemporaries profited directly and indirectly from their writings – Spenser sought support at court, for example, while Shakespeare made his living in the theater – Milton never earned much money from his publications. Instead, he lived off the money he earned from investments and, when he worked as a teacher, from his school. The exception is the sizeable income Milton received while working for the Council of State as Secretary for Foreign Tongues, including his lodgings for two years in the Palace of Whitehall beginning in November 1649. But as a government employee, Milton was primarily being paid for his duties as a translator and officer of state rather than for his four official prose tracts.[47]

Milton's limited remuneration as a writer was not unique during the seventeenth century. As the Renaissance system of patronage gradually gave way to the burgeoning book trade, printers and booksellers rarely compensated authors for their efforts. Most members of the book trade would pay a writer if they expected that a work would sell well, but even in those cases the author received only a minimal fee or an agreed-upon number of complimentary copies.[48] According to the contract for the publication of *Paradise Lost*, for example, the printer Samuel Simmons agreed to pay Milton £5 for granting him the right to publish the poem and promised to pay the author another £5 along with perhaps 200 copies at the end of the first, second, and third impressions.[49] Although these sums seem modest by today's publishing standards, Simmons treated Milton fairly for the time. The contract – the earliest surviving agreement of its kind in England – outlines a mutually beneficial working arrangement.[50] The printer agreed to pay for three editions of *Paradise Lost* at a time when many members of the book trade assumed perpetual rights to publish texts without even consulting the authors.

Another name for "members of the book trade" in early modern England was Stationers. In 1557, the crown chartered the Company of Stationers, a guild of mostly printers, binders, and booksellers, who were to oversee the production and dissemination of printed communications and to forestall the publication of "certain seditious and heretical books … moving our subjects and lieges to sedition and disobedience."[51] At the same time, the government instituted a two-part system of regulation. Anyone who wished to publish a printed text had to obtain a license from a board of government-appointed officials; a member of the Stationers' Company then had to approve the text and, for a fee, enter its title and owner's name in the Company's *Register*. The law emphasized ownership, not authorship. Prior to the first copyright act in 1709, writers had almost no legal authority; a member of the Stationers' Company who obtained a copy of a work could secure legal ownership merely by publishing the book in print or paying the fee and having it officially registered.

Knowing about the seventeenth-century book trade is valuable for readers of Milton in part because it helps us to assess his practical authority over his published works. Should we attribute every comma, case change, and use of italics to Milton? Or did he abdicate all control of his writing when he turned over a manuscript to the printer? During the course of his career, Milton worked with more than ten different printing houses and more than twenty booksellers, including Humphrey Robinson and Humphrey Moseley, two of the most prominent and influential literary publishers of the period. The number of Milton's collaborations with Stationers suggests how thoroughly he was engaged with London's publishing community and how widely his works circulated. Even when Milton lived with his parents in the suburbs of Hammersmith and Horton, he maintained connections with members of the book trade; in a letter to Alexander Gil dated 4 December 1634, for example, Milton tells his former teacher to "expect me on Monday in London (God willing) among the Booksellers" (*CPW* I: 322). Later in life, Milton also continued to develop lasting friendships with Stationers. In addition to a long friendship that he formed with Matthew Simmons and his family, Milton reportedly lived for a period in 1669 or 1670 with the bookseller Edward Millington in Little Britain, another of London's centers for bookshops, and, in a letter to his friend Carlo Dati dated 21 April 1647, Milton refers to "James, the bookseller" and "his master, a most familiar acquaintance of mine" (*CPW* II: 765). Milton also seems to have befriended George Thomason, an influential collector and bookseller. Thomason owned autographed copies of Milton's publications, and Milton wrote Sonnet 14 about the death of Thomason's wife Catherine, a book lover herself who amassed an impressive library.

We should not assume, however, that Milton's friendships enabled him to control his works' printing. If writers during the seventeenth century had almost no economic or legal rights, they also typically had limited influence over their books' design and layout. In general, decisions about spelling, case, and type were the province of the printing house during the seventeenth century. Compositors would attempt to follow an author's manuscript copy, but their work could be influenced by personal preferences, honest mistakes, and house styles. A compositor might also alter a writer's words based on the availability of type or the need to fill out or "justify" a line, perhaps adding a final "e" to some words (so as to lengthen the line), or creating abbreviations or contractions (so as to shorten the line). In *Mechanick Exercises of the Whole Art of Printing* (1683–84), Joseph Moxon describes how a seventeenth-century compositor "*is strictly to follow his* Copy" but also may incorporate changes according to "*a Custom, which among them is look'd upon as a task and duty incumbent on the* Compositer, *viz. to discern and amend the bad* Spelling *and* Pointing *of his* Copy, *if it be English.*"[52] What constituted "*bad* Spelling *and* Pointing" at a time when no widely accepted standards yet existed was evidently left to the compositor's discretion. Readers of Milton – regardless of which edition they consult – should thus not build their interpretations on typographical features such as the use of upper- or lower-case letters. Despite efforts by some twentieth-century editors to portray Milton as supernaturally vigilant, we cannot distinguish his spelling, italics, punctuation, and capitalization from his compositors' preferences.

Moxon goes on to explain that each compositor should

> *be a good English Schollar at least; and that he know the present traditional* Spelling *of all English Words, and that he have so much Sence and Reason, as to* Point *his Sentences properly: when to begin a Word with a* Capital Letter, *when (to render the Sence of the Author more intelligent to the Reader) to Set some Words or Sentences in* Italick *or* English Letters, *&c.*[53]

Nothing in Milton's writings suggests that he and his books' creators deviated from such a collaborative arrangement. While some of his printed texts retain some of his personal preferences – the 1667 and 1674 editions of *Paradise Lost*, for example, mostly respect Milton's idiosyncratic spelling of "their" as "thir"[54] – Milton, even if he had wished, could not have controlled every aspect of his works' printing: after he went blind in 1652, he would have had to rely on amanuenses to compose his works and on agents to oversee the publication. Thus, a comparison of the surviving manuscript of *Paradise Lost*, Book I, with the same text in the first printed edition of 1667 reveals that members of the printing house made more than 1,000 changes in spelling and roughly 133 changes in punctuation, all apparently attempts to normalize, albeit inconsistently, Milton's manuscript.[55]

I do not mean to suggest, however, that Milton entirely ignored his books' minor details. Milton's nephew Edward Phillips recalls visiting his uncle "for some years" during the composition of *Paradise Lost* and perusing the manuscript "in a Parcel of Ten, Twenty, or Thirty Verses at a Time, which being Written by whatever hand came next, might possibly want Correction as to the Orthography and Pointing" (*EL* 73). Phillips here suggests that before Milton handed over his manuscript to the printer he understood spelling and punctuation as having a correct form, even if he did not take pains to see these details carried through in his works' published versions. We also know that Milton cared enough about his books' physical appearance to compose a Greek epigraph expressing his disapproval of William Marshall's frontispiece portrait in Milton's 1645 *Poems*. And while members of the printing house would have designed the title pages for all of Milton's books and determined, for example, how or even if the author's name would be used to attract potential buyers, presumably Milton himself provided the classical and biblical quotations that adorn some of his texts.

Some surviving copies of Milton's seventeenth-century publications contain apparently authorial, hand-written corrections, which also indicate that he cared about but could not entirely control some of his works' minor details. In a copy of *Areopagitica* at the Harry Ransom Humanities Research Center, "wayfaring Christian" has been corrected to "warfaring Christian" with one of Milton's characteristic Rs, and the Ransom Center's copy of *A Mask* has four manuscript changes that look authorial: "my" has been corrected to "by" (line 20), "at" has been corrected to "art" (line 131), "you" has been inserted between "meane" and "that" (line 417), and "reproachfull" has been replaced with "contemptuous" (line 781).[56]

This final, substantive, hand-written revision suggests that Milton did not understand publication as the final step in the creation of a text. He not only published revised and expanded versions of his prose works – *The Doctrine and Discipline of Divorce* (1643, 1644), *The Tenure of Kings and Magistrates* (1649, 1650), *Eikonoklastes* (1649, 1650), *Pro Populo Anglicano Defensio* (1651, 1658), and *The Readie and Easie Way to Establish a Free Commonwealth* (February and April 1660) – but he also continued polishing some of his poems after they were printed. In addition to changing "reproachfull" to "contemptuous" in *A Mask*, Milton revised individual words in "On Shakespeare" between 1632 and 1645, added a headnote to *Lycidas* between 1638 and 1645, fine-tuned two lines in "On the Morning of Christ's Nativity" between 1645 and 1673, and, during the same period, incorporated four additional slight adjustments in *A Mask*.

Milton also worked with Samuel Simmons to continue improving *Paradise Lost* after its first printing. As we saw in Chapter 1, Milton revised the poem in a reissue of the first edition, adding a defense of his verse and the arguments that summarize each book. Then, for the second edition, he restructured the epic from ten to twelve books, added eight lines (VIII.1–3; XII.1–5), and incorporated a few substantive changes (I.504–5, V.636–41, VIII.4, XI.485, XI.551). As with Milton's other texts, *Paradise Lost* reflects a collaborative process of creation. According to a note in the reissue of the first edition, the printer/publisher Simmons and the book's earliest readers influenced the meaning of Milton's original work by requesting that he make at least some of these revisions.[57]

But if writers had little legal, economic, or practical authority within the English book trade, they were gradually gaining new power with the increased name recognition that came with print publication. Milton represents an important figure within book trade history because his career helps to document the early modern author's emerging symbolic status. While more than half of the items published in the 1600s were anonymous, the originality and value of a printed work came to be predicated on the existence of a visible writer. Printers began to include authors' portraits in some books, and some title pages advertised books as the creation of a particular person. In the case of Milton's prose, his first three pamphlets were published anonymously, but the title page of the fourth, *The Reason of Church-Government*, reads, "By Mr. *John Milton*," presumably because the publisher John Rothwell thought Milton's name would appeal to – or at least not dissuade – prospective customers.

As for Milton's poetry, his initials first appear in print at the end of *Lycidas* in the 1638 collection *Justa Eduardo King Naufrago*, and his full name is first printed on the title page of his 1645 collection, *Poems of Mr. John Milton*. Interestingly, at a time when portraits in books most often served as memorials to deceased authors, this collection is one of four texts published during Milton's lifetime that begins with his portrait on the frontispiece; the others are *The History of Britain*, *Artis Logicae*, and some copies of *Paradise Lost*'s second edition. While all these texts contributed to Milton's contemporary reputation, the 1645 *Poems* emphasized his authorial presence more than any of his other publications (see Figure 3 on page 161). Announcing on the title page "*Printed by his true Copies*," the book then enhances this sense of authenticity by including various commendatory notices from Milton's friends and acquaintances and by framing seventeen poems with brief, biographical notes, explaining the poet's age when he wrote a specific work or the circumstance of its composition.[58] With the 1645 *Poems* – not for the last time during Milton's career – members of the book trade were helping to create and preserve his works and, in the process, they were helping to construct John Milton as author.

The civil wars

Because so many of Milton's works engage directly and indirectly with the period's religious and political conflicts, readers need to have at least a rudimentary grasp of the British civil wars and their causes. Not only Milton's Commonwealth tracts but also various of his poems reflect the political culture of the civil war period: three of his sonnets are addressed to historical figures associated with the wars (Henry Vane, Thomas Fairfax, and Oliver Cromwell); Sonnet 8 "Captain or colonel" focuses on a possible assault on London by Royalist troops in 1642; the tailed sonnet "On the New Forcers of Conscience" criticizes Presbyterian control of the English church following the formation of the Westminster Assembly; and even *Paradise Lost* and *Samson Agonistes*, as we saw in Chapter 1, may reflect Milton's contemporary experience in their depictions of failed rebellions.

But if we accept that the British civil wars played a crucial role in Milton's life and some of his writings, the wars themselves have inspired much debate and controversy: historians continue to argue about the causes of the wars and the nature of the events that they encompassed.[59] Historians disagree even about the name of the conflict, referring to it alternately as "The English Revolution," "The English Civil War," "The Great Rebellion," or "The War of the Three Kingdoms."[60] In this book, I use the plural, lower-case "wars" to designate the period's series of armed conflicts while reserving the upper-case "War" to describe each of the three major military contests. And, instead of referring to an "English" war or wars during the seventeenth century, a widely accepted convention is now to use "British" so as to indicate that the period's conflicts included not just England but also Ireland, Wales, and Scotland.

A useful sound bite for beginning to understand Britain's civil wars is that they began as a religious controversy and became a political conflict. But, as with many sound bites, this statement both illuminates and misleads. Even before the controversy about church hierarchy and the liturgy developed into a political and then military dispute, the financial structure of Charles I's court angered members of Parliament and local governors. When the king called Parliament in January 1629, he was expecting the House of Commons to raise money to subsidize the wars he was currently fighting in Spain and France. But members refused to cooperate until Charles addressed their grievances about his administration. For example, according to the Petition of Right, which Charles had approved on 7 June of the previous year, Parliament had to consent to all forms of taxation. The House objected that, without its approval, the court was continuing to collect customs revenue known as tonnage and poundage (that is, duties and taxes levied on every cask of imported wine and on every pound of imported or exported merchandise).

Incensed by what he considered Parliament's effrontery, Charles reacted swiftly: on 10 March 1629, after less than three months, he disbanded Parliament and resolved to govern without a legislature. During the subsequent period – known as the King's Personal Rule or, by his detractors, as the Eleven Years Tyranny – the king and his finance minister attempted to deal on their own with the administration's money problems by ending the country's international conflicts and more avidly pursuing sources of domestic revenue. Charles resorted to imposing new property taxes, creating monopolies, and selling knighthoods and court appointments – actions that increased Parliament's ire and further eroded the administration's popularity.

But Parliament's dissatisfaction with Charles's financial policy was not the sole reason that the House of Commons refused to work with the king in 1629. Members also had concerns about the increased emphasis on ceremonialism and the clerical hierarchy within the English church. To these members of Parliament, the doctrines instituted by one of the king's most powerful advisers, William Laud, smacked of popery. Appointed Archbishop of Canterbury in 1633 and thus the head of the English church, Laud wanted to restore the rituals that had characterized religious practices before the Reformation. He revived a more elaborate style of ecclesiastical architecture, introduced various innovations in the liturgical service – such as kneeling at each mention of Christ's name – and attempted to establish uniform religious practices in England, Ireland, Scotland, and Wales. Defending himself against the charge that the ceremonies he advocated seemed popish, Laud insisted on the "Beauty of Holiness," an allusion to Psalms 29:2 and 96:9. He believed that external worship was intimately connected to inner faith: "I found that with the Contempt of the Outward Worship of God, the Inward fell away apace, and Profanness began boldly to shew it self."[61]

Among Laud's most controversial changes was moving the communion table. The table had traditionally been set lengthwise in the center of each church as a place for parishioners to gather, but Laud ordered that it be moved to the east end of each church and set off by a rail. For Laud, the change symbolized a de-emphasis of the pulpit and sermon and a re-establishment of the sacrament as the core of the religious service. But for Laud's critics, the table's new position seemed not only to reinforce a hierarchy between clergy and laity but also to imply the Catholic doctrine of real presence, that is, the belief that the bread and wine are not mere symbols but in fact contain the body and blood of Christ. As Milton bitterly complained in *Of Reformation Touching Church-Discipline in England* (1641), Laud had made the table of communion a "Table of separation … like an exalted platforme upon the brow of the quire, fortifi'd with bulwark, and barricado, to keep off the profane touch of the Laicks, whilst the obscene, and surfeted Priest scruples not to paw, and mammock the sacramentall bread, as familiarly as his Tavern Bisket" (*CPW* I: 547–48).

Concerns about Charles's and Laud's apparently Catholic vision for the church were exacerbated by the king's marriage to a Roman Catholic, Henrietta Maria, and Charles's limited support for the Protestant cause in the Thirty Years War, the conflict then dominating continental Europe. But while conversions to Catholicism became popular at Charles's court, Laud himself was not a Roman Catholic. Instead, he appears to have belonged to a growing cadre of powerful Arminian clergymen who were challenging the Calvinist theology that had dominated the church during the reigns of Elizabeth and

James. Calvinism divides humankind into two categories, the elect and the reprobate, and asserts that each person's fate is predestined from eternity. By comparison, Arminians – named after the Dutch theologian Jacob Arminius (1560–1609) – hold that human will contributes decisively to whether a person is saved; in opposition to Calvinism's idea of limited atonement for an elect group of people, Arminians believed that Christ died for all of humankind, and each person can accept or reject God's universal grace. Although modern historians disagree about how fully the church proscribed Calvinist predestination before Laud, and some dispute the relative significance of anti-Calvinism in causing Britain's civil conflict, certainly a theological disagreement emerged over predestination during the seventeenth century. Laud systematically but carefully attempted to eliminate Calvinist speech in London, and the king issued three royal statements forbidding debate over the issue, in 1626, 1628, and 1629.[62] Milton himself came to espouse an Arminian theology, as I will show in the next section, but his was an "Arminianism of the left" or "new Arminianism," as it is sometimes named.[63] Milton agreed with Laudian theology only in its rejection of Calvinist supralapsarianism (that is, the idea that God predestined all of humankind from eternity as either saved or damned) but instead of emphasizing high-church rituals as the means of salvation, he believed that Christians had the privilege and obligation to think for themselves and to interpret the Bible by following their conscience.

As part of this underlying belief, Milton also objected to the Episcopal form of church government that Laud promulgated to enforce uniformity of worship. Returning prematurely from his European tour, Milton, as we saw in Chapter 1, wrote five pamphlets attacking the Laudian clerical hierarchy. Prelates, Milton believed, insulted the dignity of the individual and impeded each person's independent study of religion and virtue. As he sums up the issue in *Of Reformation*, prelates "in generall … have beene in *England* to our Soules a sad and dolefull succession of illiterate and blind guides: to our purses, and goods a wastfull band of robbers, a perpetuall havock, and rapine: To our state a continuall *Hydra* of mischiefe, and molestation, the forge of discord and Rebellion" (*CPW* I: 603).

Milton also did not enthusiastically support Presbyterianism, a competing system of church government that depended on church elders or "presbyters" instead of prelates.[64] In the early 1640s, however, he allied himself with the Presbyterians largely out of convenience: they were the most politically powerful group who opposed Laud's ceremonialism. Writing in 1641, Milton deemed it no "desperate hazard" for the church to embrace Presbyterianism, "a teaching and laborious Ministery," in place of Episcopacy, which, in contrast, he calls a "boisterous & contradictional hand of a temporall, earthly, and corporeall Spirituality" (*CPW* I: 613). Milton even discourages his fellow citizens from having "an unseasonable foresight" and "propounding a doubt" about a new form of church government; reform was so imperative, he felt, that they should not worry "whether a greater inconvenience would not grow from the corruption of any other discipline [than Episcopacy]" (*CPW* I: 605).

Milton would later regret that he himself did not adequately foresee the consequences of Presbyterianism. After the civil wars began, he distanced himself from his Presbyterian allies and, as we will see more fully in the next chapter, lashed out at Presbyterians who refused to hold Charles I accountable for what Milton considered the king's tyrannical actions. Milton continued to believe that religion was a deeply personal matter, not something with which the state should meddle, regardless of whether the church was controlled by prelates or presbyters. In "On the New Forcers of Conscience," probably written in late 1646, he sharply attacks Presbyterians for attempting "To force our conscience that Christ set free" and "rid[ing] us with a classic hierarchy" (lines 6–7). Presbyters, he laments, have their own "tricks," "plots and packings worse than those of Trent" (lines 13–14), by which he means that Presbyterian decrees were worse than the canons issued by the Roman Catholic council that met at Trent in the 1500s. The poem's final line, "New *Presbyter* is but old *Priest* writ large" (20), succinctly captures his profound disappointment. *Priest*, an abbreviated form of *Presbyter*, would literally be the same word if it were written out (i.e., "writ large"). Milton is saying that Presbyterianism has proven just as corrupt as prelacy and Catholicism.

Puritans are another group that modern historians sometimes introduce to explain the period's religious controversy. But the name "Puritans" in seventeenth-century England never referred to an organized religious community. Instead, it was a term, initially of abuse, for devout Protestants (they preferred "the godly") who wished to eliminate or "purify" all traces of Catholic ceremony from English worship. "Puritans" could thus include Presbyterians but came to identify more broadly any zealous, reform-minded Protestants such as Anabaptists or Congregationalists. As a loose confederation of believers, Puritans disagreed among themselves on various religious and political issues, but they came together in their advocacy of a personal interpretation of scriptures and their passionate opposition to Laud's high-church ceremonialism.

But while Puritans' beliefs lie at the center of the conflict that contributed to civil strife, ultimately the actions of Presbyterians, not Puritans, caused the political breakdown that led to war. Members of the Scottish Presbyterian church, called the Kirk, boldly defied the king's authority: they rejected both Laud's revisions to the Book of Common Prayer and the increased control over their church that Laud wanted to grant prelates. The First Bishops' War began in January 1639 and ended in June of the same year. Charles assembled an army and led it north to the Scottish border to try to put down Scottish resistance, but his troops were poorly trained and lacked discipline. Opponents of church reform, led by the Scottish gentry, quickly gained a tactical advantage as they seized the king's arsenal and secured key ports, thus preventing Charles's army from receiving supplies and reinforcements.

Outmaneuvered and overpowered, the king was forced to end the conflict and to negotiate a treaty with the Scots. Both sides understood that hostilities would probably soon resume, and Charles returned to London with the hope of redoubling his efforts. He called Parliament in 1640 to raise funds for war, bringing an abrupt end to his eleven-year Personal Rule. Members of Parliament, however, were still dissatisfied with Charles's administration – not least over the ongoing conflict with Scotland – and wanted him to address their complaints before they voted to assist with his plans. Unnerved, Charles once again peremptorily dissolved Parliament, this time after only three weeks, thus earning it the name the Short Parliament. In *Eikonoklastes* (1649, 1650), Milton criticizes Charles both for claiming that he called Parliament not out of "necessity" but "by his own chois and inclination" and for then "not enduring the delay of his impatient will" and "dismiss[ing] them and thir greevances with scorn and frustration" (*CPW* III: 350, 354).

Charles I now turned to Spain and France to secure funds, but his efforts abroad also proved futile, and the new militia that he conscripted to send north to Scotland was by most accounts even worse prepared and less disciplined than the levy that he had raised for the First Bishops' War. On 20 August 1640 the Scottish army pre-empted the king's renewed attack by invading England and seizing the town of Newcastle in the first assault of the Second Bishops' War. This war was over within a few months, a devastating loss for Charles and another blow to his political authority, not just in Scotland but also in England, Ireland, and Wales. If Scotland could resist the king's interference in its church, why couldn't these other nations similarly practice their own form of worship?

In October, Charles and the Scots negotiated a new truce, which included a provision that Scottish forces would continue to occupy parts of northern England at the cost of £850 a day for the English government. Needing the legislature's aid and in desperate need of new subsidies, the king on 3 November 1640 once again assembled Parliament – "compell'd at length both by his wants, and by his feares," as Milton put it in *Eikonoklastes* (*CPW* III: 355). The new legislature became known as the Long Parliament because it remained in session (in various forms) until its official dissolution in 1660. This time when members began voicing their grievances about Charles's administration, the king discovered that he could not so easily dissolve Parliament: its Presbyterian members were in league with the Scottish army, and they passed a series of ordinances limiting the king's authority. Within weeks of its assembly, the Long Parliament impeached the king's two chief advisers, Archbishop Laud and Thomas Wentworth, the Earl of Strafford, on charges of treason. Soon afterwards in August 1641, Parliament abolished the Courts of Star Chamber and High Commission, institutions that had been crucial for Charles I in carrying out his Personal Rule without calling a legislature. And the Triennial Act, passed in January of the same year, guaranteed that Parliament would be called at least once every three years.

Another significant issue concerning the king and Parliament during the early 1640s involved the threat to England's security of an Irish rebellion. Parliament wanted to take control of the military, but Charles refused to accept any law that would give the legislature this authority. In March 1642, Parliament passed an ordinance – without the king's approval – granting itself executive power, and Charles responded by trying to mobilize a militia for his defense. The country was at war. The king left London and on 22 August 1642 raised the standard at Nottingham Castle; in October of the same year, he arrived in Oxford, where he began to set up an alternative government.

It might initially seem surprising that Charles, despite his administration's unpopularity, nevertheless garnered enough support to challenge his opponents militarily. But a combination of groups with different political agendas coalesced to oppose the reform-minded members of Parliament.[65] The king's supporters – who became known as Royalists – did not necessarily share an enthusiastic belief in Charles I as monarch but instead believed in the institution of monarchy and seem to have shared a concomitant anxiety that religious radicals had plans for a broad, social revolution. Perhaps the Puritans did not intend to stop with reforming the church and wanted to topple all of the nation's traditional rights and institutions.

On Parliament's side, opposition to Episcopacy united Presbyterians and Independents, but this coalition did not last; religious differences led to political disagreement. Whereas Presbyterians in Parliament favored a national church and a negotiated settlement with Charles I, the Independents wished to separate church and state and wanted to continue fighting the king's forces until they were defeated on the battlefield. The First Civil War concluded in 1646 without a definitive victory for either Parliament or the king. Charles recognized that he had no hope of achieving a military victory and gave himself to Scottish commissioners, who in turn handed him over to the English

The primary military conflicts

According to most historians' accounts, the British civil wars constitute three separate armed oppositions:

The First Civil War (1640–1646)	begins with the dissolution of the Short Parliament and ends with Charles I giving himself up to the Scots
The Second Civil War (1647–1649)	begins with the Scots turning over Charles to Parliament and ends with Charles's trial and execution
The Third Civil War (1649–1651)	begins with the establishment of a new form of government called the Council of State; it ends with the Battle of Worcester as Cromwell defeats Charles's son (the future Charles II), who forms an alliance with the Scottish army

Parliament. In 1647, the Second Civil War began, prompted in part by signs of growing divisions among factions within the legislature. While Charles secretly negotiated with the Scots to establish Presbyterianism as the national religion of England in exchange for military assistance, rebellions against Parliament broke out in Wales and north-west England. None of these new uprisings ultimately proved successful, however. Oliver Cromwell, acting as Lieutenant-General, led the New Model Army in defeating key Royalist insurgencies, and the second war came to an end within two years.

Historians attribute much of Parliament's military success to the New Model Army. What made the army new was its innovative structure: the Parliament's other, smaller armies contained men with strong regional ties, but the new model, first proposed by William Waller and then advanced by Cromwell, called for a cohesive, national fighting force that would supersede soldiers' parochial affiliations. With Thomas Fairfax as its first Captain-General and Commander-in-Chief, the army eventually grew into a highly motivated and well-disciplined military unit – although the army's early success probably stemmed more from its regular pay and Royalists' tactical blunders than the soldiers' professionalism and national pride.[66] In June 1645, just months after its formation, the New Model Army won a significant and decisive victory over the Royalists at Naseby, a battle that left the king's forces decimated and that precipitated the end of the First Civil War in the following year.

The New Model Army was not popular with everyone in Parliament. After Charles turned himself over to the Scots, Presbyterians within the legislature tried to disband the army as they pursued amnesty for the king. But other, more radical members of the House of Commons, who opposed making a deal with a figure they viewed as a tyrant, succeeded in keeping the army intact. The resulting division in the legislature culminated in late 1648 when Colonel Thomas Pride, acting on orders from the Army, forcibly purged Presbyterians from Parliament. The remaining members – who became known as the Rump – voted to bring Charles to trial. The trial began on 20 January 1649. Seven days later, the king was sentenced to death, and, three days afterwards, he was executed in the afternoon of Tuesday, 30 January. Britain had become a republican Commonwealth.

Charles's popularity increased dramatically after his death, fueled in part, as we saw in Chapter 1, by the success of *Eikon Basilike*, the best-selling book that purported to contain the king's private meditations as he awaited execution. It was this book that the government asked Milton to answer in *Eikonoklastes*.[67] On the other side, Cromwell continued to gain military and political power in the late 1640s and early 1650s. An ardent advocate for the king's trial and execution, Cromwell successfully led the army to Ireland in 1649 to suppress Royalist supporters of Charles's son, the Prince of Wales. It was for this military attack, as we also saw in Chapter 1, that the new government had requested Milton to lay the groundwork in *Observations on the Articles of Peace*.

Cromwell went on to succeed Fairfax as commander-in-chief of the New Model Army when Fairfax refused to lead troops into Scotland in 1650. The Scots had brokered a new deal with Prince Charles, who imitated his father's strategy: the prince agreed to impose Presbyterianism in England if the Scottish army supported his attempt to win back the throne. Cromwell led the army against Scotland and won decisive victories at Dunbar in 1650 and Worcester in 1651, effectively ending the third and final civil war. Prince Charles fled to Paris to join his mother in exile and stayed in France for the next nine years.

Thus began the period that historians have labeled the Interregnum (literally, "between reigns"), when England lacked a reigning monarch. Unfortunately for Independents during the Interregnum, they knew the type of government that they did not want – namely, a Stuart monarchy – but they could not agree on what type of governance best suited England, Ireland, Scotland, and Wales. After the king's execution, the Rump Parliament in 1649 appointed a new executive branch, a 41-member Council of State (34 of which were members of the House of Commons); the council's function was to ensure national security and enact the foreign and domestic policies legislated by the Rump. Milton, serving as Secretary for Foreign Tongues, reported to this executive body. The Rump, however, was supposed to be only a short-term fix, and members of the

Council of State expected the Rump's members to set up a new, representative body. When the Rump's plans continued to drag, Cromwell intervened, first in an attempt to moderate between the army and the Rump about the form of the new government; then on 20 April 1653 he led a group of soldiers to expel the Rump Parliament.

Within a few months, Cromwell set up a new, smaller Council of State, comprising 13 members with himself as its head, and made provisions for a new parliament (sometimes called the Barebones Parliament) which sat for the first time on 4 July of the same year. Some of its members, however, deemed the new parliament's legal and ecclesiastical proposals too radical, and six months after its formation, members worked to dissolve the legislature and install Cromwell as the leader of Britain for life. Parliament offered Cromwell the title of king, but he refused, wanting to distance himself from the Stuart monarchy. Instead, he recommended and accepted the title of Lord Protector in part to preserve connections with the nation's constitutional past: nobles or princes in the fifteenth century had sometimes adopted this title when a monarch was deemed unfit to rule because he was still a minor.

The Protectorate under Cromwell established religious liberty within a broad national church and unified England, Ireland, Scotland, and Wales under a permanent executive council and a single elected Parliament. But republicans believed that Cromwell's lifetime appointment undermined the principles for which they had fought the civil wars, and Presbyterians and radical sectarians remained disenchanted with the new government. Working as secretary for this experimental regime, Milton in *Defensio Secunda* (1654) blends panegyric with blunt political advice; he praises Cromwell's military achievements but warns the Lord Protector that he must now conduct a more difficult "warfare of peace" and expel avarice, ambition, and luxury from his administration (*CPW* IV: 681). Milton encourages Cromwell to preserve the country's fragile political liberty by, among other things, separating church and state, allowing for more freedom of the press, and establishing public education. He also urges Cromwell and his fellow citizens to avoid Royalists' excesses: "If you begin to slip into the same vices, to imitate those men, to seek the same goals, to clutch at the same vanities, you actually are royalists yourselves" (*CPW* IV: 681).

Throughout this turbulent period, the army remained loyal to Cromwell and helped him to maintain power as Lord Protector. But this group had no such allegiance to Cromwell's son. With the death of Oliver Cromwell on 3 September 1658, his eldest son Richard began ruling as Lord Protector in his father's place, a hereditary appointment that resembled monarchical succession and further rankled with republicans and sectaries. Lacking both the army's backing and his father's political savvy, Richard Cromwell quickly proved ineffective. He remained in power a mere seven months, and the army restored the Rump Parliament in 1659. The country was on its way back to monarchy and, as we saw in Chapter 1, Prince Charles was declared King of England on 8 May 1660, thus inaugurating the Restoration of monarchy.

In trying to comprehend the high politics of the civil wars and Interregnum, we need to remember that, despite the enormity of the events described here, national issues did not shape all aspects of Milton's life or even the lives of most British citizens during this period. The wars killed approximately 62,000 people between 1642 and 1646, possibly a larger percentage of England's total population than died in World War I.[68] But local events and the daily experience of living in provincial communities – although at times influenced by national issues – may have proved more important for many British citizens than church reform or the intrigues conducted at the palaces of Whitehall or Westminster. For many communities, the experience of war manifested itself primarily in the mundane form of a greater tax burden.

The effects of the conflict remain as difficult to isolate and measure as its various interlocking causes. Did the Long Parliament move Britain closer to a parliamentary democracy, as some Whig historians claim? Or, alternatively, did the events of the 1640s produce no long-term social changes, as revisionist historians argue? Surely the larger questions that the wars raised – about, for example, Christianity, monarchy, and toleration – would continue to shape national discourse long after Charles II took power. But as the new king established a policy of absolutism more rigid than his father's, the men and women who had opposed Charles I's administration must have despaired that the events of the preceding decades achieved nothing tangible. Milton represents one of many writers who in the immediate aftermath of the conflict struggled to determine what the wars had meant, why the revolution had failed, and what, if anything, the wars had accomplished.

Theology

"I follow no … heresy or sect" (*CPW* VI: 123), Milton writes in *De Doctrina Christiana*, his unfinished theological treatise that he composed most actively in the late 1650s and that remained unpublished until after his death. It is to this work that readers turn first to understand Milton's theology. Although we also can glean significant insight into Milton's religious beliefs by studying *Paradise Lost* and various of his other works, *De Doctrina Christiana* – even in its incomplete state – contains the most comprehensive account of his views, presented in the cool, expository style of a treatise. By genre, *De Doctrina Christiana* is a systematic theology, which means that to compose it Milton followed a logical method of classification derived from the work of the French humanist Petrus Ramus (1515–72). According to this method, students should begin with general propositions and proceed deductively, through dichotomies, toward particular principles. As Milton explains his process of composition in the treatise's first chapter, he wished "to assist the reader's memory by collecting together, as it were, into a single book texts which are scattered here and there throughout the Bible, and by systematizing them under definite headings, in order to make reference easy" (*CPW* VI: 127).

In form and much of the content, Milton's treatise resembles other Protestant systematics written during the sixteenth and seventeenth centuries. Milton's nephew, Edward Phillips (*EL* 61), first pointed out the specific influence of William Ames's *Morrow of Sacred Divinity* (1642) and Johannes Wolleb's *Abridgement of Christian Divinity* (1650), and Milton himself explains that to compose his tract he early on went "carefully through some of the shorter systems of theologians" before turning his "attention to more diffuse volumes of divinity" (*CPW* VI: 119).

But if, as Gordon Campbell has discussed, Protestant systematics typically address the same subjects and cite the same proof texts, some of the doctrines in Milton's treatise are unique to his personal theology.[69] As the quotation at the start of this section indicates, readers of Milton's works cannot classify his religious beliefs according to a single church or sect. He came to arrive at his points of Reformed doctrine by working directly from scriptures, which he believed were inspired by God. He thus agreed with some widely held Christian beliefs but he also deviated in important ways from the English church and the Book of Common Prayer – although, he insisted, such deviations were not heretical:

> before the New Testament was written, the word heresy, whenever
> it was used as an accusation, was applied only to something which
> contradicted the teaching of the apostles as it passed from mouth to
> mouth … On the same grounds I hold that, since the compilation of
> the New Testament, nothing can correctly be called heresy unless it
> contradicts that. For my own part, I devote my attention to the Holy
> Scriptures alone.   (*CPW* VI: 123)

Adhering closely to this simple exegetical principle, Milton's treatise contains neither a series of citations to theologians nor a detailed explanation of his own spiritual development. Instead, as Milton announces near the start, he has focused on scriptures and endeavored to "cram my pages even to overflowing, with quotations drawn from all parts of the Bible and to leave as little space as possible for my own words" (*CPW* VI: 122).

But even as Milton appeals to the Bible's ultimate authority in formulating the doctrines of his belief, readers may be surprised by his humility. Above all, Milton in *De Doctrina Christiana* promotes "free discussion and inquiry" and encourages readers to think for themselves and "Assess this work as God's spirit shall direct you" (*CPW* VI: 121, 124). That he describes his theological treatise as "my dearest and best possession" (*CPW* VI: 121) indicates how seriously he took his beliefs, but he does not insist that readers should agree with his biblical interpretations. Instead, he wishes to impress on readers the importance of arriving at truth on their own – "to make people understand how much it is in the interests of the Christian religion that men should be free not only to sift and winnow any doctrine, but also openly to give their opinions of it and even to write about it, according to what each believes" (*CPW* VI: 122).

Arianism

One of Milton's most heterodox theological convictions was his opposition to the Trinity, the widely held belief among Christians that treats the Father, Son, and Holy Ghost as three different persons with the same essence or being. When Milton adopted this view is not clear. In 1629 in "On the Morning of Christ's Nativity," for example, Milton still seems to accept a triune deity; he describes how the Son was "wont at Heav'n's high council table, / To sit the midst of trinal unity" (lines 10–11), and even during the anti-prelatical controversy of the 1640s Milton was still envisioning a "Tri-*personall* GODHEAD" (*Of Reformation*, *CPW* I: 614). Although biblical exegetes have found support for the Trinity in various places in Scripture, the doctrine in its origin derived largely from 1 John 5:7–8, a passage sometimes called the Johannine Comma ("comma" here meaning a section or part):

> For there are three that bear record in heaven, the Father, the Word, and the Holy Ghost: and these three are one. And there are three that bear witness in earth, the Spirit, and the water, and the blood: and these three agree in one.

Modern biblical scholars have long established this verse as a forged medieval interpolation; it began as a marginal gloss and was later translated into Greek and inserted in John's first epistle. But Milton and some of his contemporaries – most notably Isaac Newton and Milton's friend the Dutch jurist Hugo Grotius – already doubted the comma's authenticity. As Milton observes in *De Doctrina Christiana*, the verse lacked sufficient textual authority: it does not appear in "the Syriac or the other two Oriental versions [of the Bible], the Arabic and the Ethiopic, nor in the majority of the ancient Greek codices. Moreover, in those manuscripts where it does appear a remarkable variety of readings occurs" (*CPW* VI: 221).

Members of the heretical Christian sect called Socinians also rejected the authority of 1 John 5:7–8, but this group went further than Milton and propounded that the Son did not exist at all until the Incarnation. Milton's heterodox Christology, by comparison, could be more properly described as Arian – that is, in accordance with the theology of Arius, an early Christian in Alexandria (*c.* 250–336). Milton took the heretical position that a Son who is said to be "begotten" cannot be self-existent and is thus not the supreme God (*CPW* VI: 263). That Milton's chapter on the Son in *De Doctrina Christiana* is by far the longest and the only one with its own preface suggests the importance that he attached to the question of the Son's divinity. Primarily, he objects to the Son's equation with God on logical grounds. Milton emphasizes that "nothing can be said of the one God that is inconsistent with his unity, and which makes him both one and not one" (*CPW* VI: 148). In multiple polemical passages in the treatise Milton returns to the same hard arithmetic to insist on a single godhead: he writes, for example, that God is "without question numerically one" (*CPW* VI: 147); that "It is quite clear that the Father alone is a self-existent God" (*CPW* VI: 218); and that "the divine essence … is always one" and "cannot possibly generate or be generated by an essence the same as itself" (*CPW* VI: 263). Milton concludes that "the Son undoubtedly comes after the Father not only in rank but also in essence" (*CPW* VI: 263), and he dismisses the Trinity as a "bizarre and senseless idea" and "an extremely absurd paradox" maintained only with "the maximum of obstinacy and argumentativeness" (*CPW* VI: 212, 218).

But if Milton in *De Doctrina Christiana* argues forcefully and at length for the Son's distinction from and inferiority to the Father, Milton's Arianism in *Paradise Lost* is not as explicit. The necessarily less direct style of presentation in an epic poem has misled some modern readers to think that Milton depicts the Son as merely subordinate to God but still co-eternal and of the same essence.[70] Most important for dispelling such a misperception is the Son's status as created in time; instead of existing eternally like God, the Son is "of all creation first" (III.383). As God explains to Adam, He Himself is "alone / From all eternity, for none I know / Second to me or like, equal much less" (VIII.405–7). While readers might be initially confused that the Son nevertheless sits "throned in highest bliss / Equal to God, and equally enjoying / God-like fruition" (III.305–7), this description applies to the Son's position, not to his nature. And, while the narrator refers to the Son as "God" in a few places in the epic, this name change only occurs when the Son goes to earth and acts as God's minister (for example, X.97–102). As Milton explains in *De Doctrina Christiana*, "The name of God is given to judges because, in a way, when they administer justice, they are God's substitutes. The Son ... was a God on both counts, as messenger and as judge ..." (*CPW* VI: 237–38).

Acting on the Father's behalf, the Son in *Paradise Lost* accomplishes a great deal: he drives the rebel angels "out / From all Heav'n's bounds into the utter deep" (VI.715–16); he is sent to create the universe and "bid the deep / Within appointed bounds be heav'n and earth" (VII.166–67); he volunteers to save humankind, exchanging his "life for life" (III.236); and, on Judgment Day, "All knees to [him] shall bow" and he "shalt judge / Bad men and angels" (III.321, 331–32). In each of these instances, however, God enables the Son's accomplishment by transferring the necessary power, virtue, grace, or judgment. God alone in the epic is described as the "omnipotent, / Immutable, immortal, infinite, / Eternal King" (III.372–74), whereas the Son must earn his exalted position and repeatedly proves himself "By merit more than birthright" (III.309).

Holy Spirit

Milton's heterodox treatment of the Holy Spirit in *De Doctrina Christiana*, while comparatively brief, underscores his rejection of the Trinity. Milton begins by denying the widely accepted idea, put forth most influentially by Augustine in *De Trinitate*, that the Holy Spirit was breathed forth or emanated by God, a coming forth that theologians referred to as the spirit's "procession" or "spiration." Milton acknowledges that Christ in John 20:22 gives the Holy Spirit to his disciples by breathing on them but then asks incredulously, "who, on this evidence, would dare to maintain, in a discussion of the nature of the Holy Spirit, that it was breathed from the Father and the Son? The terms 'emanation' and 'procession' are irrelevant to the question of the Holy Spirit's nature" (*CPW* VI: 281). Instead, Milton cautions that the Bible "says nothing about what the Holy Spirit is like, how it exists, or where it comes from" (*CPW* VI: 281). Based on his reading of scriptures, Milton concludes that the Spirit, like the Son, is neither co-eternal nor co-essential with God; on the contrary, God created the Spirit, "not by natural necessity, but by the free will of the agent, maybe before the foundations of the world were laid, but after the Son, to whom he is far inferior, was made" (*CPW* VI: 298). Again, Milton returns to the simple logic that if God is one, God cannot be two or three: "as the Spirit of God is actually and numerically distinct from

God himself, it cannot possibly be essentially one God with him whose Spirit it is" (*CPW* VI: 288).

In *Paradise Lost*, Milton refers and alludes to the Holy Spirit in various places, but it plays a much less prominent role than the Son in the epic's narrative. As in *De Doctrina Christiana*, Milton approaches the Spirit not as part of the godhead but as a way of describing God's virtue and creative power. Thus, in the proem to Book I, the speaker calls on the "Spirit" that at the world's creation "Dove-like sat'st brooding on the vast abyss / And mad'st it pregnant" (I.17, 21–22). Here the poet directly asks the Holy Spirit to "Instruct," "Illumine," and improve him ("what is low raise and support," I.19, 23). Critics may disagree whether the Holy Spirit is the same as the "heav'nly Muse" whom the speaker initially invokes (I.6) and later identifies as Urania (VII.1), but, regardless of this question, Milton does not equate the Spirit with the Father. Instead, perhaps presumptuously, Milton associates his own poetic creation with the Spirit and the creation of the world, specifically alluding to Genesis 1:2, "And the earth was without form, and void; and darkness *was* upon the face of the deep. And the Spirit of God moved upon the face of the waters." Later, Milton returns to this imagery when Raphael describes how God created the universe "by" his Son and sent along His "overshadowing Spirit and might" (VII. 163, 165). Once again, in reworking the verse from Genesis, Milton stresses the Spirit's creative virtue: "on the wat'ry calm / His brooding wings the Spirit of God outspread, / And vital virtue infused, and vital warmth / Throughout the fluid mass" (VII.234–37).

Other references to the Holy Spirit in *Paradise Lost* cast it as a gift to the descendants of Adam and Eve so that after the Fall they can spread God's word and resist further temptations. As Michael explains to Adam, God will send a "comforter … / The promise of the Father, who shall dwell / His Spirit within them" (XII.486–88). God's Spirit, Michael adds, will "guide them in all truth," endue them "with wondrous gifts," and help them to "evangelize the nations" (XII.490, 499–500). This comforter is presumably the same as what God earlier calls "My umpire conscience" that he "will place within" the descendants of Adam and Eve "as a guide" for accepting His grace (III.194–95). Perhaps more important, both God's and Michael's descriptions seem to correspond to the speaker's opening appeal to the inward-dwelling "Spirit, that dost prefer / Before all temples th' upright heart and pure" (I.17–18). God's and Michael's comments thus help to establish the high stakes that Milton sets out for himself in *Paradise Lost*. Invoking the Spirit in the proem to Book I, Milton is not only seeking inspiration for his poetic creation but also calling on the apostolic and moral authority that God's spirit can grant.

Milton's God

Probably the defining quality of Milton's God is his unknowableness, a characteristic that has no doubt contributed to some readers' dissatisfaction with the epic's theodicy. How can Milton in *Paradise Lost* "justify the ways" of a God who mostly remains invisible, sitting in judgment in the "pure empyrean … / High throned above all highth" (I.26, III.57–58)? The narrator establishes God's inaccessibility early in Book III as the angels acclaim – and distinguish between – the Father's justice and the Son's mercy:

> Thee Father first they sung omnipotent,
> Immutable, immortal, infinite,
> Eternal King; thee Author of all being,
> Fountain of light, thyself invisible
> Amidst the glorious brightness where thou sitt'st
> Throned inaccessible, but when thou shad'st
> The full blaze of thy beams, and through a cloud
> Drawn round about thee like a radiant shrine,
> Dark with excessive bright thy skirts appear,
> Yet dazzle Heav'n, that brightest Seraphim
> Approach not, but with both wings veil their eyes.   (III.372–82)

This passage effectively encapsulates the chief characteristics of Milton's God – all-powerful, undying, infinite, and ultimately beyond human understanding. Even when God sits behind a cloud, as the narrator here explains, the highest angels must cover their eyes to approach God's dazzling brilliance. I discuss Milton's depiction of God more fully in Chapter 4, but we should note in the above lines that Milton is already suggesting both the audacity and inherent limitation of his divine portrayal. He dares to include God within his epic but indicates that God defies the metaphysical reality of the epic's narrative and can never be fully comprehended, by Milton or his readers.

In *De Doctrina Christiana*, Milton also emphasizes God's unknowableness: "When we talk about knowing God, it must be understood in terms of man's limited powers of comprehension … God has revealed only so much of himself as our minds can conceive and the weakness of our nature can bear" (*CPW* VI: 133). But just as Raphael in *Paradise Lost* tries to tell Adam and Eve about the War in Heaven in terms that they will comprehend – "what surmounts the reach / Of human sense, I shall delineate so, / By lik'ning spiritual to corporal forms" (V.571–73) – so Milton himself subscribed to what theologians call a theory of accommodation; that is, Milton accepted the authority of scriptural passages that depict God in human terms. As Milton observes, for example,

God in the Bible endures grief (Genesis 6:6), feels refreshed (Exodus 31:17), and experiences fear (Deuteronomy 32:27). Milton emphasizes that we should not hesitate to accept such human-sounding qualities if God assigns them to himself, but we should not assume that such emotions are the same for human beings as they are for God: "what is imperfect and weak in us is, when ascribed to God, utterly perfect and utterly beautiful" (*CPW* VI: 136). Milton also adamantly objects to efforts by exegetes to assign additional human qualities to God to make God easier to understand. Milton's was a limited theory of accommodation, no doubt stemming from his underlying belief in the sufficiency of Scripture. God in the Bible might at times condescend to make himself conceivable to us, but "he has brought himself down to our level expressly to prevent our being carried beyond the reach of human comprehension, and outside the written authority of scripture, into vague subtleties of speculation" (*CPW* VI: 133–34).

Arminianism

Critics generally agree that Milton was Arminian, but we don't know exactly when he adopted this theology. As we saw in the preceding discussion of the civil wars, Arminians rejected the Calvinist doctrine that God predestined humankind from eternity as either saved or damned; instead, Arminians emphasized that each person can exercise free will and accept or refuse God's universal grace.[71] As late as 1644 in the second edition of *The Doctrine and Discipline of Divorce*, Milton identifies himself as a Calvinist, defending predestination from "The Jesuits, and that sect among us which is nam'd of *Arminius*," who "are wont to charge us of making God the author of sinne" (*CPW* II: 293). In the same year in *Areopagitica*, Milton continues to associate Arminians and Catholics: he writes that "many have bin corrupted by studying the comments of Jesuits" in the same way that "the acute and distinct *Arminius* was perverted meerly by the perusing of a namelesse discours writt'n at *Delf*, which at first he took in hand to confute" (*CPW* II: 519–20). While "acute" and "distinct" suggest Milton's respect for Arminius, the comparison of Arminianism with Jesuitical thinking indicates Milton's ongoing commitment to Calvinism, as does the specific choice of "perverted," a word he later uses to describe Satan in *Paradise Lost* (XII.547).

Yet part of Milton's argument against pre-publication censorship in *Areopagitica* already implies an Arminian position. As Maurice Kelley first observed, Milton's insistence on the responsibility of individual readers challenges the fundamental assumption of high Calvinism.[72] When, for example, Milton asserts, "that which purifies us is triall, and triall is by what is contrary,"

Arminianism and Sonnet 7

Milton's Sonnet 7 "How soon hath Time," probably composed around 1633, may also already intimate a burgeoning Arminian perspective:

> How soon hath Time the subtle thief of youth,
>   Stol'n on his wing my three and twentieth year!
> My hasting days fly on with full career,
> But my late spring no bud or blossom shew'th.
> Perhaps my semblance might deceive the truth,
>   That I to manhood am arrived so near,
>   And inward ripeness doth much less appear,
>   That some more timely-happy spirits endu'th.
> Yet be it less or more, or soon or slow,
>   It shall be still in strictest measure even
>   To that same lot, however mean or high,
> Toward which Time leads me, and the will of Heaven;
>   All is, if I have grace to use it so,
>   As ever in my great Taskmaster's eye.

Here the speaker overcomes his anxiety about a lack of "inward ripeness" (line 7) by recalling that, regardless of his efforts, he will receive "that same lot, however mean or high, / Toward which Time leads me, and the will of Heaven" (lines 11–12). Milton concludes the sonnet with an emphatic spondee, "All is," which suggests a Calvinist relinquishing of control: God is omnipotent, and all is decided according to God's plan. Milton, however, then immediately inserts a caesura and the conditional clause, "if I have grace to use it so" (line 13), which together suggest that he accepted some responsibility for achieving his "lot" and was not relying entirely on providence. The sonnet also underscores the importance of individual will by deviating from the expected rhyme scheme in the sestet. The egregiously irregular pattern of *cde dce* demonstrates that the poet can "use" and make his own the preordained forms – the "strictest measure" (line 10) – that he inherits.

he hardly sounds like a Calvinist (*CPW* II: 515). Or, to take another example, Milton criticizes the "foolish tongues" who "complain of divin Providence for suffering *Adam* to transgresse"; Milton argues that, on the contrary, God gave Adam "freedom to choose" so that he could demonstrate his own merit: "If every action which is good, or evill in man … were to be under … prescription, and compulsion, what were vertue but a name, what praise could be then due to well-doing" (*CPW* II: 527).

By the time Milton began compiling and composing *De Doctrina Christiana* he clearly embraced an Arminian plan of predestination. Here Milton forcefully asserts that the "object of the divine plan was that angels and men alike should be endowed with free will" (*CPW* VI: 163), and he adduces copious examples from the Bible to argue that God's foreknowledge has no external effects:

> By virtue of his wisdom God decreed the creation of angels and men as beings gifted with reason and thus with free will. At the same time he foresaw the direction in which they would tend when they used this absolutely unimpaired freedom. What then? Shall we say that God's providence or foreknowledge imposes any necessity upon them? Certainly not: no more than if some human being possessed the same foresight. For an occurrence foreseen with absolute certainty by a human being will no less certainly take place than one foretold by God … [N]othing happens because God has foreseen it, but rather he has foreseen each event because each is the result of particular causes which, by his decree, work quite freely and with which he is thoroughly familiar. So the outcome does not rest with God who foresees it, but only with the man whose action God foresees …   (*CPW* VI: 164).

Although we ought not to treat *De Doctrina Christiana* as a gloss on *Paradise Lost*, the idea Milton emphasizes here, that divine providence resembles human foreknowledge, is dramatized in the final books of his epic as Michael teaches Adam "what shall come in future days / To thee and to thy offspring" (XI.357–58). Michael "wak'st" Adam "to foresight" (XI.368), but the angel does not possess nor bestow on Adam any authority over the events that are revealed. As Adam laments the consequence of his disobedience, he concludes that "no man [should] seek / Henceforth to be foretold what shall befall / Him or his children" because "neither [his or his children's future] his foreknowledge can prevent" (XI.770–73). Adam, in other words, can control his own choices, but even with foreknowledge he cannot control the repercussions of those choices for himself or his offspring.

God's reference in *Paradise Lost* to a group of believers "of peculiar grace / Elect about the rest" (III.183–84) raises the possibility that late in life Milton continued to subscribe to some Calvinist articles and specifically accepted that extraordinary souls were saved regardless of their repentance and obedience. But this category of believers could alternatively serve only to sum up God's preceding explanation of all those souls who will be saved by God's "grace … / Freely vouchsafed" (III.174–75), as opposed to those who will be excluded from God's mercy because they refuse to repent and obey.

Certainly other passages in Milton's epic dovetail with the Arminian theology of *De Doctrina Christiana* and emphasize that both the celestial powers and Adam and Eve are free to accept or reject God's grace. God announces, for example, that he "created all th' ethereal Powers / And spirits" to be "Sufficient … though free to fall" (III.99–101), and He places complete responsibility for the angels' rebellion on the angels themselves: "Freely they stood who stood, and fell who fell. / Not free, what proof could they have giv'n sincere / Of true allegiance, constant faith or love" (III.102–4). Raphael similarly explains to Adam that the rebel angels "headlong themselves … threw / Down from the verge of Heav'n" (VI.864–65); the rebels could have preserved their happy state simply by obeying God: "firm they might have stood, / Yet fell" (VI.911–12). Satan, too, grudgingly admits in his soliloquy to the sun that he can only blame himself for his fall: "Hadst thou the same free will and power to stand? / Thou hadst" (IV.66–67).

In the case of Adam and Eve, God plainly asserts about their fall that "if I foreknew, / Foreknowledge had no influence" (III.117–18). After they eat the forbidden fruit, God reiterates to the assembled angels that humanity's sin was not His fault: "no decree of mine / Concurring to necessitate his fall, / Or touch with lightest moment of impulse / His free will, to her own inclining left / In even scale" (X.43–47). God, in other words, did not influence the choices of Adam and Eve, as he treats the balanced scales as something separate from his person and "lightest moment" signifies the most gentle pressure that could be applied on the scales' trays. According to the logic of this imagery, the scales themselves do not decree the choices made by God's creations, unless God were to tip the balance with his thumb.

Creation, matter, and the soul

In the invocation in Book I of *Paradise Lost*, the speaker recalls "In the beginning how the heavens and earth / Rose out of Chaos" (lines 9–10). Here, in short, is Milton's rejection of the orthodox doctrine of *creatio ex nihilo* ("creation out of nothing") in favor of a Platonic notion of *creatio ex Deo* ("creation out of God"). Milton believed, in other words, that "some sort of matter" must have existed prior to the world's creation (*CPW* VI: 307), and he concludes that God created all things out of this unformed matter, what in *Paradise Lost* he calls God's "dark materials" (II.916).

Once again, Milton's theological treatise provides a lucid explanation of the reasoning behind his heterodox belief. Milton begins with Genesis 1:1, "In the beginning God created the heaven and the earth." He notes that the past tense of the Hebrew verb "to create" (*bara*) always means "to make out of something," and he argues that merely by definition creation requires a material cause – or, more simply put, that something cannot come from nothing. The matter needed for creation, Milton thus deduces, must have always existed, either separate from God, which Milton believed was impossible, or having originated from God Himself. As God is "the first, absolute and sole cause of all things" (*CPW* VI: 307), Milton concludes that God must be the material cause for all creation. That is, all things come not just "from God" but also "out of God" (*CPW* VI: 310).

Milton in *De Doctrina Christiana* goes on to argue that the original matter was good and "contained the seeds of all subsequent good … It was in a confused and disordered state at first, but afterwards God made it ordered and beautiful" (*CPW* VI: 308). Milton seems to develop this doctrine in *Paradise Lost* by depicting the "confused and disordered state" of original matter as the realm of chaos through which Satan flies on his way to earth. While the personified figure Chaos assists Satan in his search for God's newly created world, the realm over which Chaos holds sway is at least neutral and more likely seems morally good.[73] The realm contains pure potential, "neither sea, nor shore, nor air, nor fire, / But all these in their pregnant causes mixed / Confus'dly" (II.912–14). Admittedly, the adverb "Confus'dly" sounds pejorative, and Milton's description of chaos as a "vast immeasurable abyss / Outrageous as a sea, dark, wasteful, wild" (VII.211–12) sounds more threatening than constructive. But this realm serves an essential divine function: it houses the raw materials that God acts upon to form all created things. As Milton succinctly describes it, chaos is "The womb of Nature and perhaps her grave" (II.911). Here the Son takes God's "golden compasses" to "circumscribe / This universe" (VII.225–27), and here God, "th' Almighty Maker," can return if he ever wishes "to create more worlds" (II.915–16).

Milton also emphasizes that God alone represents the principal cause in all acts of creation. This position, which stems from Milton's opposition to the Trinity, is the other crucial feature of his theory of creation. In contrast to the widely held belief that the Son was the joint cause of all created things, Milton relegates the Son to a secondary role: "the Son is only he *through* whom all things are, and is therefore the less principal cause" (*CPW* VI: 302). We can piece together the sequence of creation in *Paradise Lost* as follows: God first created the Son (III.383–84), then the ethereal powers (V.835–39), and then our universe (VII.163–67). In the latter two acts, the Son participates prominently, but only as God's instrument and not as God himself. Focusing in *De Doctrina Christiana* on Colossians 1:15 and 1:18, Milton explains that "Christ is not called merely the *beginning of creation*, but *the beginning of God's creation*, and that can only mean that he was the first of the things which God created. How, then, can he be God himself?" (*CPW* VI: 302, 303).

In Chapter 4, I will discuss more fully Milton's material theory of creation and its implications for the specific depictions in *Paradise Lost* of Satan and Adam and Eve, but we should note here that Milton's understanding of creation may have also influenced two of his heterodox beliefs about the soul: mortalism and traducianism.

The mortalist heresy contends that the soul dies with the body. Having done away with the Catholic concept of Purgatory, Protestants had to explain what happens to a person's soul after death but before the last judgment. Most Protestants, following Calvin, believed that the soul is immortal and returns to God after death.[74] But Milton in *De Doctrina Christiana* offers instead a mortalist explanation, which seems to reflect the material philosophy that underpins his depiction of the "embryon atoms" that God uses to create in *Paradise Lost* (II.900). Milton once again posits an intimate connection between body and soul: he argues that with the body's death the soul also dies and remains dormant until its resurrection on Judgment Day. Milton writes in *De Doctrina Christiana* that he can state this doctrine so emphatically because he finds support for it throughout the Bible – in "virtually innumerable passages" (*CPW* VI: 400). But once again he also relies on logic to justify his belief: "what could be more absurd than that the part which sinned most (i.e., the soul), should escape the sentence of death; or that the body, which was just as immortal as the soul before sin brought death into the world, should alone pay the penalty for sin by dying although it had no actual part in the sin?" (*CPW* VI: 401).

Milton's theory of matter also probably led him to adopt a traducianist view of the soul. In contrast to the orthodox doctrine of creationism, which posits that God gives each human being at birth a freshly created soul, Milton argues that parents must pass along their souls to a child because they pass along original sin: "if sin is transmitted from the parents to the child in the act of generation, then the πρῶτον δεκτικὸν or original subject of sin, namely the rational soul, must also be propagated by the parents" (*CPW* VI: 321). Milton, as we have seen, came to embrace an Arminian doctrine of free will, but he did not find free will incompatible with the inescapability of hereditary sin. He explains the latter in material terms: because the human soul is contained in all parts of the body and "wholly in any given part of that body," the soul of "the parents, or at least of the father," must be present in all human seed – "that intimate and most noble part of the body" – and thus transmitted in the act of generation to the unborn child (*CPW* VI: 321–22). Each person is born in a sinful state, in other words, because each soul already bears the effects of the parents' sins. Echoing his discussion of the universe's creation, Milton sums up his materialist philosophy to justify the traducianist heresy: "Nearly everyone agrees that all form – and the human soul is a kind of form – is produced by the power of matter" ("*ex potentia materiae*") (*CPW* VI: 322).

Atonement

Milton in *Paradise Lost* adopts the widely accepted practice among Protestants of borrowing juridical language to describe the salvation of humankind as a legal transaction. According to this model, the Son represents the advocate of humans, and God the judge. Thus in Book III of *Paradise Lost*, God pronounces, "Die he or Justice must; unless for him / Some other able, and as willing, pay / The rigid satisfaction, death for death" (210–12). Similarly, in *De Doctrina Christiana*, Milton writes, "Christ … submitted himself voluntarily, both in life and in death, to the divine justice, in order to suffer all the things which were necessary for our redemption" (*CPW* VI: 438).

Given Milton's staunch anti-trinitarianism, such full-throated support for the atonement may seem surprising. The traditional thinking behind the atonement – most influentially put forth by the medieval theologian Anselm (*c.* 1033–1109) – is that God had to become human to make amends for the enormity of the fall of Adam and Eve. But if Milton, as we have seen, repeatedly insists that the Son is not the supreme God, how could he have believed that Jesus was both God and man? The vagueness of the explanation in *De Doctrina Christiana* is matched only by Milton's apparent confidence in it. He asserts that Christ somehow contained a "mutual hypostatic union of two natures, … of two essences, of two substances and consequently of two persons." For Milton, "It is quite certain this is so," but, he adds, "We do not know how it is so, and it is best for us to be ignorant of things which God wishes to remain secret" (*CPW* VI: 424). Readers of Milton might not expect such a learned author to accept so willingly the limits of his knowledge, but in *De Doctrina Christiana* he sounds pleased with the divine mystery:

> How much better for us, then, to know only that the Son of God, our Mediator, was made flesh and that he is called and is in fact both God and man … As God has not revealed to us how this comes about it is much better for us to hold our tongues and be wisely ignorant.   (*CPW* VI: 424)

Perhaps more surprisingly, whereas Milton arrived gradually at some of his heretical doctrines – most notably, as we have seen, his Arianism and Arminianism – he espoused a consistent position on the paradox of Christ's humanity and divinity. We find him defending the atonement not only in *Paradise Lost* and *De Doctrina Christiana* but also as early as "Upon the Circumcision," probably composed around 1633.

Less settled and more controversial in Milton's thinking was the means by which individuals can secure salvation. Milton asserts in the opening chapter of Book II of *De Doctrina Christiana*, "What chiefly constitutes the true worship of God is eagerness to do good works" (*CPW* VI: 637). However, he offers an antinomian interpretation of "good works" – that is, a person's actions need not conform to the Ten Commandments, but instead should be based on faith:

> Thus if I keep the Sabbath, in accordance with the ten commandments, when my faith prompts me to do otherwise, my precise compliance with the commandments will be counted as sin ... or unlawful behavior. It is faith that justifies, not compliance with the commandments; and only that which justifies can make any work good.   (*CPW* VI: 639)

This religious principle may seem inconsistent with the emphasis on the authority of scriptures in the rest of *De Doctrina Christiana*.[75] If, as we have seen, Milton's method in his theological treatise was to "cram my pages even to overflowing, with quotations drawn from all parts of the Bible" (*CPW* VI: 122), we would not expect him to suggest suddenly that an individual's faith trumps God's word. Yet Milton in this chapter of *De Doctrina Christiana* clearly qualifies the significance of the Bible, what he calls "the external authority for our faith," and favors instead the internal "Spirit," which he deems the "pre-eminent and supreme authority" and "the individual possession of each man" (*CPW* VI: 587). In contrast to the scriptures, which, he notes, sometimes contain various errors – "particularly the New Testament, has often been liable to corruption and is, in fact, corrupt" (*CPW* VI: 587) – the illumination of the Spirit comes directly from God and should thus guide each believer.

Milton's argument here begins to explain his dissatisfaction with organized religion and church hierarchy; he believed that anyone who follows the internal Spirit of God has the same authority for understanding truth and need not rely on bishops or a prescriptive prayer book to know what to believe and think. Aside from the scriptures, he proposes, all other outward forms of religious authority encroach on the internal presence of God: "if anyone imposes any kind of sanction or dogma upon believers against their will, whether he acts in the name of the church or of a Christian magistrate, he is placing a yoke not only upon man but upon the Holy Spirit itself" (*CPW* VI: 590).

Milton's appeal in *De Doctrina Christiana* to the supreme authority of an internal Spirit dovetails with a wide range of ideas in his works – from the invocation to the Spirit in Book I of *Paradise Lost*, to his encouraging of readers to devise their own doctrines at the start of *De Doctrina Christiana*, and to his willingness to challenge church authority in his anti-prelatical and divorce tracts. But Milton probably takes this conviction the furthest in *Areopagitica* as he argues that people must think for themselves: "A man may be a heretick in the truth; and if he beleeve things only because his Pastor sayes so, or the

Assembly so determins, without knowing other reason, though his belief be true, yet the very truth he holds, becomes his heresie" (*CPW* II: 543). Here Milton suggests not only the supreme authority of the individual conscience but also the wrongheadedness of following instead an earthly power – even when that power is leading a person toward God's truth. As Milton repeatedly demonstrates in his own theological treatise, he was willing to deviate from accepted doctrine by carefully studying Scripture and following his own inner conscience. True religion, as he contends in *Areopagitica* and shows in the assembly of his personal theology in *De Doctrina Christiana*, depends on a combination of "reason" and "belief." The only heresy for Milton is the doctrine arrived at without both of these.

Chapter 3

Prose

Shortly after the Restoration, Charles II seems to have offered Milton a position in the new government. The details of the proposal remain sketchy, but that three versions of the anecdote survive from three different sources suggests that it contains some truth. According to Milton's friend and former student Cyriack Skinner, Milton "was visited at his house on Bun-hill [see Figure 1] by a Chief Officer of State, and desir'd to imploy his Pen on thir behalfe" (*EL* 32). This account echoes the version of events that the eighteenth-century scholar Thomas Newton heard from Milton's widow. She reportedly said "that her husband was applied to by message from the King, and invited to write for the Court."[1] The third version of the incident comes from the eighteenth-century biographer Jonathan Richardson, who learned about it from Henry Bendish, the son of one of Oliver Cromwell's granddaughters. Richardson's account is the most specific: "Soon after the Restoration the King Offer'd to Employ this Pardon'd Man as his Latin Secretary, the Post in which he Serv'd *Cromwell* with So much Integrity and Ability" (*EL* 280).

The value of knowing about the king's offer – regardless of the episode's exact details – lies in part in what it implies about Milton's contemporary reputation as a prose-writer. Even after vociferously defending regicide and impugning Charles I's character, Milton was deemed such a commanding or at least capable writer of prose that Charles's son could have plausibly put aside the author's republican past and employed his talents on behalf of the restored monarchy. Skinner specifically introduces the anecdote to make this point: he wishes to show that Milton in his later years "was ... farr from being reckon'd disaffected" (*EL* 32). Newton and Richardson, however, emphasize instead Milton's unwavering principles. According to these early biographers, both Milton's widow and Cromwell's great-grandson recalled the king's offer and Milton's decision to turn it down as evidence of the author's integrity. Milton's widow remembered her husband's "answer was ... that such a behaviour would be very inconsistent with his former conduct, for he had never yet employed his pen against his conscience."[2] And Bendish reportedly said that "*Milton* Withstood the Offer; the Wife press'd his Compliance. *Thou art in the*

Right (says he) *You as Other Women, would ride in your Coach; for Me, My Aim is to Live and Dye an Honest Man*" (*EL* 280).

The story of Milton's job offer after the Restoration provides a fitting introduction to a discussion of his prose works: the anecdote not only reminds us of the poet's formidable polemical abilities but also suggests the idealism behind his political tracts. Milton sometimes wrote for money, as when he worked for the government during the Interregnum, but, so far as we can tell, he always wrote according to his conscience. His own self-deprecating assessment of his prose-writing as the product of merely his "left hand" (*CPW* I: 808) – a criticism based on unfavorable references to left-handedness in the Bible (e.g., Matthew 25:33) – belies how seriously he approached prose and how deeply he cared about the subjects he addressed. As we saw in Chapter 1, Milton intruded into prose works such as *The Reason of Church-Government Urg'd against Prelaty* and *Pro Populo Anglicano Defensio Secunda* to meditate on his life and writings. He did so not just because he perceived a rhetorical advantage to writing about himself in public texts but because he had a personal investment in the debates in which he participated.

This chapter focuses on the meaning and significance of Milton's major prose works, grouped chronologically by the controversies and subjects that interested him: church government, divorce, free speech, and the Commonwealth. The following discussion addresses both Milton's motives and the tracts' historical contexts; other topics include the rhetorical strategy of individual arguments and the contemporary impact of Milton's efforts. Today, beginning readers of Milton may be most interested in his prose for what it reveals about his life and poetic aspirations. But collectively these texts provide a fascinating glimpse into the culture's concerns and illustrate the evolution of both Milton's writing style and his religious and political thinking.

Anti-prelatical tracts

Within less than a year, between May 1641 and April 1642, Milton wrote five pamphlets criticizing the English church's Episcopal power structure. This issue might not seem compelling to modern readers, but Milton and his contemporaries felt that much was at stake in the controversy, and ultimately, as discussed in Chapter 2, the question of how best to worship God and organize the church contributed to the outbreak of civil war in the middle of the seventeenth century. The controversy reached back to the reign of Elizabeth I (1558–1603), who responded to a growing diversity of religious opinions by permitting greater latitude in the practices of individual congregations.

Elizabeth's successor, however, had little tolerance for religious diversity. James I (1603–25) wholeheartedly endorsed an Episcopal form of church government and interpreted critiques of Episcopacy as a threat to his supreme authority as the head of church and state. "No bishop, no king!" James famously asserted at the Hampton Court Conference, which he convened in 1604 to respond to calls for church reform. Summing up his reaction to the reformers, the king threateningly added, "I will make them conform themselves, or else will *harrie* them out of the land, or else do worse, *only hang them*."[3]

The church controversy centered on Episcopacy versus Presbyterianism. Episcopacy is a hierarchical form of church government controlled by a polity of ecclesiastical dignitaries called bishops – or, as Milton preferred to call them, prelates. In the English system, the king appointed two archbishops (of York and Canterbury), who then appointed an additional twenty-four bishops, each of whom had sacramental and political authority over a designated group of parishes known as a diocese. For some English Christians, including Milton, this system too closely resembled the organization of the Catholic Church and granted bishops too much power over the laity. Presbyterians offered some of the loudest calls for reform: they disapproved of the top-down Episcopal hierarchy and favored more local control of religious matters. In Presbyterianism, each congregation is governed by both its own ministers and one or more elected laymen called elders or presbyters. Congregations are then grouped into districts and overseen by an assembly or "presbytery" comprising all the ministers and some representative elders.

During the reign of Charles I (1625–49), Presbyterian reformers met with even greater resistance than under James I. With the appointment in 1633 of William Laud as Archbishop of Canterbury, opponents of Episcopacy were treated as enemies of the state and "Separatists from the Church of *England*"; Laud forced many of them to leave Britain for the Netherlands or the New World.[4] If Presbyterians were upset that the Reformed church still seemed too Catholic, Laud's zealous insistence on the significance of ceremony and external worship did nothing to allay those concerns. On the contrary, instead of trying to placate Presbyterians and integrate them within the English church, Laud enhanced the authority of bishops and thus reaffirmed the church's commitment to Episcopacy. Standing on the scaffold in 1645 after being found guilty of treason, Laud remained resolute in his position on church authority: "I have not found … any one sin [in me], which deserves death by any known law of this kingdom."[5]

Milton in his five so-called anti-prelatical tracts opposed Episcopacy primarily because he felt that it interfered with the right and responsibility of individual believers to follow their conscience and interpret Scripture for themselves. Thus he complains in his first treatise, *Of Reformation Touching Church-Discipline in England* (May 1641), that bishops treat the laity like "lay dogs" and "give over the earnest study of vertue, and godlinesse as a thing of greater purity then they [the laity] need, and the search of divine knowledge as a mystery too high for their capacity's, and only for Churchmen to meddle with" (*CPW* I: 547, 548). Milton argues that the laity should not allow bishops "the whole managing of our salvation" and should instead pursue divine knowledge on their own through a careful study of scriptures (*CPW* I: 548). While he admits that "some Books [of the Bible], and especially some places in those Books ... remain clouded," he believes "that which is most necessary to be known is most easie; and that which is most difficult, so farre expounds it selfe ever, as to tell us how little it imports our *saving knowledge*" (*CPW* I: 566).

Milton in *Of Reformation* also criticizes prelates as "followers of this World" (*CPW* I: 532) for extending their authority to secular matters and for what he perceived as a preoccupation with material wealth. He objects to the bishops' extravagant churches, exorbitant fees, and costly prelatical courts. He associates this worldliness with the Laudian emphasis on external worship – what Milton bitterly attacks as "the new-vomited Paganisme of sensuall Idolatry" (*CPW* I: 520) – and argues that Laud's policy was part of a broader effort to denigrate spirituality, to "draw downe all the Divine intercours, betwixt *God*, and the Soule, yea, the very shape of *God* himselfe, into an exterior, and bodily forme," which Milton identifies as essentially Catholic (*CPW* I: 520).

Part of Milton's critique of the prelates' worldliness focuses on a royal statement, *The Kings Majesties Declaration to His Subjects Concerning Lawfull Sports to be Used*, first published in 1618 by James I and reissued on 21 May 1633 by Charles I. This royal publication, which became known as the *Book of Sports*, lists "all lawfull Recreation" permitted by the king on Sundays and other holy days, "Such as dauncing, either men or women, Archery for men, leaping, vaulting" and "May Games, Whitson Ales, and Morris-dances, and the setting up of May-poles."[6] While the declaration insists that such recreations should be undertaken "without impediment or neglect of Divine Service," Milton, like other contemporary reformers, felt that such pastimes profaned religious days and were being used by the king and his bishops to distract citizens from independently pursuing spiritual matters.[7] Milton argues that the Sabbath should instead be kept holy "[so] that we might have one day at least of seven set apart wherein to examin and encrease our knowledge of God, to meditate, and commune of our Faith, our Hope, our eternall City in Heaven, and to quick'n, withall, the study, and exercise of Charity" (*CPW* I: 589).[8] Milton proposes a simple solution: he urges his countrymen to follow the model of Reformed churches on the Continent and, in place of prelates, to elect pastors to oversee the congregations. As he more forcefully puts it, he wants to "cut away from the publick body the noysom, and diseased tumor of Prelacie, and come from Schisme to *unity* with our neighbour Reformed sister Churches" (*CPW* I: 598).

Milton's next pamphlet, *Of Prelatical Episcopacy* (June or July 1641), develops the same argument as he replies to two tracts defending Episcopacy written by Joseph Hall, Bishop of Exeter, and James Ussher, Archbishop of Armagh. As with Milton's first anti-prelatical treatise, *Of Prelatical Episcopacy* is remarkable for its scornful tone and rhetorical brilliance. Principally, Milton argues that the scriptures have sole authority in the question of church government, and he takes pains to show that the ancient church fathers – "that indigested heap, and frie of Authors" (*CPW* I: 626) – are comparatively unreliable. Milton's contempt for the unthinking resort to tradition represents a recurrent theme in his polemical writings. In this case, he compares the consulting of ancient tradition to "vaine foraging after straw" (*CPW* I: 627) and, more vividly, "searching among the verminous, and polluted rags dropt overworn from the toyling shoulders of Time" (*CPW* I: 639). Instead of imbibing the "sincere milke of the Gospell," defenders of Episcopacy, he derisively adds, are "drink[ing] from the mixt confluence of so many corrupt, and poysonous waters, as tradition would have perswaded … [them] to by most ancient seeming authorities" (*CPW* I: 649).

Milton's other main argument in *Of Prelatical Episcopacy* is that the apostles were one-time followers of Christ and should not be cited as a precedent for establishing the current church's government. He agrees that the apostles appointed bishops in several churches but he rejects the argument put forth by opponents of reform that bishops were given authority over the Presbytery. On the contrary, he emphasizes, the two offices are synonymous: "that which is cleare in Scripture, that a Bishop and *Presbyter* is all one both in name, and office" (*CPW* I: 650). Thus, Milton would accept bishops as part of the church's structure so long as they were elected elders and not prelatical appointments by a civil magistrate. In other words, as the tract's title suggests, Milton opposes "Prelatical Episcopacy," not "Episcopacy" as he believes the Bible defines it.

Written in response to Hall's and Ussher's earlier tracts, *Of Prelatical Episcopacy* helps to illustrate how all of Milton's anti-prelatical prose should be seen within a wider debate about church government. This controversy – one of the period's many so-called pamphlet wars – anticipates the polemical exchanges that still today occur in a newspaper's editorial pages and through online message boards. During the seventeenth century, writers instead expressed their opinions and answered their opponents in printed arguments, counterarguments, and rebuttals.

Milton's third tract, *Animadversions upon the Remonstrants Defence* (July 1641), suggests the complex way that such debates unfolded and the harsh rhetoric that they often engendered. In *Animadversions* (the title means "censorious comments"), Milton once again opposes Bishop Hall, but this time he vehemently attacks Hall on behalf of "Smectymnuus," a group of Presbyterian clerics who defined their collective identity by combining their initials – Stephen Marshall, Edmund Calamy, Thomas Young, Matthew Newcomen, and William Spurstowe.[9] These five men had collaborated on a pair of treatises and probably invited Milton to assist them. Young, as we saw in Chapter 1, tutored Milton as a boy in Bread Street, and Newcomen and Spurstowe, Milton's contemporaries at Cambridge, likely heard the young author delivering his speech in 1627 at the college's annual vacation exercise. In *Animadversions*, Milton was specifically answering Hall's *A Defence of the Humble Remonstrance* (12 April 1641), which countered Smectymnuus's *An Answere to a Book Entitled An Humble Remonstrance* (20 March 1641), which – as its title suggests – had attacked Hall's initial publication, *An Humble Remonstrance* (13 January 1641).[10]

Milton's method in *Animadversions* is to quote a line or brief passage from Hall's *Defence* out of context and then to offer his own, often jeering reply immediately afterwards. The resulting dialogic exchange (I quote a passage in Chapter 2; see page 42) casts Milton as erudite and adamant while depicting Hall as obtuse and incapable. Primarily, Milton attacks Hall's endorsement of Episcopacy and his dependence on ancient church authorities. Milton derides the latter as an "over-awfull esteeme of those more ancient then trusty fathers whom custome and fond opinion, weake principles, and the neglect of sounder and superior knowledge … have gain'd them a blind reverence" (*CPW* I: 698). In this regard, Milton echoes the works of Francis Bacon and the Royal Society, although instead of adopting an inductive, experimental form of knowledge like the one that Bacon advocates in *The Great Instauration*, Milton emphasizes a careful reading of the Bible and the application of reason, inspired by God.

At the same time, Milton in *Animadversions* criticizes Hall personally, and in these passages Milton's indignant tone can seem relentless and petty. When, for example, Hall refers metaphorically to finding "gold in the Channell," Milton responds literally, "You have forgot that gold hath been anathematiz'd for the idolatrous use" (*CPW* I: 687), and when Hall writes, "I beseech God … that they may see good," Milton replies, "If you meane good Prelates, let be your prayer, aske not impossibilities" (*CPW* I: 732). The bishop's dismissal of "verbal exceptions" as "light froth" that "will sink alone" similarly inspires Milton's scorn:

> O rare suttlety, ... when I beseech you, will light things sink? when will light froth sink alone. Here in your phrase, the same day that heavy plummets will swimme alone. Trust this man, Readers if you please, whose divinity would reconcile *England* with *Rome*, and his philosophy make friends nature with the *Chaos* ...   (*CPW* I: 671)

Milton here exploits Hall's poor diction to cast aspersions on the bishop's credibility and to discredit Hall's Episcopal argument. In the preface to *Animadversions*, Milton tries to justify these instances of "well heated fervencie" by arguing that he must answer Hall in kind (*CPW* I: 663). Given Hall's sneaky rhetorical tactics – his "grand imposture," his "false trade of deceiving," and his "slye shuffle of counterfeit principles chopping and changing" (*CPW* I: 663) – Milton rationalizes that readers should excuse the contemptuous tone of his own rebuttal: "it will be nothing disagreeing from Christian meeknesse to handle such a one in a rougher accent, and to send home his haughtinesse well besputed with his owne holy-water" (*CPW* I: 662).

Some readers will nevertheless find Milton's style in *Animadversions* unnecessarily mean-spirited. Even when Hall in *Defence* criticizes the pope, a point on which Milton and Hall could have agreed, Milton still faults his Episcopal opponent. Following the practice of Protestant reformers who identified the papacy with Antichrist, Hall asks rhetorically, "And what saies Antichrist?" Milton caustically replies, "Ask your Brethren the Prelates that hold intelligence with him, ask not us. But is the Pope Antichrist now? good news! take heed you be not shent [i.e., reproached] for this ..." (*CPW* I: 673). The implication is not just that Episcopacy is a fundamentally papal form of church government but that Hall himself is a papist and trying to disguise his true religion.

But lest we think that the acerbic tone of *Animadversions* represented a permanent shift in Milton's polemical style, he adopted a much more subdued approach in his next tract, *The Reason of Church-Government* (late January 1642). This change in tenor probably reflected the greater respect he had for his opponents, Bishop James Ussher and the late Bishop Lancelot Andrewes.[11] The change may also have been influenced by the tract's different rhetorical context: Milton was no longer writing on someone else's behalf, as in *Animadversions*, and no longer had reason to feel protective.

Once again, Milton in *The Reason of Church-Government* attacks prelacy by focusing on logic and the scriptures; his larger argument is that the Bible does not prescribe or establish a precedent for an Episcopal church government.

Milton asserts in particular that Aaron in the Book of Exodus cannot be a pattern for Episcopacy, as was often claimed, because Aaron derived his extra authority from his position as a prince before he became a priest. And Milton argues that Christ did not prefigure kings or prelates, as Bishop Andrewes had suggested, because, among other reasons, Christ's kingdom has not yet come. Instead, Milton argues, prelacy opposes the reason of the Gospel; it confounds the principles of humility and lowliness that Christ embodied, and it has created schisms within the church.

Milton also continues to hold out hope that congregations will be revitalized when the laity is no longer excluded from church government. He reasons that "the minister of each Congregation" is "best acquainted with his own flock" and is thus in the best position of "preserving in healthful constitution the innerman, which may be term'd the spirit of the soul" (*CPW* I: 837). Such inner authority justifies, for Milton, the laity's participation in the church: he refers to the "love of God … ever kept alive upon the altar of our hearts" as "the first principle of all godly and vertuous actions in men" and describes the "pious and just honouring of our selves" as the second principle "whence every laudable and worthy enterprize issues forth" (*CPW* I: 841). This ideal of inner purity underlies, as we will see, much of Milton's prose, including *The Doctrine and Discipline of Divorce*, *Areopagitica*, and his Commonwealth publications. In the case of his anti-prelatical tracts, Milton uses this principle to argue for a more democratic approach to religious life; he describes the laity as "the rightfull Clergy of Christ" (*CPW* I: 838) and blames Catholicism and Episcopacy for denying churchgoers their dignity. In particular in *The Reason of Church-Government*, he cites Saint Paul as having given "the title of Clergy … to all God's people, till Pope *Higinus* and the succeeding Prelates took it from them, appropriating that name to themselves and their Priests only; and condemning the rest of Gods inheritance to an injurious and alienat condition of Laity" (*CPW* I: 838).

Both *Reason* and Milton's final anti-prelatical tract, *An Apology against a Pamphlet* (April 1642), contain important autobiographical digressions emphasizing his virtue and education and describing his poetic aspirations. As discussed in Chapter 1, it is in *An Apology* that Milton offers his famous formulation "he who would not be frustrate of his hope to write well hereafter in laudable things, ought him selfe to bee a true Poem" (*CPW* I: 890). Whether Milton actually lived up to this high standard, we do not know, but in summarizing his studies and forecasting his accomplishments, he was already beginning to draft the "Poem" of his life for us. His participation in the anti-prelatical controversy afforded him an opportunity to write his own life and to ensure, in terms of his axiom, that his experiences and his aspirations rhymed.

In *An Apology*, Milton specifically responds to the anonymous author of *A Modest Confutation* (1642), who had attacked Milton as a "*grim, lowring, bitter fool*" for the harsh style of *Animadversions*.[12] Milton in his reply tries to answer his detractor point by point. To the charge that he spent his youth "*in loytering, bezelling, and harlotting*" (A3r), for example, Milton describes reading and writing as his favorite pastimes. And to the insinuation that he was "*vomited out*" (A3v) of Cambridge because of some impropriety, Milton explains that he earned the respect of the Fellows at Christ's College.

An Apology, although published anonymously, accordingly contains some of Milton's most personal writing: he angrily defends the style and method of *Animadversions* – he insists, for example, on the didactic value of vehemence, satire, and "unmannerly" language (*CPW* I: 903) – and he savagely criticizes the anonymous confuter for his pedantry, misconceptions, and poor prose. *An Apology* also includes some strong political and religious arguments. Perhaps most strikingly, Milton incorporates a lengthy digression praising the Long Parliament.[13] He extols the members for their "mature wisdome, deliberat vertue, and deere affection to the publick good" (*CPW* I: 922), and he optimistically foretells that they will become "both the great reformers of the Church, and the great restorers of the Common-wealth" (*CPW* I: 924).

Milton in *An Apology* also continues to argue against Episcopacy, denouncing the "barbarous" preaching of prelates – "declaiming in rugged and miscellaneous geare blown together by the foure winds" (*CPW* I: 934) – and he criticizes once again the prelates' preoccupation with worldly power over spiritual matters. New in this tract is his argument against the Episcopacy's prescription of set prayers. Milton instead prefers natural expressions of faith, "which from a sincere heart unbidden come into the outward gesture" (*CPW* I: 941), an idea that years later he would illustrate in *Paradise Lost*. After Adam and Eve pray spontaneously and unanimously, the narrator describes them as "other rites / Observing none, but adoration pure / Which God likes best" (IV.736–38). In *An Apology*, Milton not only opposes prescribed prayer because it "hinders piety" and "weaken[s] the spirituall faculties" (*CPW* I: 937), but he also finds fault with the English liturgy currently in use because of its Catholic tenor, excessive use of call and response, and general lack of passion "whereto the soule might soar upon the wings of zeale" (*CPW* I: 939).

Milton's emphasis of the natural expression of religious zeal and an individual's "sincere heart" helps to illustrate that *An Apology* – like all his writings about church government – is more "anti-prelatical" than "pro-Presbyterian." Milton supported the Presbyterian cause in his early prose, but he did so as the most expedient way of challenging Episcopacy and not because he had a long-term commitment to a Presbyterian theology. As we saw in Chapter 1,

Presbyterian members of Parliament gravely disappointed Milton during the civil wars by refusing to support the king's trial and execution, and even earlier, as we will see in the next section, he grew disillusioned with Presbyterians in the Westminster Assembly who did not defend the rights of individual congregations to choose their own form of church government. Milton over time came to view Presbyterianism and Episcopacy as equally bad and began to pursue his own personal theology (see "Theology" in Chapter 2). In his anti-prelatical writings, we glimpse this religious independence in its inchoate form as he emphasizes the authority of the individual conscience and challenges both tradition and high-ranking members of the clergy in defense of the laity. Already in the 1640s he was favoring "obedience to the Spirit of God" rather than "the faire seeming pretences of men" as "the best and dutifull order that a Christian can observe" (*CPW* I: 937).

Reading Milton's anti-prelatical tracts as a group also reveals that he had already developed a vigorous rhetorical style. Readers who are not interested in the controversy about the structure of the early modern church can thus still appreciate how his early writing on this subject is in various ways poetical: Milton repeatedly incorporates striking images and colorful, often extended metaphors to belittle his detractors and to develop his biblical and logical arguments. Thus, he does not simply refer to the prelates' greed but instead attacks "the many-benefice-gaping mouth of a Prelate" with "his canary-sucking, and swan-eating palat" (*Of Reformation*, *CPW* I: 549). Or, to argue that opponents of church reform fear the plain meaning of scriptures, Milton imagines a landscape of truth and error: "they seek the dark, the bushie, the tangled Forrest, they would imbosk: they feel themselvs strook in the transparent streams of divine Truth, they would plunge, and tumble, and thinke to ly hid in the foul weeds, and muddy waters, where no plummet can reach the bottome" (*Of Reformation*, *CPW* I: 569). Here Milton depicts prelates as sea monsters whose dwelling in darkness symbolizes their error and whose avoidance of the fishermen's "plummet" presumably suggests their godlessness through a veiled allusion to Christ as a fisher of men (Matthew 4:19).

Even in *The Reason of Church-Government*, which, as we have seen, has a more moderate style, Milton is still capable of graphic imagery and virulent polemic. He attacks prelacy as "a distill'd quintessence, a pure elixar of mischief, pestilent alike to all" (*CPW* I: 858) and compares England's Episcopal church government to a "great Python" that has been "bred up and nuzzl'd" by bishops' worldly ambitions, "a masse of slime and mud, the sloathful, the covetous and ambitious hopes of Church-promotions and fat Bishopricks" (*CPW* I: 858). And Milton concludes the tract by vehemently beseeching Parliament to eradicate Episcopacy: "rain down your punishing force upon this godlesse and oppressing government: and bring such a dead Sea of subversion upon her, that she may never in this Land rise more to afflict the holy reformed Church, and the elect people of God" (*CPW* I: 861).

Or, to take one last example, Milton compares prelacy to a severe winter, which destroys "all noysome and rank weeds" as well as "wholesome herbs, and all fresh dews" (*CPW* I: 785). For Milton, prelacy is worse than winter because a repressive church government destroys true religion (flowers) but lets bad faith (weeds) continue to grow: the bishops "let out freely the ill, and keep down the good, or else keepe downe the lesser ill, and let out the greatest." Milton anticipates a spring that will bring an end to the country's spiritual malaise – the bishops' "violent & hidebound frost" – and will usher in a period of renewed freedom, "when the gentle west winds shall open the fruitfull bosome of the earth thus over-girded by your imprisonment, then the flowers put forth and spring, and then the Sunne shall scatter the mists, and the manuring hand of the Tiller shall root up all that burdens the soile without thank to your bondage" (*CPW* I: 785). In contrast to the church's oppression – which Milton conveys with the words "over-girded," "imprisonment," "burdens," and "bondage" – this pastoral imagery evokes a prelapsarian state of almost effortless fecundity. This new edenic state, Milton suggests, can be achieved on earth. In *Paradise Lost* the angel Michael also promises Adam and Eve that they can attain an earthly paradise after the Fall (XII.587), but Michael warns that they cannot depend on religious institutions: the angel explains that "Wolves shall succeed for teachers, grievous wolves, / Who all the sacred mysteries of Heav'n / To their own vile advantages shall turn" (XII.508–10). In the 1640s, by comparison, we find Milton still holding out hope for the possibility of a public remedy for humankind's fallen condition. As his wintry metaphor suggests and as he emphasizes in all his anti-prelatical tracts, the crucial first step is to reform the nation's church.

Divorce pamphlets

Just as Milton in his anti-prelatical tracts was lending his voice to a larger controversy about church government, his four pamphlets defending divorce can be understood in the context of a broader cultural debate about the indissolubility of marriage. Various English writers published their positions on divorce – both for and against – during the first two decades of the seventeenth century, and even earlier, as we will see, a bill for the reformation of ecclesiastical law had come before Parliament and included a proposal to allow divorce with the right to remarry.

The Western prohibition against divorce can be traced to the late twelfth century when the Catholic Church began to define marriage as a sacrament. Although the indissolubility of marriage did not become canon law until 1563 at the Council of Trent, the church's medieval doctrine had long before established that a husband and wife could only dissolve a valid marriage by the death of one of the spouses. If a spouse committed adultery or any other offense that made cohabitation undesirable, the church allowed the innocent spouse the right to "separation from bed and board" (in Latin, *a mensa et thoro*), but in these cases the couple still remained legally married and were expected to remain faithful to each other.

Possible exceptions to the Catholic divorce doctrine included marriages that were not consummated or in which one of the spouses was not a Christian, but both of these situations were rare. The other, more well-known exception to the Catholic doctrine was an ecclesial annulment. In these cases, a nuptial contract could be dissolved if a pre-existing circumstance invalidated the marriage and showed in effect that the sacrament had never taken place. Petitions for annulments in England during the medieval and early Renaissance period also appear to have been rare.[14] But if, for example, one of the spouses could show that she or he was pressured into marriage or lacked the requisite maturity to make such a commitment, an ecclesial tribunal could annul the contract, and the spouses were free to marry other people.[15]

Almost all Protestant theologians rejected the Catholic divorce doctrine. By the end of the sixteenth century all Protestant courts – Swiss, German, Scottish, Scandinavian, and French Protestant – had legalized divorce with the right to remarry for the innocent spouse, and some Protestant marriage courts allowed both parties to marry again.[16] Continental reformers also criticized the Catholic doctrine of *a mensa et thoro*, arguing that it constituted a divorce because it abrogated the purpose of matrimony. Reformers cited most of the same biblical texts, in particular Matthew 19:9, in which Christ seems to assert that divorce should be allowed in cases of sexual infidelity: "Whosoever shall put away his wife, *except it be for fornication*, and shall marry another, committeth adultery" (emphasis added).

Reformers, however, believed that divorce should be allowed only as a last resort and only in situations where reconciliation was impossible. Consequently, very few divorces were granted in Protestant nations. According to one estimate, the annual divorce rate in most jurisdictions during the sixteenth century was roughly 0.02 per 1,000 people; by comparison, the divorce rate in the United States in 2001 was more than 247 times greater.[17] Even in the infrequent cases where divorce was allowed, Protestant theologians tried to impose guidelines and restrictions on couples. Luther, for example, advised a delay of six months to a year before a spouse could remarry, "otherwise it would have the evil appearance that he was happy and pleased that his spouse had committed adultery and he was joyfully seizing the opportunity to get rid of this one and so practise his wantonness under the cloak of the law."[18]

Luther was one of the harshest critics of the Catholic Church's canon law on divorce, and, although early in his career he had reservations about permitting divorce except for adultery, he also came to support divorce in cases of impotency and desertion.[19] Calvin maintained a more conservative position: he argued that the only valid reason for dissolving a marriage was adultery, although some of his writings suggest that he may have also accepted desertion and religious disparity as valid grounds for divorce.[20] Among the other leading reformers, Martin Bucer was probably the most permissive. A German theologian and the author of *De Regno Christi* – parts of which Milton translated into English in 1644 – Bucer expanded the possible reasons for divorce to include leprosy, impotency, insanity, and emotional incompatibility.[21]

Bucer's support for Henry VIII's wish to divorce his first wife ultimately came to influence efforts to reform England's ecclesiastical law.[22] England and Ireland were the only countries in the sixteenth century in which a Reformed national church continued to adhere to the Roman Catholic doctrine prohibiting divorce. Ironically, Henry VIII (1491–1547) had broken with the Catholic Church in 1533 precisely because he wanted to dissolve his first marriage. When the Catholic Church refused to annul the king's marriage to Catherine of Aragon on the basis that she had been married to his brother Arthur – a degree of kinship for which, an added layer of irony, the Church had previously granted the king a special dispensation – Henry VIII secretly married Anne Boleyn and declared himself the supreme head of the English church.

Yet the separated English church did not deviate from the Catholic doctrine on the indissolubility of marriage, and most English theologians supported the prohibition of divorce. In 1552 a bill for the reformation of ecclesiastical law, *Reformatio Legum Ecclesiasticarum*, came before Parliament and included a proposal to allow divorce with the right to remarry under a broad range of circumstances – adultery, desertion, "deadly hostility," and "the crime of ill treatment" (the latter was defined as "a man is cruel to his wife and displays excessive harshness of word and deed").[23] If it had passed, the new law would have given England the most liberal divorce policy in Europe. But Parliament discussed the new marriage provisions only briefly, and the changes were never approved. When the church's canon law was later published in 1604, it permitted only separations *a mensa et thoro* with the added conservative proviso that "here shale be a caution and restraint inserted … that the parties so separated shall live chastely and continently; neither shall they, during each other's life, contract matrimony with any other person."[24]

The English government did not take any further action to legalize divorce until more than sixty years later. Beginning in 1670, four years before Milton's death, Parliament established a secular divorce policy whereby couples could obtain divorces in cases of adultery. Thus, in March 1698, Parliament granted Charles Gerard, the Second Earl of Macclesfield, a divorce from his wife Anna, who was accused of committing adultery. This type of formal legislative act to dissolve a marriage was uncommon, however: between 1670 and 1749, only sixteen acts were passed, and almost all were granted to men.[25] The English Parliament did not approve a more general law legalizing divorce until the nineteenth century, and the specific policy that Milton advocated was not passed until the late twentieth century when the Divorce Reform Act of 1969 began allowing divorce in cases of irreconcilable differences.[26]

Some English writers before Milton had defended divorce. William Tyndale, for example, probably best known today for being the first to translate parts of the Bible into English, supported divorce for desertion and adultery, as did Thomas Cranmer, Archbishop of Canterbury. Cranmer initially had opposed divorce but later, reporting on the case of William Parr, Marquis of Northampton, and his wife, Lady Anne, Cranmer cited Matthew 19 in arguing that the couple's divorce should be allowed.[27] And while the Catholic writer Thomas More as Lord Chancellor had opposed Henry VIII's efforts to annul his first marriage, More in *Utopia* (1516) includes divorce with remarriage for the injured spouse as a feature of his fictional island, not only in cases of "adultery or intolerably bad behaviour," but also "occasionally … by mutual consent … on grounds of incompatibility."[28]

In the first half of the seventeenth century in England, the debate about divorce seems to have intensified.[29] In the preceding decades, publications about the subject may have been suppressed by the Archbishop of Canterbury, John Whitgift (1583–1604). Edmund Bunny, for example, claimed to have written his book opposing divorce in 1595, but he had to wait "a good while together" for the archbishop to allow its publication.[30] Bunny's *Of Divorce for Adulterie* ultimately appeared in 1610, one of a spate of theological treatises – some for and some against divorce – published under Whitgift's successors, Richard Bancroft (1604–11) and George Abbot (1611–33). Not surprisingly, most of the tracts that defended the English doctrine of marriage's indissolubility were written by bishops or other clerics holding high ecclesiastical office; presumably these men had earned their prestigious positions because they accepted the church's policies.[31] Writing against divorce were Godfrey Goodman, Bishop of Gloucester; John Prideaux, Bishop of

Worcester; Anthony Sparrow, Bishop of Exeter; John Fell, Bishop of Oxford; John Howson, Bishop of Oxford and then Durham; and Lancelot Andrewes, Bishop of Ely and then Winchester.

But whereas these bishops argued for the indissolubility of marriage by focusing almost exclusively on Scripture – in particular Matthew 19 and 1 Corinthians 7 ("Let not the wife depart from her husband") – writers who supported divorce tended to address the social benefits of allowing couples to separate legally. Seventeenth-century defenders of divorce – such as William Ames, William Perkins, Henry Smith, and William Whatley – still incorporated a considerable amount of biblical exegesis in their tracts, but a discussion of justice and the best way to structure society complemented these writers' interpretations of Scripture.[32]

Still, even with the new social emphasis, the most liberal arguments for divorce in seventeenth-century England continued to focus on cases of desertion and adultery. In other words, no one before Milton exceeded the already widely accepted position taken by Continental Protestants during the preceding century. As the historian Roderick Phillips has observed, an inconsistency emerged in the works of English reformers: writers increasingly considered the importance of a family and the companionate qualities of marriage, but their arguments for allowing divorce continued to emphasize a couple's sex life.[33]

Milton's divorce tracts are significant in part because he was the first writer to pursue the logical implications of the Puritans' ideal of companionate marriages and strong families. He thus broadened the valid reasons for divorce to include emotional incompatibility, defended the rights of both spouses to remarry (not just the victim of an unfaithful spouse), and argued that the right to dissolve a marriage should be transferred from ecclesiastical or civil courts and rest solely with the spouses themselves. As we saw in Chapter 1, Milton had personal reasons for writing about divorce after his first wife, Mary Powell, deserted him for three years and went to live with her parents. But if Milton was motivated in part by his own marital problems, he nevertheless developed an argument that reached not just beyond his own circumstances but beyond the terms advocated by other contemporary writers.

To understand the ambitious nature of Milton's divorce tracts, we need to begin with his definition of matrimony. Again and again, he describes marriage as "a meet and happy conversation" (*CPW* II: 246), a metaphor that implies reciprocity, if not equality, as it treats the two spouses as mutual participants in an intellectual and emotional relationship. Milton accordingly objects to the emphasis on adultery in Protestant marriage laws because sexual activity is not related to the fundamental purpose of matrimony. He bases this part of his argument on Genesis 2:18, "And the LORD God said, It is not good that the man should be alone; I will make him an help meet for him." Here, Milton notes, God expressly institutes marriage as a cure for the "evill of solitary life" and mentions reproduction only afterwards (in Genesis 3:16), "as being but a secondary end in dignity, though not in necessitie" (*CPW* II: 235). To restrict divorce to cases of adultery, Milton thus reasons, overstates the importance of sex – "affirms the bed to be the highest of marriage" (*CPW* II: 269) – and elevates "the disappointing of an impetuous nerve" over the "ingenuous grievance of a minde unreasonably yoakt" (*CPW* II: 249). For Milton, the desire to satisfy an "irrationall heat" (*CPW* II: 249) is far less important than the "rationall burning" that marriage alone can remedy (*CPW* II: 251).

As in Milton's anti-prelatical prose, his tracts on divorce benefit from their vivid imagery and metaphors. Milton writes, for example, that a couple lacking a "correspondence … of the minde" must forever "grind in the mill of an undelighted and servil copulation" (*CPW* II: 326, 258) and will be "two carkasses chain'd unnaturally together …, a living soule bound to a dead corps" (*CPW* II: 326). But also, as in his writings about prelacy, Milton relies chiefly on logic and scriptures to make his point. To take one example: he builds part of his argument on the definition of marriage that he takes from Genesis 2:18. He asserts that a bad marriage does not provide "solace and delight" (*CPW* II: 235) and, in fact, must be worse than loneliness: "the continuall sight of … [a spouse's] deluded thoughts without cure, must needs be … a daily trouble and paine of losse" (*CPW* II: 247). He then reasons that a marriage that does not meet its God-given purpose is not a valid marriage. He concludes that divorce should therefore be allowed because, according to God's law, incompatible couples are not actually married.

Milton published his first divorce tract, *The Doctrine and Discipline of Divorce*, on 1 August 1643, and six months later on 2 February 1644 he published a greatly expanded, revised edition. Like other seventeenth-century defenders of divorce, he attempts to address the possible social benefits of allowing the dissolution of bad marriages:

> peace and love, the best subsistence of a Christian family will return
> home from whence they are now banisht; places of prostitution will be
> lesse haunted, the neighbours bed less attempted, the yoke of prudent and
> manly discipline will be generally submitted to, sober and well order'd
> living will soon spring up in the Commonwealth.   (*CPW* II: 230)

In some places in the divorce tracts, Milton argues by analogy that an "ill mariage" resembles an "ill Government" (*CPW* II: 229), no doubt alluding to the mismanagement that occurred under the administration of Charles I. But, as the above passage illustrates, Milton also believed that bad marriages had real consequences for the nation. Such unions, he insists, are "hurtfull and distrac-tive" not just to "the house" but also to "the Church and Common-wealth" (*CPW* II: 318).

Yet, aside from occasionally acknowledging the benefits to society of allowing divorce, most of *The Doctrine and Discipline of Divorce* focuses on Milton's legal reasoning and his explication of Scripture. In this regard, he sounds more like the bible-quoting bishops who argued against divorce than the social-minded Puritans who defended a spouse's right to dissolve an adul-terous marriage. Milton's argument is threefold: he attempts to show that the Old Testament allows divorce for reasons other than adultery; he insists that Christ's comments about marriages agree with the Law of Moses; and he wishes to show that prohibiting divorce, beyond the specific exceptions stipulated by Moses, contradicts the reason behind the Law.

Milton proceeds like a skilled literary critic, carefully interpreting individ-ual words and verses from the Bible. As in the anti-prelatical tracts, he bases his authority on "the firm faith of a knowing Christian" (*CPW* II: 282), but he also establishes two key interpretive principles: context and charity. In the former case, he argues against reading scriptures too broadly: "there is scarce any one saying in the Gospel, but must be read with limitations and distinctions, to be rightly understood"; correctly interpreting Christ's words, he adds, "requires a skilfull and laborious gatherer; who must compare the words he finds, with other precepts, with the end of every ordinance, and with the general *analogy* of Evangelick doctrine" (*CPW* II: 338). Milton introduces the principle of charity, by comparison, to guard against reading the Bible too literally and "resting in the meere element of the Text" (*CPW* II: 236). Readers should instead begin with the premise that God is good and just and intends goodness and justice for his creatures. In this regard, Milton's method differs from the practice of literary critics because he encourages readers not to aspire to an objective analysis of scriptures but to approach the text with benevolence and forbearance. As Milton plainly puts it, "the way to get a sure undoubted knowledge of things, is to hold that for truth ... which accords most with charity" (*CPW* II: 340).

Thus, when Paul writes, "It is better to marry then to burne" (1 Corinthians 7:9), Milton interprets "burn" generally so that the verse justifies divorce for more than "the meer motion of carnall lust" and "the meer goad of a sensitive desire" (*CPW* II: 250, 251). Following the principle of charity, Milton inter-prets the passage in terms of Adam's innocent request for a help-meet and asserts that *to burn* encompasses "the desire and longing to put off an unkindly solitarines by uniting another body, but not without a fit soule to his in the cheerfull society of wedlock" (*CPW* II: 251). He similarly interprets Moses' words in Deuteronomy 24:1, "When a man hath taken a wife, and married her, and it come to pass that she find no favour in his eyes, because he hath found some uncleanness in her: then let him write her a bill of divorcement, and give it in her hand, and send her out of his house." For this verse, again following the principle of charity, Milton observes that "uncleanness in her" in the original Hebrew means "*nakednes of ought, or any reall nakednes*: which by all the learned interpreters is refer'd to the mind, as well as to the body" (*CPW* II: 244). He thus concludes that Moses permitted divorce for both adultery and incompatibility, just as Paul recognized the importance of comfort and solace as the foundation for all marriages.

Milton then turns to Christ's statement about divorce in Matthew 5:32, "But I say unto you, That whosoever shall put away his wife, saving for the cause of fornication, causeth her to commit adultery: and whosoever shall marry her that is divorced committeth adultery." Some readers, Milton notes, will argue that "the words of Christ are plainly against all divorce, except in cases of fornication" (*CPW* II: 281). But here, stressing his first interpretive principle of not reading scriptures too broadly, he insists that we must contextualize Christ's speech "by considering upon what occasion every thing is set down: and by comparing other Texts" (*CPW* II: 282). Milton suggests that Christ was exaggerating for rhetorical effect in addressing the Pharisees: "Christ meant not to be tak'n word for word, but like a wise Physician, administring one

Allegory of Custom and Error

In the following passage from the start of the revised edition of *The Doctrine and Discipline of Divorce*, Milton sets out one of the foundational principles of his prose and, in particular, his argument defending divorce. He objects to relying unthinkingly on custom instead of making independent choices using one's reason and conscience. This passage also illustrates how Milton in his early prose incorporated figurative language to enrich his ideas and how he used long, complex sentences that seem more appropriate to oral delivery than writing. One strategy for understanding Milton's sometimes cumbersome syntax is to read passages such as the following one aloud. (I have modernized the spelling and punctuation for the sake of clarity.)

> If it were seriously asked – and it would be no untimely question, Renowned Parliament, select Assembly – who of all teachers and masters that have ever taught, hath drawn the most disciples after him, both in religion and in manners, it might be not untruly answered, Custom.
> Though Virtue be commended for the most persuasive in her theory, and Conscience in the plain demonstration of the spirit finds most evincing, yet whether it be the secret of divine will, or the original blindness we are born in, so it happens for the most part that Custom

still is silently received for the best instructor. Except it be because her method is glib and easy, in some manner like to that vision of Ezekiel, rolling up her sudden book of implicit knowledge for him that will to take and swallow down at pleasure, which proving but of bad nourishment in the concoction, as it was heedless in the devouring, puffs up unhealthily a certain big face of pretended learning, mistaken among credulous men for the wholesome habit of soundness and good constitution, but is indeed no other than that swollen visage of counterfeit knowledge and literature, which not only in private mars our education but also in public is the common climber into every chair where either religion is preached or law reported, filling each estate of life and profession with abject and servile principles, depressing the high and heaven-born spirit of man far beneath the condition wherein either God created him or sin hath sunk him.

To pursue the allegory, Custom being but a mere face, as echo is a mere voice, rests not in her unaccomplishment until by secret inclination she accorporate herself with Error, who being a blind and serpentine body without a head, willingly accepts what he wants and supplies what her incompleteness went seeking. Hence it is that Error supports Custom, Custom countenances Error.

Here Milton begins by addressing members of Parliament and the Westminster Assembly. He asserts that when choosing a possible teacher, most people will blindly follow custom instead of virtue and their own conscience because custom is so readily available and requires so little effort. He compares the practice of accepting what others have done to an act of eating (rather than reasoning). Specifically, he alludes to the biblical verse in which the prophet Ezekiel has God's will revealed to him on a scroll that he is then commanded to eat (Ezekiel 2:8–3:3).

Milton pursues this alimentary metaphor by then comparing custom to junk food: it goes down easily but provides no nourishment. The specific side-effect of consuming custom is that it causes the eater's head to swell – it gives consumers "a certain big face of pretended learning" – a symptom that symbolizes the vanity of people who pretend to know a great deal but who merely imitate what has been previously done. Such arrogance, Milton adds, is often mistaken for real knowledge, which explains why custom is ruining the country's education, law, and religion: teachers, lawyers, and clerics who cannot think for themselves often misinform and mislead.

Milton concludes his allegory of Custom by describing it as a mere face, a symbol of the superficiality of heedlessly following tradition. Custom allows bad judgments to appear with a good face ("We've always done things this way …," a defender of custom might say) even though such judgments lack rational support ("… but I have no idea why"). That Error's snake-like body props up Custom alludes to the serpent from Genesis, while Error's blindness symbolizes the ignorance that leads to accepting conventions unthinkingly. As Milton neatly conveys in his final sentence, the only justification for relying on custom is error, and the only good face that can be put on error is an appeal to custom. Here Milton's use of chiasmus underscores the symbiotic nature of error and custom's destructive marriage, an apt image to introduce a tract about bad relationships, which Milton then goes on to argue should be dissolved.

excesse against another to reduce us to a perfect mean" (*CPW* II: 282–83). Milton explains that Christ gave "this rigid sentence against divorce" only to counteract the Pharisees' extravagant behavior – "as when we bow things the contrary way, to make them come to thir naturall straitnes" (*CPW* II: 283). Working from Matthew 5:17–20, Milton notes that Christ himself pledged that he would not contradict the Old Testament – "that he came not to abrogate from the Law *one jot or tittle*, and denounces against them that shall so teach" (*CPW* II: 283). Milton goes on to argue that Christ's reference to "fornication" could mean "actual adultery" (*CPW* II: 337) or, following the more charitable reading of this verse by the Dutch theologian Hugo Grotius, it could signify "a continual headstrong behaviour, as tends to plain contempt of the husband" (*CPW* II: 335) or "diverse obvious actions, which either plainly lead to adultery, or give such presumption wherby sensible men may suspect the deed to be already don" (*CPW* II: 337). Milton thus concludes that the New Testament, like the Law of Moses, permits divorce in cases of sexual infidelity as well as emotional incompatibility.

In his next tract, *The Judgement of Martin Bucer* (6 August 1644), Milton did not develop his reasons for defending divorce. Instead, he attempted to fortify his earlier argument by translating into English sections of a treatise by the German theologian Martin Bucer (1491–1551). Milton claimed to have come across Bucer's works only three months after the publication of the second edition of *The Doctrine and Discipline of Divorce*, thus emphasizing that he had not been influenced by Bucer's reasoning. Surprised and pleased to find an authority who supported his position, Milton translated into English parts of Bucer's tract in the hope of answering his own detractors. He wished to use Bucer as a type of celebrity endorsement, "as my complete suretie and testimonial, if Truth be not the best witnes to it self, that what I formerly presented to your reading on this subject, was good, and just, and honest, not licentious" (*CPW* II: 439).

The Judgement of Martin Bucer is perhaps more significant for today's readers of Milton because it hints at his growing disillusionment with Presbyterianism. Whereas in early 1644 Milton addressed the second edition of *The Doctrine and Discipline of Divorce* "To the Parlament of England, with the Assembly" (*CPW* II: 222), by the time he published *The Judgement of Martin Bucer* he only addressed Parliament.[34] In the intervening three months, he seems to have become disenchanted with the Westminster Assembly, a body of divines, dominated by Presbyterian clergy, whom the Long Parliament had appointed to supervise the reorganization of the English church. Milton in the preface to *The Judgement of Martin Bucer* refers disparagingly to "the scanty and unadequat and inconsistent principles of such as condemn others for adhering to traditions, and are themselves the prostrate worshippers of Custom"

(*CPW* II: 439). Here he may have specifically had in mind Presbyterians in the Assembly who opposed a compromise form of church government proposed by a group of Independent ministers. Published under the title *An Apologetical Narration* on 3 January 1644, the compromise proposal called for a middle way between Presbyterian church government and the less structured, more tolerant approach to organizing the English church favored by radical sects. When some members of Parliament sided with the authors of *Apologetical Narration* and argued that England's national church should tolerate dissenters and allow congregations to govern themselves according to the members' consciences, Presbyterians in the Assembly were outraged. They believed this policy granted individual congregations too much freedom – but that was precisely the type of liberty that Milton's argument in his anti-prelatical treatises had warranted. In contrast to the Presbyterians' position, Milton, as we have seen, emphasized the laity's authority and argued for the power of an individual conscience.

Milton may have had other, more personal reasons for his growing dissatisfaction with Presbyterianism. Not only had Presbyterian clergy attacked the arguments for reform that he presented in his anti-prelatical tracts, but also Presbyterians in Parliament may have been behind efforts to have *The Doctrine and Discipline of Divorce* formally censored. As we saw in Chapter 1, for example, a Presbyterian divine, Herbert Palmer, addressed both houses in August 1644 and called for Milton's first divorce tract to be publicly burnt.

Part of Milton's response to such criticism was to devote his third treatise on divorce to refuting one of his detractors. *Colasterion* (4 March 1645) – the name literally means a place or instrument of punishment – addresses (and dresses down) an anonymous writer who in November of the previous year had published a pamphlet criticizing *The Doctrine and Discipline of Divorce*. Milton explains that he had to settle for this writer "since no worthier an adversary makes his appearance" (*CPW* II: 729), and, as in *Animadversions* and *An Apology*, Milton sustains this caustic tone, systematically and sometimes savagely attacking the anonymous critic's character and argument. When, for example, the critic claims not to understand Milton's reference to a "fit conversing Soul," Milton asks incredulously, "What should a man say more to a snout in this pickle, what language can be low and degenerat anough?" (*CPW* II: 747). Or, when the anonymous author announces that he does not understand Milton's reference to the "gentlest" purpose of marriage, Milton scornfully replies, "how should hee, a Servingman both by nature and by function, an Idiot by breeding, and a Solliciter by presumption, ever come to know, or feel within himself, what the meaning is of gentle?" (*CPW* II: 741).

On the same day that *Colasterion* was published, Milton's final divorce tract also appeared. *Tetrachordon* is arguably more important than Milton's preceding two treatises for what it reveals about the development of his thinking. Among its most notable features, *Tetrachordon* includes a fuller discussion of women's role in marriage. Although Milton subtitled *The Doctrine and Discipline of Divorce* as "Restor'd to the good of both Sexes" (*CPW* II: 234), none of his earlier tracts had much to say about the spouses' relative rights or authority. On the one hand, much of Milton's discussion in *The Doctrine and Discipline of Divorce* is predicated on a reciprocal model of marriage, and he attributes the grounds for divorce to a blameless incompatibility. On the other hand, Milton in some passages in *The Doctrine and Discipline of Divorce* accepts a hierarchy of gender in which women are inferior to men. He asserts, for example, that whether to dissolve a marriage should be decided privately, according to "the will and consent of both parties, or of the husband alone" (*CPW* II: 344).

This same tension occurs in *Tetrachordon* but here Milton more fully considers women's relative power. Milton still posits a blameless incompatibility as the reason to allow divorce, but his language in some of these passages – perhaps influenced by his own recent marital difficulties – suggests that a wife's willfulness and hostility may be to blame for failed marriages.[35] Yet, if Milton continued to believe in men's authority over women, he also supported a more egalitarian model of marriage than can be found in the Bible. He accepted Paul's pronouncement "that the head of every man is Christ; and the head of the woman is the man" (1 Corinthians 11:3), but Milton then adds, "Nevertheless man is not to hold her as a servant, but receives her into a part of that empire which God proclaims him to, though not equally, yet largely, as his own image and glory" (*CPW* II: 589). Milton also acknowledges that some women are superior to some men and thus should have authority over their husbands: "if she exceed her husband in prudence and dexterity, and he contentedly yeeld, for then a superior and more naturall law comes in, that the wiser should govern the lesse wise, whether male or female" (*CPW* II: 589).

In addition to this more sustained consideration of women's authority, Milton in *Tetrachordon* elaborates his defense of divorce. Perhaps most obviously, he supplements the scriptural grounds from *The Doctrine and Discipline of Divorce* by citing more supporting authorities. Especially in the last section of *Tetrachordon*, he piles on one testimonial after another. He claims that he adds such citations reluctantly and concedes that "multiplicity of Authors" does "not solidly fetch the truth, … nor argue a thing false by the few that hold so" (*CPW* II: 692). Nevertheless, he cites some three dozen writers and councils to bolster his position on the dissolubility of marriage. He begins with theologians from early Christianity – such as Ambrose, Augustine, Basil, Jerome, Justin Martyr, Origen, Lactantius, and Tertullian – and includes twenty scholars and reformed clerics who also supported his argument, most notably Bucer, Cranmer, Fagius, Grotius, and Peter Martyr.

Milton in *Tetrachordon* also revises part of the scriptural argument from his earlier prose. As we saw in Chapter 1, the title of his fourth divorce tract literally means "four-stringed," which the subtitle then explains: "Expositions upon the foure chiefe places in Scripture which treat of Mariage, or nullities in Mariage" (*CPW* II: 586). The four places in question describe God's institution of marriage (Genesis 1:27–28 and 2:18, 23–24), Moses' rules on divorce (Deuteronomy 24:1–2), Christ's answers to the Pharisees on divorce and marriage (Matthew 5:31–32 and 19:3–11), and Paul's delineation of rules for spouses (1 Corinthians 7:10–16).

Milton, as in his anti-prelatical tracts, again argues against reading the Bible too strictly. Instead of adhering to the "dead letter" of Mosaic Law, he aspires to follow "the guidance of … [Christ's] living Spirit" (*CPW* II: 588) and to discover the scriptures' most charitable meaning, "if alwayes not writt'n in the characters of the law, yet engrav'n in the heart of man by a divine impression" (*CPW* II: 588). Milton applies this loose interpretive principle to a passage that he had discussed in *The Doctrine and Discipline of Divorce* in which Christ responds to the Pharisees: "Moses because of the hardness of your hearts suffered you to put away your wives: but from the beginning it was not so" (Matthew 19:8).[36] In his earlier tract, Milton had devised a somewhat complicated and limited reading that depended on the statement's situational context. Milton interpreted Christ as saying that "many licentious and hard-hearted men" abused the law of Moses and divorced their wives for insignificant reasons; Moses "suffered" them to do so because he wished to preserve divorce – a "just and lawfull privilege of remedy" – for the "good men" who genuinely found themselves in bad marriages (*CPW* II: 307).

But in *Tetrachordon*, Milton now observes that "hardness of hearts" can mean either "a stubborne resolution to doe evil," as he had previously interpreted the phrase, or "the imperfection and decay of man from original righteousnesse" (*CPW* II: 661–62). This latter meaning simplifies Milton's interpretation and broadens the passage's significance. Christ no longer refers only to hard-hearted men, such as the Pharisees, but to all of humankind, imperfect since Adam and Eve's first act of disobedience. Thus, when Christ adds "from the beginning it was not so," Milton now explains that this clause refers to the perfect lives of Adam and Eve before the Fall, not to the period before Moses delivered the law to his people.

Milton also develops his new interpretation of Matthew 19:8 into a fuller theory of natural law. Focusing on "from the beginning it was not so," he distinguishes between primary and secondary laws of nature. Whereas the primary law of nature applied only to Adam and Eve in the garden before the Fall, God introduced the secondary law – of which the permission to divorce is one part – after the Fall as a remedy for "our imperfet and degenerat condition" (*CPW* II: 661). Milton specifically refers to the latter type of natural law, arrived at through reason, as the "secondary law of nature *and of nations*" (*CPW* II: 661, emphasis added) because he believes that it should provide the foundation for human justice.[37] As Milton reasons, "the whole juridical law and civil power is only suffer'd under the Gospel, for the hardnes of our hearts" (*CPW* II: 662). In other words, civil law can be justified only in so far as it corresponds to the secondary law of nature, as described in the Bible, and thus allows humankind to cope with and find relief from the consequences of its fallen state.

This idea, as we will see at the end of this chapter, is significant for Milton's later writings. Whereas in *Tetrachordon* Milton uses the equation of natural and civil law to support divorce, he later applies this theory in his Commonwealth prose to justify the rights of a people under a monarch. Following the implications of his earlier argument, Milton will suggest that people should have the right to dissolve not only a bad marriage but also a relationship with a bad king.

Areopagitica (1644)

It was public reaction to Milton's position on divorce that prompted him to publish *Areopagitica* in November 1644. Responding to calls that his divorce tract should be censored, Milton decided to take up his pen on behalf of freedom of the press. As Milton himself acknowledged in *The Doctrine and Discipline of Divorce*, self-interest often lies behind attempts to effect social change: "when points of difficulty are to be discusst, appertaining to the removall of unreasonable wrong and burden from the perplext life of our brother, it is incredible how cold, how dull, and farre from all fellow feeling we are, without the spurre of self-concernment" (*CPW* II: 226).[38] In Milton's own case, his defense of divorce, published without a license two years earlier, provided the "spurre" he needed to address the government's regulation of the book trade, in particular the system that required authors to obtain a license before publishing their works.

But even before the divorce controversy, Milton supported the free circulation of ideas. In *Animadversions*, he asserts that "nothing is more sweet to man" than the "liberty of speaking" (*CPW* I: 669), and in *The Reason of Church-Government* he anticipates that "the honest liberty of free speech from my youth" will serve "as the best treasure, and solace of a good old age" (*CPW* I: 804). Years later, in *Pro Populo Anglicano Defensio Secunda* (1654), he continues to hold a principled belief in free expression. He warns Oliver Cromwell not to institute a similar form of pre-publication censorship, proposing that the newly titled Lord Protector should "permit those who wish to engage in free inquiry to publish their findings at their own peril without the private inspection of any petty magistrate, for so will truth especially flourish" (*CPW* IV: 679).

Milton in *Defensio Secunda* goes on to explain his reasons for writing *Areopagitica* in somewhat idealistic terms. He recalls that he specifically wished to show "that the judgment of truth and falsehood, what should be printed and what suppressed, ought not to be in the hands of a few men (and these mostly ignorant and of vulgar discernment) charged with the inspection of books, at whose will or whim virtually everyone is prevented from publishing aught that surpasses the understanding of the mob" (*CPW* II: 626). That Milton here equates the discerning of "truth and falsehood" with "what should be printed and what suppressed" suggests the landmark nature of *Areopagitica*'s argument. In 1644 he anticipated the central role that the printing press would come to play and allied its unfettered operation "with truth, with learning, and the Commonwealth" (*CPW* II: 488). Some modern readers have even come to regard *Areopagitica* as a manifesto of individual liberty. Milton eloquently defends both the free circulation of knowledge and the right and privilege of thinking for oneself. "[A]bove all liberties," he appeals to Parliament, "Give me liberty to know, to utter, and to argue freely according to conscience" (*CPW* II: 560).

But Milton in *Areopagitica* was also directly addressing the period's specific publishing conditions. As he explains near the start of the tract, he did not oppose all censorship; he only wanted the Parliament to judge "over again that Order which ye have ordain'd *to regulate Printing*," by which he presumably meant the Licensing Order passed on 16 June 1643 (*CPW* II: 490–91). The new law stipulated, as Milton summarizes, "*That no Book, pamphlet, or paper shall be henceforth Printed, unless the same be first approv'd and licenc't by such*, or at least one of such as shall be thereto appointed" (*CPW* II: 491). This Licensing Order represented Parliament's attempt to re-establish control of the book trade following the temporary collapse of the government's system in 1640. With the assembly of the Long Parliament in November of that year, England experienced its first period of unrestricted publication since 1476 when William Caxton introduced printing in Westminster. The elimination of the Courts of Star Chamber and High Commission in July 1641 meant that members of the book trade no longer feared royal prosecution for publishing a work that could be deemed scandalous or seditious. The quantity of English publications consequently soared: the total number of published items leapt from 625 in 1639 and 848 in 1640 to 2,034 in 1641 and 3,666 in 1642.[39]

The Long Parliament responded to this outpouring of printed matter with a series of laws that revived key provisions from the intrusive regulations favored by the Stationers' Company and characteristic of Tudor and Stuart control of the press. Parliament specifically wanted to curtail the "many false forged, scandalous, seditious, libelous, and unlicensed Papers, Pamphlets, and Books to the great defamation of Religion and government."[40] The 1643 Licensing Order did not include the threat of corporal punishment, an important part of previous legislation under Charles I, but the new government still attempted to establish a rigid protocol for overseeing printed publications. Under the new law, Presbyterian censors replaced Episcopal licensers, and Parliament assumed the position formerly held by the king.

We should not overstate, however, the extent of the Long Parliament's interference. Although some authors and printers may have found the government's laws regulating the book trade to be repressive, the licensing system under the Long Parliament seems never to have been strictly enforced.[41] The government tried to prosecute anyone who repeatedly published unlawful works, or, as in Milton's case with his divorce tracts, anyone who took egregiously controversial positions or whose works elicited official complaints. But the quantity of manuscripts that the government's thirty-four licensers would have been expected to examine must have necessitated in practice no more than a cursory review of some tracts. As Milton observes in *Areopagitica*, "there cannot be a more tedious and unpleasing journey-work, a greater losse of time ... then to be made the perpetuall reader of unchosen books and pamphlets, oftimes huge volumes" (*CPW* II: 530). And with only a little initiative, authors and printers could have circumvented the Long Parliament's order, either by inserting a controversial passage in a book after it was officially licensed, or, as Milton did with his unlicensed divorce tract and *Areopagitica*, by simply ignoring the law altogether. In 1644, the year *Areopagitica* was printed, only 20 percent of the published books and pamphlets were registered, which suggests that in many cases owners did not bother to obtain official approval.[42] Presumably, the mere existence of pre-publication licensing discouraged some writers from even attempting to take controversial works to press, but we cannot know how often such self-censorship occurred or with what frequency licensers redacted or expunged a passage they deemed unacceptable from a work that they then approved.

Milton's argument in *Areopagitica* emphasizes both the effrontery of Presbyterian interference and the impracticality of the government's policy. Even an author who was not trying to skirt the law, Milton notes, would be grossly inconvenienced if he had to seek approval for every late revision: "what if the author shall be one so copious of fancie, as to have many things well worth the adding, come into his mind after licensing, while the book is yet under the Presse…[?]" (*CPW* II: 532). Milton also faults the government's order because it will require licensers to redact individual passages in books that "are partly usefull and excellent, partly culpable and pernicious"; the labor of making so many separate "expurgations, and expunctions" would "ask as many more officials … that the Commonwealth of learning be not damnify'd" (*CPW* II: 529).

As various critics have noted, Milton's concern about Presbyterians in Parliament seems to underpin his broader opposition to pre-publication licensing in *Areopagitica*. Given that Presbyterians, striving to consolidate their power within Parliament, had the most to gain from the Licensing Order of 1643, Milton may have advocated less regulation for the book trade in order to limit Presbyterian control of the government.[43] As the radical writer William Walwyn complained in *A Compassionate Samaritane* (1644), the "Ordinance for licensing of Bookes, which being intended by the Parliament for a good and necessary end …, is become by meanes of the Licensers (who are Divines and intend their owne interest) most serviceable to themselves."[44] Like Walwyn, Milton may have wanted a freer press in order to give voice to opponents of Presbyterianism and thus to thwart calls for a settlement with Charles I.

Certainly in *Areopagitica* Milton emphasizes his dissatisfaction with Presbyterians for beginning to resemble prelates. What was only intimated in *The Judgement of Martin Bucer* finds much fuller expression here. Although Episcopacy was not formally abrogated until 9 October 1646, prelates were excluded from the House of Lords as of 13 February 1642, and the abolition of the Star Chamber in 1641 had eliminated their authority for censoring books. With the revival of licensing, Milton in *Areopagitica* warns, "Episcopall arts begin to bud again" and the country will suffer "a second tyranny over learning" (*CPW* II: 541, 539). He repeatedly underscores the Long Parliament's hypocrisy for adopting a system of regulation just as rigid as the restrictions that the Episcopal church government had imposed on learning: "He who but of late cry'd down the sole ordination of every novice Batchelor of Art, and deny'd sole jurisdiction over the simplest Parishioner, shall now at home in his privat chair assume both these over worthiest and excellentest books and ablest authors that write them" (*CPW* II: 540). Milton argues that the 1643 order "will soon put it out of controversie that Bishops and Presbyters are the same to us both name and thing" (*CPW* II: 539), an idea that he reiterates, as we have seen, in "On the New Forcers of Conscience," in which he laments that "New *Presbyter* is but old *Priest* writ large" (line 20).

Even Milton's decision to title his treatise *Areopagitica* after the highly respected Athenian court that met on a hill named Areopagus was in part an attempt to encourage Parliament not to repeat the prelates' policies. Just as the Greek orator Isocrates had appealed in his similarly titled tract for the Areopagus to reform itself and live up to its reputation as virtuous and fair-minded, so Milton was trying to persuade England's government to follow the Areopagus's classical precedent and to return to the ideals that initially distinguished the Long Parliament from Charles I's administration. Milton wanted the new government, as he puts it in *Areopagitica*, to demonstrate "what difference there is between the magnanimity of a trienniall Parlament, and that jealous hautinesse of Prelates and cabin Counsellours that usurpt of late" (*CPW* II: 488–89).

Presbyterian calls for reconciliation with the king also likely influenced Milton's acceptance of some censorship. Although in principle he may have believed in the value of regulating the book trade, the specific language that he uses to propose limited censorship seems intended as a critique of the king's administration. Most notably, Milton's rejection of "a rigid externall formality" as a "grosse conforming stupidity" (*CPW* II: 564) forcefully alludes to efforts by Charles I and Laud to restore and make uniform the elaborate rituals that characterized religious worship before the Reformation.[45] Immediately after dismissing "a rigid externall formality," Milton in *Areopagitica* introduces his exceptions to what should be freely published:

> Yet if all cannot be of one mind, as who looks they should be? this doubtles is more wholsome, more prudent, and more Christian that many be tolerated, rather then all compell'd. I mean not tolerated Popery, and open superstition, which as it extirpats all religions and civill supremacies, so it self should be extirpat, provided first that all charitable and compassionat means be us'd to win and regain the weak and the misled: that also which is impious or evil absolutely either against faith or maners no law can possibly permit, that intends not to unlaw it self.   (*CPW* II: 565)

Commentators such as Ernest Sirluck are no doubt correct that Milton here refers to Roman Catholicism as an exception to his argument for toleration;[46] in particular, the description of "open superstition" as "extirpat[ing] all religions and civill supremacies" echoes the language used by other seventeenth-century pamphleteers who also tried to impose limits on what should be tolerated.

Milton's argument in *Areopagitica*

Milton divides *Areopagitica* into four parts. He begins by discussing the history of licensing so as to "lay before" Parliament that "the inventors of it to bee those whom ye will be loath to own," namely Roman Catholics (*CPW* II: 491). In contrast to ancient Athens, Sparta, and Rome, which censored only blasphemous and libelous writing after it was published, the popes of Rome "extended their dominion over mens eyes, as they had before over their judgements, burning and prohibiting to be read, what they fansied not" (*CPW* II: 501–2).

Milton then discusses reading in general and the need to allow the publication of both good and bad books. He argues that the only way to prove one's virtue is to know evil and still to choose good – as he memorably asserts, "I cannot praise a fugitive and cloister'd vertue, unexercised & unbreath'd" (*CPW* II: 515) – and he concludes that the best way to "scout into the regions of sin and falsity" is by "reading all manner of tractats, and hearing all manner of reason" (*CPW* II: 517).

In the third section of *Areopagitica*, Milton shows that Parliament's Licensing Order fails to suppress the books the government wished to control, namely "scandalous, seditious, and libellous Books" (*CPW* II: 491). Here he also argues that "all recreations and pastimes, all that is delightfull to man" would have to be regulated because these things could equally "corrupt the mind" (*CPW* II: 523), a prospect that he considers ridiculous and impractical.

Milton concludes his argument by discussing the ways that licensing will make people not just less knowledgeable but less perceptive. The government's current system of censorship, he argues, will result in "the discouragement of all learning, and the stop of Truth, not only by disexercising and blunting our abilities in what we know already, but by hindring and cropping the discovery that might bee further made both in religious and civill Wisdome" (*CPW* II: 491–92). Even the most judicious licensers, Milton argues, would merely reinforce the status quo and "let passe nothing but what is vulgarly receiv'd already" (*CPW* II: 534). English citizens would come to depend on their ministers instead of thinking for themselves.

Milton also emphasizes in the tract's final section that people must achieve spiritual knowledge through their own hard work. Someone who "beleeve[s] things only because his Pastor sayes so, or the Assembly" may be a "heretick in the truth" (*CPW* II: 543). In other words, some people may know "the truth" because a religious or civil authority has told it to them, but these people are as bad as heretics because they cannot understand what they have been told. Like a math teacher who insists that students must show their work, Milton believes that the right answers are essential but so are the right means of arriving at them.

But we also need to remember that the answer to Milton's question about a forced uniformity ("as who looks they should be?") would have included the English church under Laud. In this context, "tolerated Popery" – as opposed to simply "popery" – is not a synonym for "open superstition" but more likely refers to Laudian ritual under an Episcopal form of church government. In Milton's view, to insist that such ceremonialism determined a person's salvation was tantamount to tolerating Catholicism, and books espousing such a belief should not be freely printed.

I do not mean to suggest, however, that Milton's political circumstances entirely shaped his argument in *Areopagitica*. Alongside the tract's practical objections to the government's licensing policy, Milton argues that allowing a select group of agents – whether Stationers or licensers – to oversee the book trade will lead "primely to the discouragement of all learning, and the stop of Truth" (*CPW* II: 491). This part of *Areopagitica* sounds more idealistic, concerned less with Presbyterians in Parliament than with an abstract principle of liberty. In a series of extended poetic images – a characteristic, as we have seen, of his early prose – Milton emphasizes the dynamic nature of pursuing "religious and civill Wisdome" (*CPW* II: 492). He compares truth to a "streaming fountain" whose waters must flow "in a perpetuall progression" (*CPW* II: 543); to a "flowry crop ... sprung up and yet springing daily in this City" (*CPW* II: 558); and to a virgin, "hewd ... into a thousand peeces," whose "lovely form" must be actively "gather[ed] up limb by limb" (*CPW* II: 549).

As this last metaphor suggests, Milton tries to counter the government's idea of restricting control of the book trade by advocating instead a more inclusive process that depends on various gatherers. In contrast to Presbyterians, "who perpetually complain of schisms and sects, and make it such a calamity that any man dissents from their maxims" (*CPW* II: 550), Milton extols the value of open discussion and constructive disagreement: "Where there is much desire to learn, there of necessity will be much arguing, much writing, many opinions" (*CPW* II: 554). In another of the tract's extended metaphors, he compares the pursuit of knowledge with constructing "the house of God," for both require various, differently skilled people, "some cutting, some squaring the marble, others hewing the cedars" (*CPW* II: 555). Here Milton also puns on contemporary fears of "sects and schisms" within the English church by insisting that to construct the physical temple "there must be many schisms and many dissections made in the quarry and in the timber" (*CPW* II: 566, 555). Milton points up the need for tolerating a diversity of Christian opinions and suggests that individual efforts will lead to a greater collaborative achievement: "out of many moderat varieties and brotherly dissimilitudes that are not vastly disproportionall arises the goodly and the gracefull symmetry that commends the whole pile and structure" (*CPW* II: 555).

This ideal of a collaborative construction is not limited to writers; commentators often overlook that Milton includes both printers and readers within the social process that he promulgates. In various places in *Areopagitica*, he focuses on an author's authority, as in the tract's most often quoted passage, in which he describes a "good Booke" as "the pretious life-blood of a master spirit, imbalm'd and treasur'd up on purpose to a life beyond life" (*CPW* II: 493). Perhaps influenced by his own legal difficulties, Milton repeatedly addresses the ways that the law demeans "the free and ingenuous sort" whose "publisht labours advance the good of mankind" (*CPW* II: 531). He complains, for example, that the licensing order implies that members of Parliament "distrust the judgement & the honesty" of authors, casting them as mere "Grammar lad[s]" and "boy[s] at school" (*CPW* II: 531).

But elsewhere in *Areopagitica* Milton hints at the perspectives of printers, publishers, and booksellers, and emphasizes the need for their cooperation to create and circulate books. His singling out of a parliamentary order from 29 January 1642 suggests his respect for agents of material production; as Milton loosely paraphrases, the order required that "the Printers and the Authors name, or at least the Printers be register'd" (*CPW* II: 569). Even Milton's metaphor of differently skilled artisans constructing God's temple could suggest the division of labor in a printing house and include members of the book trade as part of the social process of authorship. "[L]earning is indetted," Milton more plainly asserts near the end of *Areopagitica*, to the "honest profession" of bookmaking (*CPW* II: 570).

Trying to establish the significance of books near the start of the tract, Milton alludes to the myth of Cadmus: "I know they [books] are as lively, and as vigorously productive, as those fabulous Dragons teeth; and being sown up and down, may chance to spring up armed men" (*CPW* II: 492). But even here Milton hints that authors do not work in isolation. If we recall that Cadmus was credited with inventing the use of letters to signify speech sounds (or, according to some traditions, introducing the alphabet into Greece), he represents a material agent on whom authors depend to create their texts. When Milton writes that books are as "lively" and "vigorously productive" as Cadmus's "fabulous Dragons teeth" (*CPW* II: 492), he conjures the image of letters as the life-giving seed that books preserve. Only when "sown up and down" in readers' minds, can the words stored in books give birth to – "chance to spring up" – people "armed" with an author's insights (*CPW* II: 492).

Milton's allusion to Cadmus thus also includes readers within the social process of acquiring knowledge that the government's licensing policy threatened to impede. Authors and printers, he believed, depend on a book's audience for their work to have lasting value. Milton accordingly compares a good reader to "a good refiner" who "can gather gold out of the drossiest volume," even using "errors" – when they are "known, read, and collated" – for "the speedy attainment of what is truest" (*CPW* II: 513, 521). Like Psyche sifting through

Venus's "confused seeds," readers must "cull out, and sort asunder" the good ideas found in books (*CPW* II: 514).

This part of *Areopagitica* echoes other seventeenth-century discussions of reading as a laborious searching and gathering. Perhaps most immediately, Milton's metaphor suggests Francis Bacon's indictment of scholastic reading in *The Advancement of Learning* (1605). Bacon compares "schoolmen" to spiders, spinning ideas out of their heads, "admirable for the fineness of thread and work, but of no substance or profit"; Bacon instead wants readers who will weigh what they read with what they observe, and "hunt" in books "after the weight of matter, worth of subject, soundness of argument, life of invention, or depth of judgment."[47]

Milton in *Areopagitica* pushes this idea of active reading further. Most notably, personifying truth as a dismembered virgin raises the stakes for readers' engagement with an author's and printer's work; Milton's violent imagery suggests the tremendous responsibility he accords a book's audience. He wants readers who will persevere, "imitating the carefull search that *Isis* made for the mangl'd body of *Osiris*" by "gathering up limb by limb" the "dissever'd peeces" of Truth "scatter'd" through various pamphlets and books (*CPW* II: 549, 550–51). If, as Sabrina Baron has argued, Milton in *Areopagitica* ultimately emerges less as an opponent to censorship and more as "the proponent of the freedom to read," equally important is the obligation that Milton believes readers have: they must work hard and think for themselves.[48] Because "the knowledge and survay of vice is in this world so necessary to the constituting of human vertue," readers must cultivate good reading habits: "how can we more safely, and with lesse danger scout into the regions of sin and falsity then by reading all manner of tractats, and hearing all manner of reason" (*CPW* II: 516–17)? Milton introduces metaphors of digesting food and compounding medicine to emphasize readers' power and responsibility. Whereas "Bad meats will scarce breed good nourishment in the healthiest concoction," a "discreet and judicious Reader" can digest even "bad books," making them useful "to discover, to confute, to forewarn, and to illustrate" (*CPW* II: 512). He adds that books also resemble "usefull drugs and materialls wherewith to temper and compose effective and strong med'cins" (*CPW* II: 521). This comparison once again suggests the potential that books contain and the work that they require: readers must first transform a text into something useful, then apply it in their pursuit of knowledge.[49]

Yet, lest we overstate Milton's ideas about readers' authority, we need to remember that, for all Milton's open-mindedness and forward thinking in *Areopagitica*, his willingness to serve as a government licenser just five years after the tract's publication seems to qualify further his arguments for readers' freedom.[50] Milton was also inclined to elevate the status of readers in general, not necessarily the actual readers who purchased his own poetic and prose works. The year before he died, Milton in *Of True Religion* (1673) was still urging his readers "to read duly and diligently the Holy Scriptures" (VIII: 433) and still hoping readers would peruse books critically "to examine their Teachers themselves" (VIII: 435). But Milton could also respond harshly to readers of his works whom he considered impertinent or ill-prepared. When readers of the first edition of *Paradise Lost* wondered why the poem did not rhyme, he added a sharp critique of their expectations, dismissing "the jingling sound of like endings," and when readers objected to the logic and morality of his divorce tracts, he wrote two sonnets satirizing such hostile reactions as the "barbarous noise ... / Of owls and cuckoos, asses, apes and dogs."[51] The problem with his divorce tracts, he would later explain, was that he should not have written in English, "for then I would not have met with vernacular readers, who are usually ignorant of their own good, and laugh at the misfortunes of others" (*CPW* IV: 610).

If we are looking for consistency in Milton's words and deeds, it may lie not in an idealized notion of a free press but in an ongoing commitment to the social process of pursuing knowledge that he describes in *Areopagitica*. In practice and in principle, Milton throughout his career depended on other people in the creation and circulation of his texts. Returning, for example, to the note on the verse that he added to *Paradise Lost*, we discover that he wrote it only after the request of the printer Samuel Simmons and that Simmons, on behalf of the "many" who "desired it," also asked Milton to compose the arguments that summarize each of the epic's books.[52] Often, as with *The Doctrine and Discipline of Divorce*, Milton attempted to accommodate readers' responses by working with printers and booksellers to publish revised versions of his prose tracts. When readers failed to live up to Milton's high expectations, he tried harder in each expanded edition to map out the preparation and effort he required of them.

Milton also envisioned his own writing as part of a larger cooperative endeavor – the building of God's temple, as he describes it in *Areopagitica*. Thus in his theological treatise, *De Doctrina Christiana*, Milton promotes "free discussion and inquiry" (*CPW* VI: 121); he does "not urge or enforce anything upon [his] own authority" but instead tells readers to think for themselves and "Assess this work as God's spirit shall direct you" (*CPW* VI: 121, 124). Or, to take a more well-known example, when Eve in *Paradise Lost* separates from Adam to garden alone, she argues, "what is faith, love, virtue unassayed / Alone, without exterior help sustained?" (IX.335–36). Critics frequently note that Eve is paraphrasing the crucial point in *Areopagitica* that virtue must be tested; as we have seen, Milton in 1644 specifically explains that he "cannot praise a fugitive and cloister'd vertue, unexercis'd & unbreath'd, that never sallies out and sees her adversary" (*CPW* II: 515). But, as Joan Bennett has astutely observed, the second part of Eve's argument for working alone is faulty: Adam's "exterior help" would not limit Eve's virtue or compromise her free will.[53] Eve does not sin until she eats the fruit, but here she fails to understand that arriving at truth is both an individual endeavor and a collaborative process, and that she and Adam should "sustain" each other as they decide whether to work together or apart.

That Milton stages the scene preceding the fall of humankind by dramatizing one of *Areopagitica*'s core principles is significant. In the years following the tract's publication, he may have agreed to work as a government licenser, and his faith in readers may have sometimes waned, but he still believed in the need for collaboration. In both *Areopagitica* and *Paradise Lost*, Milton continues to emphasize that "Where there is much desire to learn, there of necessity will be much arguing, … many opinions" (*CPW* II: 554).

Commonwealth prose

This section focuses on the group of political treatises that Milton authored during the civil wars and Interregnum to defend the English revolution on behalf of the new government. "Commonwealth" refers to the country's new political structure: from 1649 to 1660, England's monarchical government was replaced by a Parliament and an executive Council of State.[54] The tracts that Milton wrote during these eleven years demonstrate both his radical political thinking and his thorough engagement with the period's major political events. Nine of Milton's works from these years deserve special attention: *The Tenure of Kings and Magistrates*, *Eikonoklastes*, his three Latin defenses, *A Treatise of Civil Power*, *Considerations Touching the Likeliest Means to Remove Hirelings*, *The Readie and Easie Way to Establish a Free Commonwealth*, and *Brief Notes upon a Late Sermon*.

Arguably Milton's most important Commonwealth tract is his first, *The Tenure of Kings and Magistrates*, published on 13 February 1649, then published in a revised and expanded edition sometime before 30 September of the same year. The tract's theoretical justification for deposing and punishing a monarch represents a significant contribution to early modern political theory. Milton posits a reciprocal relationship between a king and his people:

> since the King or Magistrate holds his autoritie of the people, both
> originally and naturally for their good in the first place, and not his

own, then may the people as oft as they shall judge it for the best, either choose him or reject him, retaine him or depose him though no Tyrant, merely by the liberty and right of free born Men, to be govern'd as seems to them best.   (*CPW* III: 206)

Milton, in other words, was challenging the prevailing theory of the divine right of kings, embraced by both Tudor and Stuart monarchs, perhaps most notably by James I in *Basilikon Doron* (1599). Milton rejects outright the idea that kings are answerable only to God; he calls it a violation of law and reason: "For if they may refuse to give account, then all cov'nants made with them at Coronation; all Oathes are in vaine, and meer mockeries, all Lawes which they sweare to keep, made to no purpose" (*CPW* III: 204). Most remarkably, Milton expands the justification for deposing a ruler and maintains that, even if a king is not a tyrant, the people have the natural right to keep or depose him because they give him his power.

This part of *Tenure*'s argument follows the logic of Milton's divorce tracts. Like a nuptial contract between a husband and wife, the political contract between a king and his people should not be sustained if it no longer fulfills its God-given purpose – solace against loneliness, in the case of a marriage, and the public good, in the case of a monarch. Whereas Milton had previously used an ill-managed government as an analogy for understanding an ill marriage, he now pursues the comparison in the opposite direction: just as bad marriages should be dissolved, so bad rulers should be deposed. A nation's people, he argues, can depose their king because they are authorized by God "as Maisters of Family in thir own house" (*CPW* III: 237).

Milton derived his contractual theory of government from his concept of the secondary law of nature, which, as we saw in the discussion of his divorce tracts, he believed God gave to humankind to cope with its fallen state. Milton begins with the premise that God creates all people with the same authority: "No man … can be so stupid to deny that all men naturally were borne free, being the image and resemblance of God himself, and were by privilege above all the creatures, born to command and not to obey" (*CPW* III: 198–99). Milton's natural law theory thus justifies the limits of a monarch's authority and the rights of the people. If a king breaks his contract with his subjects, they have the right to depose and punish him because by nature they are equally free (*CPW* III: 254). As Milton repeatedly insists, "Justice is the onely true sovran and supreme Majesty upon earth," not a king or magistrate (*CPW* III: 237).

The logical and scriptural emphasis of Milton's argument in *Tenure* echoes the polemical strategy in his anti-prelatical and divorce writings, but new to this tract is his more restrained prose style. Milton no longer incorporates vivid imagery and elaborate metaphors to enhance his argument. Instead, perhaps due to the sensitivity of his subject – *Tenure* appeared two weeks after Charles I's execution and four days after his burial at Windsor – Milton prefers a less poetic style and a less passionate tone. He never mentions Charles I by name in *Tenure*, and he argues almost politely, more like an impartial scholar than an irate partisan.

Also, Milton's argument in *Tenure* remains limited in significant ways. As David Loewenstein has observed, Milton may take a radical position in defending revolution, but he never resolves his populist argument with the fact that he is attempting to defend an unrepresentative government – the Rump Parliament and the army, the two bodies that had put the king on trial.[55] Readers might also reasonably question Milton's broad appeal to a law of nature for determining whether a king has violated his contract with his people. While Milton contends that a ruler – "be he King, or Tyrant, or Emperour" – should be subject to "the Sword of Justice" if he has massacred his subjects or made secret deals to attack cities or countries (both of which, he believed, Charles I had done), Milton never spells out a practical method for evaluating whether a king should be retained or deposed (*CPW* III: 197). Instead, he suggests that such judgments should be made on a case-by-case basis according to "the Law of nature and right reason" (*CPW* III: 197). This general formulation points up Milton's unwavering belief in the power of reason informed by divine guidance – "right reason" re-occurs, for example, in *Paradise Lost* (VI.42, XII.84) – but the vagueness of his language in *Tenure* betrays his argument's impractical idealism. As Merritt Hughes has noted in his survey of published responses to the civil wars, writers with diverse political positions similarly appealed to "natural law" and the "public good" (*salus populi*) to defend their convictions. The army, for example, tried to use the law of nature to justify purging Presbyterian members from Parliament who supported the king, while, on the other side, Presbyterians attempted to use the law of nature to bolster their support for the divine right of kings. By the middle of the seventeenth century, writers cited the doctrine of the law of nature with greater frequency but less clarity; the concept was quickly devolving, Hughes observes, into "a transcendent principle of essentially emotional appeal."[56]

But if parts of *Tenure* remain unsettled, Milton offers a clear and forceful critique of Presbyterians, the other crucial emphasis of the tract's argument. *Tenure*, more than *Areopagitica*, demonstrates Milton's growing disenchantment with the group he had supported in the early 1640s in his anti-prelatical prose. He concedes that "very many" Presbyterians are "good and faithfull Christians" (*CPW* III: 238), but he adds in disgust that the same Presbyterian ministers who had so vehemently criticized and waged war against the king now "plead for him, pity him, extoll him, protest against those that talk of bringing him to the tryal of Justice" (*CPW* III: 193). In some of the tract's sharpest language, he denounces Presbyterians as "Mercenary noisemakers," "prevaricating Divines," and "Ministers of sedition" (*CPW* III: 236, 232). He believed the king was still guilty of the tyrannical crimes that were at the heart of the civil conflict – that is, Charles I had levied war against his people and Parliament – and thus the king should still be held accountable. In contrast, Presbyterians appeared to be motivated by self-interest in their shifting response to the monarch. They initially opposed the king, Milton alleges, "while the hope to bee made Classic and Provincial Lords led them on, while pluralities greas'd them thick and deep" (*CPW* III: 196). But once Charles had agreed to accept a Presbyterian church government in Scotland and to establish the same system in England, the Presbyterians favored a negotiated settlement and opposed putting the king on trial.

Milton's disappointment with Presbyterians becomes a recurrent theme in the subsequent tracts he wrote in his official capacity as Secretary for Foreign Tongues. As we saw in Chapter 1, his first government assignment, *Observations on the Articles of Peace* (16 May 1649), again highlights Presbyterian hypocrisy, and in his next major prose work, *Eikonoklastes*, Milton continues to denounce Presbyterians, "whose lips preserve not knowledge, but the way ever op'n to … [their] bellies" (*CPW* III: 553).

Yet *Eikonoklastes* has comparatively less to say about the inconsistency of the country's religious leaders; here Milton concentrates on justifying the regicides for putting Charles I on trial and finding him guilty of treason. Published on 6 October 1649, nine months after *The Tenure*, *Eikonoklastes* represents a thoroughgoing rebuttal of *Eikon Basilike: The Portraiture of His Sacred Majesty in His Solitudes and Sufferings* (1649), a widely popular book that purported to contain Charles I's prayers and private meditations while in prison awaiting trial. Milton in *Eikonoklastes* deploys the same method that had been so successful in *Animadversions*: he quotes passages from *Eikon Basilike* and follows each with a detailed rebuttal. But whereas in his earlier tract Milton was openly contemptuous of his opponent, in *Eikonoklastes* he adopts a measured tone, more appropriate to a recently deceased monarch whose book resembles a memorial more than a polemic.

Milton in *Eikonoklastes* seems to have understood the difficulty of his appointed task. Beginning with an elaborate frontispiece portrait depicting Charles I kneeling and gazing toward heaven, *Eikon Basilike* appealed to contemporary readers' raw emotions; it sought to dispel the notion of tyranny by portraying the late king as a benevolent, misunderstood martyr. Milton's strategy for his rebuttal was to turn the strength of the book's style into a weakness: he treats the performative power of *Eikon Basilike* as a symptom of its dishonesty and contends that the book – whose title literally means "The King's Image" – represents a mere image, "a civil kinde of Idolatry" (*CPW* III: 343). Milton thus casts himself as an *eikonoklastes*, or in modern spelling an iconoclast (literally, "destroyer of images"), and sets out to break apart the book's false depiction and expose the truth behind the royal façade. He shows, for example, how the king in *Eikon Basilike* pleads that he "*had rather not rule then that his people should be ruin'd*," but, Milton observes, "yet above these twenty yeres [Charles I] hath bin ruining the people about the niceties of his ruling" (*CPW* III: 498). Or when the king claims that he "*oft'n prayd that all on his side might be as faithfull to God and thir own souls, as to him*," Milton bitterly counters, "But Kings, above all other men, have in thir hands not to pray onely but to doe. To make that prayer effectual, he should have govern'd as well as pray'd" (*CPW* III: 531). Milton repeatedly attempts to show the difference between the king's seductive words and "his own farr differing deeds" (*CPW* III: 347).

One of Milton's most striking and most controversial criticisms of *Eikon Basilike* was that Charles I had cribbed a prayer, spoken by the character Pamela, from Philip Sidney's *Arcadia* and presented it "word for word" as one of his own personal meditations (*CPW* III: 362). While this point looks ahead, as Mark Rose has noted, to the first Copyright Act of 1709, Milton seems less concerned with the issue of plagiarism than with the fact that the king "shark'd" a prayer from a secular romance instead of addressing God sincerely, "of his own proper Zeal" (*CPW* III: 367, 364).[57] In this regard, Milton revisits the argument from his anti-prelatical tracts against set prayers and in favor of natural expressions of faith. But the vehemence of Milton's criticism of the king's misuse of Pamela's prayer – and the strident Royalist counterarguments that it prompted – also suggests a larger political concern. Long before 1649, as Milton must have known, disenfranchised Royalists had composed supplements and sequels to Sidney's unfinished romance in an attempt to ally themselves with the *Arcadia*'s chivalric values and Sidney's reputation as a charismatic aristocratic hero.[58] Thus when Milton in *Eikonoklastes* complains that the author of *Eikon Basilike* was trespassing against "human right, which commands that every Author should have the property of his own work reserved to him after death as well as living" (*CPW* III: 365), he was opposing in part the way that Royalists used Sidney for ideological purposes. The "good caution" (*CPW* III: 362) that Milton advocates represents an exhortation for readers to approach *Arcadia* as a fictional work by Sidney rather than accept its compatibility with the late king's cause.

Today readers of *Eikonoklastes* will probably be struck most by the rigor and thoroughness of the book's overarching argument: Milton painstakingly refutes *Eikon Basilike*, chapter by chapter, citing a wealth of supporting documents and authorities and explaining at each point the political events alluded to by Charles. Yet, based on the ongoing popularity of *Eikon Basilike* and the relative lack of interest that Milton's *Eikonoklastes* seems to have garnered, we may detect a fundamental miscalculation on Milton's part. His reasoned and well-researched argument could not compete with the more visceral response that the king's book prompted. Whereas *Eikon Basilike* continued in print throughout the seventeenth century, *Eikonoklastes* appeared in only one other edition in Milton's lifetime.

When on 8 January 1650 the Council of State next called on its Secretary for Foreign Tongues "to prepare something in answer to the book of Salmasius," Milton had learned his lesson.[59] In *Pro Populo Anglicano Defensio* ("The Defense of the English People"), published on 24 February 1651, Milton draws largely on scriptures to construct a detailed moral justification for deposing a tyrant; as in *Tenure*, his basic premise remains that kings derive their authority from the people, who are naturally free. But in *Defensio* Milton sloughs off the moderate tone of *Tenure* and *Eikonoklastes*, recapturing instead the scorn and wit – albeit not the poetic style – that characterized much of his early prose. The specific book that the Council wanted Milton to answer was *Defensio Regia pro Carolo I* ("The Royal Defense of Charles I" [1649]), written by the celebrated European scholar Claudius Salmasius. As Milton's nephew Edward Phillips characterized the conflict, Milton was "our little *English David*" opposing the "great *French Goliah*, to whom he gave such a hit in the Forehead, that he presently staggered, and soon after fell" (*EL* 70). Milton achieved his victory over Salmasius by adopting the same zealous thoroughness on display in *Eikonoklastes*. Point by point, he challenges and outdoes Salmasius's scholarship, exposing inconsistencies and oversights in the great writer's logic and research. At the same time, Milton attacks Salmasius personally, deriding everything from his Latin grammar to his marriage and manhood. "[T]he improvised effusions of any blabbermouth who makes rhymes while standing on one leg would be far more deserving of publication," Milton sneers, adding, "I personally despise and mock you; for it would be far beneath the dignity of the English nation herself to take any general notice of such a boring little weevil as you" (*CPW* IV: 334, 339). So it goes for almost two hundred pages.

Milton maintains this indignant tone as he continues his polemical defense of the new government in two more Latin tracts, *Pro Populo Anglicano Defensio Secunda* ("The Second Defense of the English People"), published on 30 May 1654, and *Pro Se Defensio* ("Defense of Himself"), published the following year on 8 August. Of all Milton's Latin prose, his second defense is probably most often consulted by students and scholars because it contains a long auto-biographical digression in which Milton defends his experience and character. Once again, the Council of State had commissioned Milton as Secretary for Foreign Tongues to respond to a printed critique of the English government. But the anonymous pamphlet *Regii Sanguinis Clamor* ("The Cry of the Royal Blood" [1652]) not only attacks Parliament and the army for the "horrible crime" of executing Charles I – "Compared with this, the crime of the Jews in crucifying Christ was nothing" – it also singles out Milton as the author of *Defensio*.[60] The treatise's objective was both to refute Milton's first defense and to persuade Continental monarchies to look unfavorably on England's new government.

The scurrilous nature of the personal attack that Milton suffers in *Clamor* arguably warrants his autobiographical comments in the second defense. The author of *Clamor* devotes the final chapter to belittling "That Foul Rascal John Milton," and in various other passages he criticizes Milton as a "loathsome executioner," a "monster of a man," and an "insignificant piece of mud."[61] Milton in his second defense accordingly argues that he was not expelled from Cambridge, as the author of *Clamor* suggests, and he systematically answers the other charges made against him: he defends his parents, boyhood, early education, university experience, international travel, and publication record. Milton even finds it necessary to defend his blindness against the charge in *Clamor* that he lost his sight as divine punishment for writing in support of regicide:

> I call upon Thee, my God, who knowest my inmost mind and all my thoughts, to witness that (although I have repeatedly examined myself on this point as earnestly as I could, and have searched all the corners of my life) I am conscious of nothing, or of no deed, either recent or remote, whose wickedness could justly occasion or invite upon me this supreme misfortune. As for what I have at any time written …, I likewise call God to witness that I have written nothing of such kind that I was not then and am not now convinced that it was right and true and pleasing to God. And I swear that my conduct was not influenced by ambition, gain, or glory, but solely by considerations of duty, honor, and devotion to my country.   (*CPW* IV: 587)

Most remarkable about *Defensio Secunda*, however, may be that Milton balances the type of sincere apologia illustrated in the above passage with coarse puns, lofty panegyric, savage satire, and candid political advice. *Defensio Secunda* represents Milton's most accomplished Latin prose, a dexterous blend of various styles, by turns cautionary, censorious, laudatory, bawdy, and erudite. He praises various English leaders and foreign dignitaries, including the revolutionaries John Bradshaw, Thomas Fairfax, and Oliver Cromwell, and, perhaps to show that he did not disapprove of all monarchs, he includes a tribute to Queen Christina of Sweden, "whose devotion to the liberal arts and to men of learning has never been surpassed" (*CPW* IV: 556). But, in another example of the tract's diverse style, Milton interrupts his extended panegyrics with a blunt warning for Cromwell, newly appointed as Lord Protector: "Consider again and again how precious a thing is this liberty which you hold, committed to your care, entrusted and commended to you by how dear a mother, your native land" (*CPW* IV: 673).

Milton's final Latin defense, *Pro Se Defensio*, is a simpler tract and reveals far less about Milton than his *Defensio Secunda*. The title specifically alludes to Milton's effort to defend the rhetorical strategy that he deployed in his second defense. Because the Protestant cleric Alexander More added a preface to *Clamor* and supervised and corrected the press work, Milton in *Defensio Secunda* had treated More as the book's author. We now know that *Clamor* was in fact written by the Royalist priest Peter Du Moulin, but in *Pro Se Defensio*, Milton adamantly upholds his choice of More as author, despite new evidence that he had received to the contrary. Milton thus made, according to some critics, the "worst mistake of his public career."[62]

But if the objective of *Pro Se Defensio* seems fairly specific and of limited interest to modern readers, Milton's final Latin defense is nevertheless valuable for its detailed discussion of authorship. Milton justifies calling More the author of *Clamor* according to the type of collaborative writing that, we have seen, commonly occurred in the seventeenth century.[63] For Milton, "author" includes all the people who cooperate in producing a text; he thus attacks More, the alleged writer, as well as its printer, Vlacq, and the other anonymous participants who helped to produce the critique. Echoing *Areopagitica*'s defense of collaborative learning, Milton threatens that he can assign responsibility for a text to any of its collaborators, regardless of their particular involvement:

> If I find that you wrote or contributed one page of this book, or even one versicle, if I find that you published it, or procured or persuaded anyone to publish it, or that you were in charge of its publication, or even lent yourself to the smallest part of the work, seeing that no one else comes forth, for me you alone will be the author of the whole work, the culprit and the crier.   (*CPW* IV: 712–13)

Reports of More's scandalous misconduct, combined with the punning potential of his name (*morus* is Latin for "foolish"), made him a rhetorically ideal candidate for Milton to attack as the author of *Clamor*, but Milton in the above passage implies that, if he had known the book's other contributors, they would have shared responsibility for its authorship, as the printer Vlacq does. Milton cites Justinian to support this logic: "If any, to the infamy of another, shall write, compose, or publish any libel or poem or history, or with evil intent shall cause any such to be done," then that person "shall be considered and punished as the author" (*CPW* IV: 713).

Admittedly, Milton's definition of an author in *Pro Se Defensio* ignores an important distinction: he never addresses the question of who was primarily responsible for *Clamor*. As Milton discovered with *Clamor*, identifying all of a book's collaborators is difficult, and pinpointing each person's contribution is sometimes impossible. His argument is therefore more theoretical than practical, but it nevertheless has provocative implications for reading Milton's own works and, more generally, studying early modern literature. We could, for example, apply his inclusive theory of authorship to *Responsio ad Apologiam Anonymi* (1652), a prose work in which Milton collaborated with his nephew John Phillips, or to *An Answere to a Book Entitled An Humble Remonstrance* (1641), a pamphlet by Smectymnuus for which Milton probably wrote the postscript.

Milton composed his remaining Commonwealth tracts – as he did *Pro Se Defensio* and *Tenure* – without the benefit of a formal government position. No longer writing at the request of the Council of State, he instead shared his opinions as a concerned and deeply engaged private citizen. Ill health and other longer projects – namely, *De Doctrina Christiana* and *The History of Britain* – may have temporarily limited Milton's political publications after 1655. But in the final, increasingly unstable years of the Interregnum following the death of Oliver Cromwell, Milton returned to political prose with renewed energy and a growing sense of desperation.

In mid-February 1659, Milton published *A Treatise of Civil Power in Ecclesiastical Causes*, which he addressed to the new Parliament under Cromwell's son Richard. This brief tract underscores Milton's radical religious convictions: he argues that neither the civil government nor ecclesiastical authorities should attempt by outward force to control believers' inward faith and conscience. Here we see the natural development of Milton's critique of England's church government from the early 1640s; individual believers, he once again insists, should be guided by the Holy Spirit and their own reasoned reading of the scriptures, regardless of whether "the visible church with all her doctors gainsay" (*CPW* VII: 248). Milton also emphasizes the idea from *Areopagitica* that believers should follow their "inward perswasive motions" and engage in a "free and lawful debate at all times by writing, conference or disputation" (*CPW* VII: 261, 249). He correspondingly downplays the significance of external authorities: "none can judge or determin here on earth, no not church-governors themselves against the consciences of other beleevers" (*CPW* VII: 244). Civil power in particular, he argues, violates "the fundamental privilege of the gospel, the new-birthright of everie true beleever, Christian libertie" (VII: 262).

Milton's next tract, *Considerations Touching the Likeliest Means to Remove Hirelings out of the Church* (August 1659) develops a similar argument. Milton continues to oppose a hierarchical national church as he warns the restored Rump to reduce the number of paid ministers or "hirelings." Although he concedes that these ministers should receive a "due recompense or reward," he objects to the large sums that the laity were required to dole out to support the clergy: "That which makes it so dangerous in the church, and properly makes the *hireling*, a word always of evil signification, is either the excess thereof, or the undue manner of giving and taking it" (*CPW* VII: 278–79). Milton especially opposes tithes, a tax collected by the church of one-tenth of the laity's income, which had become a point of contention during the civil wars. In 1659 various petitions continued to come before Parliament to abolish this fee. Milton argues that the payment of tithes as stipulated in Leviticus had been abandoned under the Gospel, and he wishes that English ministers could imitate Christ and his apostles by "looking for no recompence but in heaven" (*CPW* VII: 303). While Milton also offers some practical solutions for eliminating tithes – he recommends, for example, that the state establish public libraries and free education for ministers – above all he insists that civil support for a church's ministry demeans Christian liberty (*CPW* VII: 289). As in his anti-prelatical tracts and *Areopagitica*, Milton foregrounds the spiritual authority of an individual conscience reading the Bible: the "studie of scripture," he asserts, is "the only true theologie," adding that "certainly it is not necessarie to the attainment of Christian knowledge that men should sit all thir life long at the feet of a pulpited divine" (*CPW* VII: 306, 302).

On the eve of the Restoration, Milton composed three other short prose works about the government's civil and ecclesiastical problems: *A Letter to a Friend, Concerning the Rupture of the Commonwealth* (20 October 1659); *Proposalls of Certaine Expedients for the Preventing of a Civil War* (between 27 October and 24 December 1659); and *The Present Means, and Brief Delineation of a Free Commonwealth* (between 23 February and 4 March 1660). None of these works were printed during Milton's life, and it is not clear how finished Milton judged the surviving manuscripts to be. All three focus on possible ways to maintain the Commonwealth and forestall the country's return to monarchy – or, as Milton puts it, "to save us from approaching ruine … [b]eing now in Anarchy …" (*CPW* VII: 329). Milton in all three tracts calls for "the settling of som firme & durable government," either a senate or general council of state, instead of "single government by any one person," which he considers the "common enemie, gapeing at present to devour us" (*CPW* VII: 336, 331).

Milton eloquently pursued the same position in his next tract, *The Readie and Easie Way to Establish a Free Commonwealth*, arguably his most important piece of political prose from the late 1650s. As England's Commonwealth government was collapsing, Milton hurriedly published the first edition of *The Readie and Easie Way* in late February 1660; then, attempting to respond to the country's rapidly changing political situation, he produced a fully revised and greatly expanded second edition in the first week of April. The tract is remarkable both for Milton's fiery rhetoric and for his unwavering conviction. He argues that England should not revert to the limitations of personal liberty that come with monarchy – what he deems a return to "a Lent of Servitude" in

---

The poetry of *The Readie and Easie Way*

Milton in *The Readie and Easie Way* boldly returns to the fierce, poetic style of his earlier English prose. The passionate peroration in the second edition ranks among his most notable accomplishments. He brings his argument into sharp focus and in the final lines exhorts his readers:

> Thus much I should perhaps have said though I were sure I should have spoken only to trees and stones; and had none to cry to, but with the Prophet, *O earth, earth, earth!* to tell the very soil it self, what her perverse inhabitants are deaf to. Nay though what I have spoke, should happ'n (which Thou suffer not, who didst create mankind free; nor Thou next, who didst redeem us from being servants of men!) to be the last words of our expiring libertie. But I trust I shall have spoken perswasion to abundance of sensible and ingenuous men: to som perhaps whom God may raise of these stones to become children of reviving libertie; and may reclaim, though they seem now chusing them a captain back for *Egypt*, to bethink themselves a little and consider whether they are rushing; to exhort this torrent also of the people, not to be so impetuos, but to keep thir due channel; and at length recovering and uniting thir better resolutions, now that they see alreadie how open and unbounded the insolence and rage is of our common enemies, to stay these ruinous proceedings; justly and timely fearing to what a precipice of destruction the deluge of this epidemic madness would hurrie us through the general defection of a misguided and abus'd multitude. (*CPW* VII: 462–63)

Here Milton uses biblical and metaphorical language to denigrate public sentiment for monarchy and to advance his reasons for maintaining England as a commonwealth. He specifically casts the supporters of kingship as faithless

Israelites who sinfully prefer the servitude of their Egyptian captivity – "chusing them a captain back for *Egypt*" – over a path to the Promised Land. That he allies himself with the "Prophet" who cried "*O earth, earth, earth*" both elevates his own stature while further debasing his opponents. Milton is comparing himself to the prophet Jeremiah who angrily called out to the earth as he cursed Jeconiah (also called Coniah), the banished King of Judah and the worthless son of the evil King Jehoiakim, clearly meant in the context of *The Readie and Easie Way* to evoke Charles I and his exiled son, the future Charles II.

The natural imagery in this passage encapsulates Milton's sense of England's political crisis: an extended water metaphor ("rushing," "torrent," "deluge") disparagingly describes the swelling, heedless support that monarchy has garnered. Instead of falling impetuously over "a precipice of destruction," the people of England, according to Milton's metaphor, should "keep thir due channel," a potentially paradoxical image for retaining their hard-won liberty.

With the passage's second metaphor, Milton compares insensible readers to stones, emphasizing the resistance that he fears his ideas might meet. He hopes that he can persuade an "abundance of sensible and ingeneous men" to support the Commonwealth, but he recognizes that, as in the parable of the sower, his words may fall on stony ground and fail to take root (see Matthew 13:5). That he then aspires to turn these "stones" into "children of reviving libertie" may allude to either Ezekiel, who had a vision of dry bones being revived by his preaching (Ezekiel 37), or John the Baptist, who also referred to "stones" and "children" while encouraging the Pharisees and Sadducees to repent (Matthew 3:8–9).[64] Pairing "expiring libertie" with "reviving libertie" effectively summarizes the choice that Milton believes England now faces. Just as he allusively raises his own stature to that of a prophet – Jeremiah, Ezekiel, or John the Baptist – he encourages his readers to use their reason and faith so as to distinguish themselves from the "misguided and abus'd multitude."

which the king "must be ador'd like a Demigod" (*CPW* VII: 408, 425). He also appeals once again to the law of nature – "truly and properly to all mankinde fundamental" – as he affirms the justice of having tried and executed Charles I (*CPW* VII: 413). New in the tract's second edition is a proposal for an alternative senate modeled on the Areopagus or Sanhedrin, but primarily in both versions of *The Readie and Easie Way* Milton warns against an impending loss of freedom – "the deluge of … epidemic madness" (*CPW* VII: 463) – that will come with a return to monarchy. Milton insists that the majority opinion should not prevail "where main matters are in question" (*CPW* VII: 415). Popular sentiment might support a return to monarchy, but Milton values above everything else "liberty of conscience" which, he explains, "monarchie and her bishops both fear and hate" (*CPW* VII: 456, 458). He argues that it is more just for a minority to compel the majority to retain their rights than for the majority to force the minority to forfeit their freedom: "They who seek nothing but thir own just libertie, have alwaies right to winn it and to keep it, when ever they have power, be the voice never so numerous that oppose it" (*CPW* VII: 455).

Reading *The Readie and Easie Way* today, we should not underestimate Milton's courage. He was continuing to write openly on behalf of the Commonwealth – his name or initials appear on the title pages of both editions – even as public sentiment for restoring Charles II was cresting and the restored Long Parliament clearly began to prepare for a return to monarchy. Although General George Monck, the commander-in-chief of the army, had announced at the beginning of 1660 that he would support maintaining a commonwealth, Monck's decision to reinstate the Presbyterian members of Parliament whom the army had forcibly removed in 1648 all but ensured the end of republicanism and the return of Charles II. The restored MPs had been originally purged, as we saw in Chapter 2, because they did not wish to put the king on trial; by the time that the second edition of *The Readie and Easie Way* was published, these members had already called for new elections and pointedly omitted the Rump's proposal that all members needed to oppose monarchy.

By the time Milton wrote his next and final Commonwealth tract, he must have realized the increasing likelihood that the republican government would fail. Published shortly after the second edition of *The Readie and Easie Way* in early April 1660, *Brief Notes upon a Late Sermon* has a more specific focus. The tract mostly attacks Matthew Griffith, a Royalist minister and former chaplain to Charles I. Griffith had delivered and published a sermon in which he cast Charles II as a divinely chosen leader, who, like Samson, would unexpectedly take vengeance on God's enemies, namely, Presbyterians and Independents who had opposed Charles I. Milton in *Brief Notes* responds to Griffith by returning to the type of personal assault and scriptural refutation that, as we have seen, characterized so many of Milton's earlier tracts. But while Milton continues to argue that Charles I was justly removed from power and espouses once again the ideal that the people or their representatives have the right to make their own law – "If a people be put to warre with thir King for his misgovernment, and overcome him, the power is then undoubtedly in thir own hands how they will be governd" (*CPW* VII: 481) – he for the first time seems to accept that England will return to monarchy. He offers the desperate concession that, if his fellow citizens insist on a return to kingship, England's new leader should at least not be the son of a vanquished tyrant:

> if we will needs condemn our selves …, despairing of our own vertue, industrie and the number of our able men, we may then, conscious of our own unworthiness to be governd better, sadly betake us to our befitting

> thraldom: yet chusing out of our own number one who hath best aided the people, and best merited against tyrannie.   (*CPW* VII: 482)

Under such a leader, Milton tries to persuade himself, perhaps the country would not be permanently ruined: "the space of a raign or two we may chance to live happily anough, or tolerably" (*CPW* VII: 482).

As we know, Milton's arguments on behalf of individual liberty and the Commonwealth proved to no avail: England returned to monarchy a month later in May 1660 as Charles II triumphantly succeeded his father. Milton soon found himself in hiding and briefly imprisoned, no doubt living in fear of Royalists' reprisals. He did not entirely abandon political prose, however. In the year before he died, Milton once again argued for religious freedom in *Of True Religion, Heresy, Schism, Toleration* (March or April 1673). Responding to the withdrawal on 8 March 1673 of the Declaration of Indulgence, a royal statute that had temporarily suspended all penal ecclesiastical laws and allowed Protestant nonconformists to apply for licenses to worship publicly, Milton made the case for tolerating all manner of Protestants. Nonconformists may incorrectly interpret the Bible, he reasoned, but only Catholics are heretical because they alone reject the sole authority of Scripture: "Heresie is in the Will and choice profestly against Scripture; error is against the Will, in misunderstanding the Scripture" (*CPW* VIII: 423).

But, even as Milton in *Of True Religion* reiterates the principle of toleration and open discussion that he had memorably articulated in *Areopagitica* – he again writes, for example, "that all controversies being permitted, falshood will appear more false, and truth the more true" (*CPW* VIII: 438) – in his later years, as we will see in the next chapter, he would mostly turn to poetry. Perhaps the fiery tone and passionate rhetoric of *The Readie and Easie Way* anticipates this change. Or perhaps he discovered that he preferred the more expansive and more subtle register of poetry to express himself following the defeat of republicanism. Whatever the motive, even long after the country returned to monarchy Milton continued to compose in verse, writing his three long masterpieces – *Paradise Lost*, *Paradise Regained*, and *Samson Agonistes* – in further pursuit of his political and religious ideals.

Chapter 4

Poetry

Two years before the publication of *Paradise Lost*, Milton gave a hand-written copy of his epic to a former student. Thomas Ellwood was an earnest, 26-year-old Quaker who for approximately seven months in 1652 had met daily with the blind author and read to him in Latin while Milton interjected occasional explanations and corrections. Later, in April 1665, as the plague began raging in London – it ultimately killed more than 75,000 people[1] – Ellwood helped his former teacher move to a cottage in Chalfont St. Giles, a safe distance outside the city.

It was at this cottage, which still stands today, that Milton two months later gave Ellwood the manuscript of *Paradise Lost*. He invited Ellwood to take it home and come back with his opinion. Ellwood recalled that when he returned, Milton and he discussed the epic:

> He asked me how I liked it, and what I thought of it, which I modestly but freely told him: and after some further Discourse about it, I pleasantly said to him, Thou hast said much here of *Paradise lost*, but what hast thou to say of *Paradise found*? He made me no Answer, but sate some time in a Muse; then brake off that Discourse, and fell upon another Subject.[2]

Months later, after Ellwood's release from prison where he had been incarcerated for his religious beliefs, he visited the author again. Milton showed him *Paradise Regained* and "in a pleasant Tone said to me, *This is owing to you: for you put it into my Head, by the Question you put to me at* Chalfont; *which before I had not thought of*."[3]

This anecdote about Ellwood provides a revealing glimpse into Milton's process of writing. The modern scholarly editions in which Milton's poems are often reproduced give his work tremendous authority but necessarily obscure the circumstances that shaped his words and ideas. Published with solemn dustjackets and adorned with footnotes and prefaces, Milton's poems can resemble unalterable monuments more than living works that might have been otherwise. Readers may understandably feel daunted by poems that seem to have sprung from the author's head like Sin in *Paradise Lost*, "shining heav'nly fair" and fully developed (II.757).

But Ellwood's narrative reminds us that Milton wrote his poems over time and occasionally sought other people's opinions. Not only did his blindness necessitate that he rely on friends and acquaintances to transcribe *Paradise Lost*, but, as the revisions by various hands in the surviving manuscript of Book I illustrate, many people assisted Milton in amending his epic. Admittedly, Ellwood's recollection of his specific exchange with Milton may sound naïve: *Paradise Lost* in its final form clearly addresses "Paradise found," and Milton's sitting "some time in a Muse" before changing the subject could indicate that he was searching for a polite way to deflect his former student's criticism rather than meditating on Ellwood's suggestions. Yet Ellwood by all other accounts was perceptive, and we have no reason to doubt his understanding of his conversation with his former teacher. Why would Milton have bothered to share the poem with Ellwood years before its publication if he did not intend to take seriously Ellwood's ideas? In particular, we do not know how close to the final version the manuscript was that Milton shared with him. Perhaps Ellwood's comment prompted Milton to say more about "Paradise found" in his epic, adding, for example, Michael's pronouncement that Adam and Eve after the Fall can find a "paradise within … happier far" (XII.587). Certainly Milton's assertion that Ellwood inspired him to write *Paradise Regained* corresponds to the other information we have about the author's willingness to accept people's ideas. It also fits with Milton's description in *Areopagitica* of collaborative learning, which he compares to the construction of a temple, "some cutting, some squaring the marble, others hewing the cedars" (*CPW* II: 555).

Although this chapter has more to say about the content of Milton's individual poems than his process of composition, Ellwood's anecdote usefully suggests that even Milton's greatest poetic works should be read as having been produced in conversation – not just with Milton's muse but also with his friends, his predecessors, and his circumstances. Primarily, the chapter will address the imagery, motifs, and structures of Milton's poetry while also including close readings of a few passages to illustrate his poems' subtlety and complexity. The chapter focuses on Milton's three long poems – *Paradise Lost*, *Paradise Regained*, and *Samson Agonistes* – as well as five of his early masterpieces: "On the Morning of Christ's Nativity," *L'Allegro*, *Il Penseroso*, *A Mask Presented at Ludlow Castle*, and *Lycidas*. It also addresses Milton's sonnets and his first printed collection, the 1645 *Poems*. All of the material covered here should be read in conjunction with the information about context and genre in the preceding chapters; readers may thus need to consult the index to find related discussions of individual works. The chapter's broader aim is to show that the most rewarding way to read Milton's poetry is critically, paying close attention to the music of his verse and the richness of his language. Readers should accordingly follow Ellwood's example: we need to focus on what Milton openly says and question what he might only imply.

"On the Morning of Christ's Nativity" (1629)

That "On the Morning of Christ's Nativity," sometimes called the Nativity Ode, comes first in both Milton's 1645 and 1673 collections suggests Milton's and his publishers' awareness of its excellence. Printed at the start of both volumes, the poem signals Milton's ambition as a Christian poet. Here, the layout announces, is the nativity of a great talent.

Various other English and Continental lyrics about Christ's birth were published during the seventeenth century, most notably Torquato Tasso's "Nel giorno della Natività" (1621), Ben Jonson's "A Hymn on the Nativity of My Savior" (1640), Robert Herrick's "An Ode of the Birth of Our Savior" (1648), Henry Vaughan's "Christ's Nativity" (1650), and Richard Crashaw's "In the Holy Nativity of Our Lord God" (1652). But Milton's ode remains unique in its emphasis on the significance of Christ's birth for supplanting ancient beliefs and defining human history. Milton achieves this effect in part by artfully manipulating the depiction of time. The ode, as its title indicates, focuses on the morning of Christ's birth, but it also describes or alludes to the creation of the world, the "age of gold" (line 135), the Crucifixion, Judgment Day, and Moses' receiving of the Ten Commandments. The ode's year of composition, 1629, printed following the title in Milton's first collection, provides yet another possible frame of reference and underscores the author's precocity. Collapsing all these temporal events within a poem entitled "On the Morning of Christ's Nativity" suggests that this single occurrence encompasses and gives meaning to all other significant moments in history. With the birth of Christ, Milton seems to say, everything changes.

Milton, though, balances the ode's more audacious, prophetic gestures with humbler and quieter intonations. Thus, when he imagines the holy music that accompanies Christ's birth transporting humankind back to a prelapsarian state – "Truth and Justice then / Will down return to men, / Orbed in a rainbow" – he abruptly breaks off his hopeful vision, as if realizing that he has gotten ahead of himself: "But wisest Fate says no, / This must not yet be so, / The babe lies yet in smiling infancy" (lines 141–43, 149–51). Similarly, in the opening stanzas, the poet beseeches his muse to "run" and arrive first at the Christ child: "Have thou the honor first," he commands (lines 24, 26), encouraging his muse to "prevent" the "star-led wizards," which can mean that he wants her to precede the three wise men or, more boldly, that he wants her to frustrate or hinder them (lines 23, 24).[4] But when the speaker then imagines his muse placing "thy humble ode … / … lowly" at the infant's "blessèd feet" (lines 24–25), his tone sounds respectful, almost timid. This reverential gesture virtually abases the speaker as he grants his muse ownership of the poem (he calls it "thy," not "my," ode) and turns the ambition inherent in his wanting to be first into an expression of zeal more than ego.

Fittingly for a poem about such a momentous event, the stanza structure of the Nativity Ode is unique. Each of the opening four stanzas contains six decasyllabic lines capped with an alexandrine, rhyming *ababbcc*, a verse called rhyme royal but here with an extra foot in the final line. Milton had used this form before in "On the Death of a Fair Infant," probably about the death of his sister's daughter, and he would attempt it again with less success in "The Passion," his unfinished poem about Christ's sufferings. However, the elaborate stanzas in the remaining part of the Nativity Ode, labeled "The Hymn," have no precedent in English literature, and Milton himself never again used this structure. Each stanza contains two lines of six syllables (hexameter), one line of ten syllables (pentameter), two more lines of six syllables, another line of ten syllables, a line of eight syllables (octameter), and a concluding line of twelve syllables (an alexandrine). The rhyme scheme is *aabccbdd*.

In narrative terms, the Nativity Ode comprises five main sections: it begins with an invocation (stanzas 1–4, numbered separately), describes nature and its anticipation of Christ's birth (stanzas 1–8), celebrates the accompanying immortal music and its effects (stanzas 9–17), catalogues the disempowering of the ancient gods (stanzas 18–26), and concludes with an image of the sleeping infant and attending angels (stanza 27). Among the poem's most striking features is the amount of space that Milton devotes in the fourth part to the suddenly obsolete pre-Christian gods. Milton dramatizes the falseness of ancient religions by describing how, with the arrival of Christ, the Greek, Roman, Hebrew, Phoenician, and Egyptian gods must "Troop to th' infernal jail" (line 233). The nativity of Christ not only overwhelms sinful Nature – "in awe to him" she doffs "her gaudy trim" and tries to "hide her guilty front with innocent snow" (lines 32–33, 39). Christ's birth also silences the fraudulent pagan deities: "The Oracles are dumb, / No voice or hideous hum / Runs through the archèd roof in words deceiving" (lines 173–75).

Milton then emphasizes Christ's potency by contrasting the poem's long list of pagan gods with the simple image of a tiny "infant's hand" (line 222). Even as God lies sleeping in his "swaddling bands," he can still "control" and fill with dread "the damnèd crew" of ancient deities (line 228). Milton would face this

question again in his poetry: how to incorporate in a Christian work his knowledge and admiration of pre-Christian literature? The detail that he lavishes on
the pagan gods suggests his intense enthusiasm for antiquity even as he rejects
the gods' validity, and we should note that he seems to treat the classical gods
differently than other ancient idols. He emphasizes the "weeping," "plaint," and
"loud lament" of the departing Greek and Roman deities (lines 183, 191), in
contrast to the unwept vanishing of the other pagan gods, whom he describes
as "dismal," "brutish," and "sullen" (lines 205, 210, 211). Milton may be let-
ting go of the classical past in the Nativity Ode, but he does so slowly, almost
reluctantly.

L'Allegro and Il Penseroso (1631)

The most important feature of *L'Allegro* and *Il Penseroso* is that Milton wrote
them as companion pieces. These two lyric poems were published twice in
Milton's lifetime, in 1645 and 1673, and both times they appeared together,
L'Allegro followed by *Il Penseroso*. Milton envisioned some of his other works
in relationship to each other: he wrote two poems about the mail-carrier
Hobson, two sonnets on his divorce tracts, four poems on the Gunpowder
Plot, and two poems about the Roman singer Leonora. Also, *Paradise Regained*
and *Samson Agonistes* were published together in 1671 and seem to share a
precise, intertextual relationship.[5] In *Pro Populo Anglicano Defensio Secunda*,
Milton raises the possibility that he even conceived some of his prose works as
companion pieces; he emphasizes, if only in retrospect, that his divorce tracts,
Of Education, and *Areopagitica* address three types of domestic liberty (*CPW*
IV: 624).

In the case of *L'Allegro* ("The Joyful One") and *Il Penseroso* ("The
Contemplative One"), however, their interrelationship is more fundamental
to their meaning. In part, the pairing of these subjects represents an amusing
exercise. Milton first celebrates mirth, then extols the merits of melancholy,
as if to demonstrate his rhetorical agility; he can argue both positions equally
well, using the same form, iambic tetrameter couplets. In this regard, the
poems reflect the polemical atmosphere of Milton's university training with
its emphasis on oratorical exercises and disputation. Students were expected
to argue in support of arbitrary positions, such as whether day is better than
night or whether learning brings more blessings than ignorance.

But *L'Allegro* and *Il Penseroso* also pose a serious poetic choice: did Milton
have a mirthful or melancholic disposition? Did he aspire to write playful or serious poetry? Some readers may be tempted by the order in which

the poems were printed, the greater length of *Il Penseroso*, and the second poem's apparently more definitive final lines to infer that Milton was arriving at melancholy. He seems to stage his poetic maturation as he takes leave of his younger, occasional lyrics; looks forward to writing an epic; and in the end aspires to "something like prophetic strain," meaning a divinely inspired melody (line 174).

Yet, a careful reading suggests that Milton was striving for a different conclusion. Each poem contains potentially ambivalent passages that gently question the speaker's enthusiastic endorsement of the disposition that he describes. The "secret shades" where Saturn and his daughter Vesta conceive the goddess Melancholy, for example, hint at the impropriety of their incestuous relation (line 28), while *Il Penseroso*'s Catholic imagery also may undermine, for Milton, the speaker's contemplative mood: Melancholy is personified as a "pensive nun" (line 31), and the speaker later seeks out a Catholic church whose cloister and stained glass windows provide only "a dim religious light" (line 160). By comparison in *L'Allegro*, the speaker's description of the music he enjoys – "winding bout," "wanton heed," and "giddy cunning" – sounds vertiginous and vaguely threatening (lines 139–41), while his pursuit of "unreprovèd pleasure free" in the company of two goddesses as they wait for the sun to rise introduces the possibility of sexual promiscuity (line 40). That each poem contains intimations of discontent seems to invite a reconsideration of the alternative disposition.

Further complicating the likelihood that Milton favored melancholy over mirth is the complex interrelationship between the two poems. *L'Allegro* and *Il Penseroso* have much in common: most obviously, both have Italian titles, depict idealized landscapes, personify their respective dispositions, refer to the myth of Orpheus, and so on. The two poems also include a series of artful, sometimes subtle contrasts. *L'Allegro* begins at the break of day and continues through night, whereas *Il Penseroso* begins at night and continues through a (cloudy) day; in *L'Allegro*, the speaker goes "walking not unseen" (line 57), whereas in *Il Penseroso* the speaker does in fact "walk unseen" (line 65); in *L'Allegro*, the speaker gladly hears the lark's "startl[ing]" song at the break of day (line 42), whereas in *Il Penseroso* he enjoys instead the "sweetest, saddest" song of the nightingale (line 57); and so on.

The cumulative effect of all these cross-references and echoes is that *L'Allegro* and *Il Penseroso* seem to present a both-and relationship more than an either-or choice. Like the two intertwined strands of a DNA molecule, the poems cannot be separated without altering what they are. The force of their aesthetic and philosophical value lies in how they engage with each other; the reward of reading each poem comes from experiencing them together and discovering their various intertextual allusions that often defy a simple, one-to-one correspondence.

And just as the two poems derive their power in conversation with each other, Milton suggests that the two dispositions do not exist separately: life's mirthful moments help to define and enhance melancholy periods – and *vice versa*. Correspondingly, the modes of poetry that the two dispositions reflect are complementary, not contradictory, so that, for example, both light-hearted and serious moments occur in Milton's three long poems. Milton may have progressed from writing pastoral poetry to a biblical epic, but he never entirely relinquished the themes of his early, occasional verse – and these early poems already anticipate the subjects and dialogic style of his more serious, mature poetry.

A Mask Presented at Ludlow Castle (1634)

As we saw in Chapter 2, a masque is a genre of dramatic, courtly entertainment that combines music, poetry, dance, and spectacle, held together by a slight, often allegorical plot. In 1634, The earl of Bridgewater, John Egerton, commissioned Milton to write a masque for Michaelmas night, 29 September, in celebration of the earl's reunion with his family and his formal installation as Lord President of the Council of Wales. The earl's new position came with considerable authority and prestige: as President, he would oversee a prerogative court empowered to keep law and order throughout Wales and the border counties. The celebration that he and his family hosted on 29 September was his official introduction to the region and the first opportunity for the region's people to honor their new leader.

Milton responded to the occasion with *A Mask Presented at Ludlow Castle* (sometimes called *Comus*, beginning with eighteenth-century stage adaptations). Milton's masque tells a simple, magical story: three children on their way home become separated in the woods. One of them, the Lady, is captured by an evil enchanter, Comus, who binds her to a chair and tries to persuade her to drink a potion that will turn her into one of his animal-headed acolytes. She resists, and ultimately her two brothers rescue her with the aid of an Attendant Spirit and Sabrina, a virgin river goddess. In 1634, the chief performers were the Earl of Bridgewater's three children – Lady Alice, age fifteen; Lord Brackley, age eleven; and Thomas Egerton, age nine. Although the identities of the people who portrayed Comus and Sabrina remain unknown, the Attendant Spirit was performed by Milton's friend Henry Lawes, a court musician who also served as the Egerton children's music tutor. Lawes wrote the songs for *A Mask* and over the next few years shared manuscript copies of the work with friends and acquaintances before overseeing its print publication in 1637.

Various other dramatic works seem to inform the broad contours of Milton's masque. Perhaps most obviously, he seems to have borrowed elements of the plot from Shakespeare's *A Midsummer Night's Dream* (c. 1595), which focuses on magical transformations and young people lost in a wood, as well as from George Peele's *An Old Wives' Tale* (1595), which depicts two brothers trying to rescue their sister from an evil sorcerer.[6] Milton adapted the character Comus from Greek mythology. Komos, the son of and cup-bearer to Bacchus, was a god of revelry, drink, and sexual indulgence. Ben Jonson's *Pleasure Reconciled with Virtue* (performed in 1618) also included a version of the Greek deity, but in Jonson's masque Comus only appears briefly and represents festivity and gluttony in contrast to Milton's more richly imagined depiction of a seductive enchanter.

Yet, if Milton in *A Mask* imaginatively develops his source material – adding, for example, Circe as Comus's mother – first-time readers might be struck by the work's limitations more than its innovative style. Although *A Mask* has more in common with early modern drama than most masques from the period, it is not a play. Readers who expect the type of ambitious plotting and complex characters found in, say, the works of Shakespeare or Christopher Marlowe should turn instead to *Paradise Lost*. With *A Mask*, Milton's goals were more modest. Working with non-professional actors and within the limited space of Ludlow Castle's Great Hall, he was trying first and foremost to delight and compliment the earl and his family.

This does not mean that *A Mask* is as simple as it might initially appear. Milton, as we saw in Chapter 2, adds philosophical and psychological depth to the Lady's and her brothers' plight by adapting the convention of an antimasque to amplify the danger that Comus poses (see pages 43–44). At stake for the Lady is not just whether she will drink from Comus's cup but whether she has the requisite virtue and moral education to withstand what his offer symbolizes. If she gives in to temptation and drinks, her face will be "changed / Into some brutish form of wolf, or bear, / Or ounce, or tiger, hog, or bearded goat" (lines 69–71). Comus's victims, the Attendant Spirit adds, do not realize that they have been transformed and "boast themselves more comely than before, / And all their friends and native home forget" (lines 75–76). These details imply that the Lady by drinking would be giving in to her animal instincts, relinquishing her godly reason, and losing both her perception of reality and her relationship to her aristocratic family and their moral values.

That Milton focuses *A Mask* on the specific moral value of chastity also distinguishes his drama from other contemporary English masques. We do not know whether to attribute this theme to Milton or the earl, but clearly Comus's threat and the Lady's power are sexual. The two brothers, for example, describe their fears for their sister in physical terms: they expressly worry about "some ill-greeting touch" (line 406) and the wood's "rude burs and thistles" (line 352), and they fear that their sister will be trapped "within the direful grasp / Of savage hunger, or of savage heat" (lines 357–58). The Elder Brother goes on to explain that his sister can protect herself because she possesses the "hidden strength" of "chastity": "She that has that, is clad in complete steel" (lines 418, 420, 421). And in the Lady's response to Comus – a passage not included, interestingly, in the two manuscripts of *A Mask* that survive from Milton's lifetime (lines 779–806) – the Lady vehemently defends her virtue as the "sun-clad power of Chastity" (line 782). Then, as she gets carried away, she goes further, citing not just her purity but "the sage / And serious doctrine of Virginity" (lines 786–87).

This sexual theme and the masque's rich allegorical details have proven remarkably pliable to modern literary critics, who have devised various, provocative interpretations of the drama's characters and plot. Some critics, for example, have focused on Comus's threat to the Lady's chastity to support a psycho-biographical reading. According to this way of thinking, the central conflict between the Lady and Comus dramatizes a pre-Oedipal or Oedipal scenario. These readings foreground Comus's fixation on his mother: when he first hears the Lady's song – her "divine enchanting ravishment" – he immediately thinks of his own mother's singing, "I have oft heard / My mother Circe ..." (lines 245, 252–53). Psychological interpretations are also based on two key biographical facts. Milton's nickname at Cambridge was "the Lady of Christ's," and, after graduating with an MA, he went home to live with his parents instead of entering a career.[7] Thus, Milton might have unconsciously identified with the character named "the Lady" in *A Mask* as she spends most of the action stuck to her seat. Milton in 1634 was also apparently stuck, unsure what to do with his life.

According to a pre-Oedipal reading, the excessive rhetoric that characterizes the standoff between Comus and the Lady represents the young Milton's own sense of maternal dependence in his paralyzed state. That Comus, a character arguably defined by his mother's influence, prevents the Lady from getting out of her chair would accordingly correspond to Milton's feelings of being subsumed by his own mother.[8] Milton resembles the Lady in *A Mask*, in other words, because a fit of the mother prevented him, like her, from acting, although in the Lady's case her fit is allegorized in the form of Comus.

The Oedipal reading, by comparison, posits that Milton was trapped within the classic psychological dilemma of wanting to possess his mother but being forbidden to do so. In this case, Comus's attraction to the Lady would signify the healthy resolution of the Oedipal dilemma – namely, finding a surrogate for the mother in an available sexual object. But because Comus represents an evil character, Milton seems to be stubbornly resisting his own healthy psychological development and denying his desire and sexuality. This denial, according to one critic, might have served as the basis for Milton's artistic inspiration, a so-called "sacred complex" underlying his greatest works.[9]

Other critics also foreground Comus's sexual threat and the Lady's power of chastity, but they offer instead historical interpretations of Milton's court drama. Barbara Breasted, for example, was among the first to suggest that the notorious scandal within the Earl of Bridgewater's extended family influenced the details of Milton's text.[10] The brother-in-law of the earl's wife, the second Earl of Castlehaven, was tried, convicted, and executed for committing and inciting multiple rapes and acts of sodomy against his wife and servants. Could Milton's masque – specifically the depiction of the Lady's resistance to Comus's temptation – be an attempt to repair the family's reputation, which had been damaged by the trial and the Earl of Castlehaven's beheading?

Leah Marcus has alternatively found striking parallels between Milton's masque and the contemporary case of Margarey Evans, a fourteen-year-old girl who in 1631 was raped by the roadside in Herefordshire.[11] Despite taking the extraordinary step of appealing for justice to the Privy Council – of which the Earl of Bridgewater was a member – Evans was never able to prove her case, and her attacker was never convicted. Could Milton in *A Mask* be dramatizing on a higher plane some elements of Evans's story and admonishing the council members in attendance at Ludlow for failing to administer justice and for lacking Sabrina's compassion?

Still other critics have argued that Milton was trying to impart a more general moral lesson to the masque's original aristocratic audience.[12] In some places in *A Mask* Milton egregiously compliments the earl and his family. Near the start, for example, the Attendant Spirit describes the earl as "A noble peer of mickle trust and power" who has nursed "his fair offspring ... in princely lore" (lines 31, 34). Similarly, at the conclusion, the spirit praises the exemplary education that the earl and his wife have provided for their children, "so goodly grown / Three fair branches of your own" (lines 968–69).

Yet, as even a superficial reading of the masque reveals, the earl's three children overcome temptation and find their way "through hard assays / With a crown of deathless praise" only because they receive considerable assistance (lines 972–73). The Lady should be admired for resisting Comus, and the brothers could be complimented for bravely challenging the sorcerer, but ultimately the three children fail to capture Comus, and the Lady does not rescue herself. First the Attendant Spirit learns from a "certain shepherd lad / Of small regard to see to" that to conquer Comus the brothers will need a "small unsightly root" of "divine effect" (lines 619–20, 629, 630). Then, to rescue the Lady from her seat, the brothers will require help from Sabrina, whom Meliboeus, the "soothest shepherd that e'er piped on plains," had first mentioned to the Attendant Spirit (line 823).

All these details are potentially symbolic. The description of the shepherd lad suggests that he represents a true, humble pastor, while the plant's "divine effect" seems to figure God's assistance or, more specifically, a Christian way of knowing, as the plant allows its bearers to see through Comus's deceptions and to resist his spells. The details about Meliboeus, by comparison, suggest that he is an artist figure and, because the story of Sabrina derives chiefly from *The Faerie Queene*, he may stand for Spenser and represent a type of the true poet.

If we then piece together these symbols, Milton in *A Mask* was telling the earl and the aristocratic audience at Ludlow not to take their power for granted and to supplement their moral education with the ministry of God's word and the power of poetry. Without divine and poetic guidance, in other words, they will remain children lost in a dark, dangerous wood. The final part of the Lady's rescue also fits such a reading. That she requires the help of Sabrina, a personified purifying river, could indicate another way that Milton was instructing the ruling class to go beyond their own experience: they can rule effectively only if they also draw on the region and its natural resources.

Yet, regardless of which interpretive approach readers favor – psychological, historical, moral, or something else – it is important that Comus ultimately escapes. Milton in *A Mask* seems to suggest that the "riot and ill-managed merriment" (line 172) that Comus embodies cannot be entirely contained. *A Mask* thus looks forward to a key idea from *Paradise Lost*: Satan, like Comus, succeeds only in heaping further punishment on himself, but within the epic's narrative the danger that he represents is never eliminated. The Elder Brother eloquently anticipates the logic of Milton's mature theodicy:

> ... this I hold firm,
> Virtue may be assailed, but never hurt,
> Surprised by unjust force, but not enthralled,
> Yea even that which mischief meant most harm,
> Shall in the happy trial prove most glory.
> But evil on itself shall back recoil,
> And mix no more with goodness, when at last
> Gathered like scum, and settled to itself,
> It shall be in eternal restless change

> Self-fed and self-consumed; if this fail,
> The pillared firmament is rottenness,
> And earth's base built on stubble.   (lines 588–99)

Milton in *Paradise Lost* will develop this idea of evil recoiling back on itself and, through the allegorical characters of Sin and Death, will depict how evil can literally be "Self-fed and self-consumed."

More generally, Milton in *A Mask* was rehearsing the basic plot of his epic: Comus tempts the Lady with an enchanted cup, whereas Satan persuades Eve to eat the forbidden fruit. But, in *A Mask*, freed from the constraints of following the Genesis narrative, Milton imagines a woman who successfully resists her tempter. He thus diverges not just from the plots of other early modern court masques but also from the familiar biblical story. As opposed to Eve, the Lady heroically withstands Comus's seduction through her intelligence, her sacred vehemence, and the ministrations of a female protector.

Lycidas (1638)

Even if Milton had never written his three great long poems, he would still be read today because of *Lycidas*. It remains one of the most forceful pastoral poems written in English and one of the most compelling meditations on death and vocation in any language. As with many of Milton's early poems, he wrote *Lycidas* for someone else and, in the tradition of Greek and Continental Latin odes, then used the occasion to reflect on his own concerns and ambitions. On 10 August 1637, Edward King, a classmate of Milton's for six years at Christ's College, had drowned tragically in a shipwreck on the Irish Sea as he was traveling from Chester Bay to visit his family in Ireland. When King's university friends decided to publish a memorial volume, *Justa Eduardo King Naufrago* ("Obsequies for Edward King," 1638), Milton agreed to contribute a poem.

Although some critics have doubted the sincerity of Milton's friendship with King because of *Lycidas*'s impersonal pastoralism, the headnote that Milton added when the poem was reprinted in 1645 and 1673 refers to the young men's attachment. It begins, "In this Monody the Author bewails a learned Friend, unfortunately drown'd in his Passage from *Chester* on the *Irish* Seas, 1637" (*CPMP* 120). In addition to calling King Milton's "Friend," the note uses "bewails," which suggests a loud lament or great sorrow; and Milton's nephew Edward Phillips recorded separately that his uncle "had contracted a particular Friendship and Intimacy" with King "for his great Learning and Parts."[13] We also know that Milton and King had much in common. Although King was three years Milton's junior, both wrote poetry, both intended to take Holy Orders and become clerics, and both had delayed their plans apparently to prepare themselves better for the ministry. King's premature death would have understandably rattled the young Milton: how could he avoid thinking about the possibility of his own death and his own unfulfilled ambitions?

Lycidas traces the speaker's spiritual development as he questions the meaning of life and tries to understand why his friend died so young. In what follows, I briefly paraphrase the main ideas of each verse so that readers can more confidently explore on their own the nuances of Milton's allusions and imagery. The separate, supplementary discussion of patterns of imagery (see box on pages 154–55) demonstrates how Milton uses specific motifs to dramatize the speaker's progression from anger to grief to consolation.

For most of the poem, the speaker is an "uncouth swain" (line 186), meaning an unskilled or unknown shepherd or laborer. Initially, he sounds angry. He lashes out at nature, shattering the leaves on a group of shrubberies – laurel, myrtle, and ivy – all of which Milton has apparently chosen because they have classical associations with writing poetry and, in contrast to the swain's deceased friend, Lycidas, these three plants are evergreens. The speaker specifically announces that he has "come to pluck" the shrubberies' berries "harsh and crude, / And with forced fingers rude, / Shatter your leaves before the mellowing year" (lines 3–5). This description evokes Lycidas's untimely demise while also suggesting the swain's outrage and, through "forced fingers rude," his sense of obligation and unpreparedness.

The second verse paragraph contains a formal invocation, as the speaker calls on the "sisters of the sacred well" (line 15), a circumlocution that emphasizes the Muses' connection with water, one of the poem's primary motifs. Then, in a poignant vignette, the swain hopes that one day a poet inspired by a Muse will similarly honor him:

> So may some gentle muse
> With lucky words favour my destined urn,
> And as he passes turn,
> And bid fair peace be to my sable shroud.
> For we were nursed upon the self-same hill,
> Fed the same flock, by fountain, shade, and rill.   (lines 19–24)

For a poet to identify with his deceased friend was not uncommon in Renaissance odes and epitaphs.[14] Here Milton suggests that he and King were good friends; Lycidas and the swain were raised together and shared similar pastoral experiences. But we should also note the modesty of the swain's specific vision: he does not necessarily aspire to immortality through verse but hopes merely that after he dies someone will walk by the urn with his ashes and wish him well.

The third and fourth verse paragraphs are among the most explicitly pastoral passages in *Lycidas*. First the speaker nostalgically recalls how he and Lycidas worked as shepherds, often rising before the sun and staying out until the first star appeared. The swain also emphasizes that he and Lycidas played music together, fancifully adding that their songs were so good that even fauns and satyrs danced to them. The fourth verse, in contrast, depicts the "heavy change" that has occurred since Lycidas has died (line 37). Through three natural metaphors, the speaker describes the loss of Lycidas's music and underscores Lycidas's youth and beauty. The swain compares the absence of his friend's song to insects destroying a rose, to parasites attacking newly weaned calves, and to an early frost killing newly blooming hawthorn shrubs.

Patterns of imagery in *Lycidas*: the case of hair

Milton incorporates various image patterns in *Lycidas* that make the poem more cohesive and help to dramatize the swain's evolving understanding of his friend's death. One overlooked image that plays a crucial role in the swain's spiritual progress is hair. Milton directly refers to hair three times: "the tangles of Neaera's hair" (line 69), Saint Peter's "mitred locks" (line 112), and Lycidas's "oozy locks" (line 175). But the image's greater resonance demonstrates the value of carefully examining the subtle details in Milton's works. The following analysis is intended as a model of the type of scrutiny that *Lycidas* rewards. Readers should question what other motifs can be identified in *Lycidas*. How does Milton develop the poem's various image patterns?

In the case of hair, Milton begins *Lycidas* by focusing on the top of the swain's head: the poet describes three evergreen crowns, the laurel, myrtle, and ivy, which, as commentators have long observed, collectively signify poetic triumph.[15] Later, when the swain laments the elusiveness of winning such a garland, Milton again alludes to hair by blaming "the blind Fury with th' abhorrèd shears," who "slits the thin-spun life" (lines 75–76). This image not only evokes Samson's famously fatal haircut, but it also associates an untimely death with the Furies and their snake-wreathed tresses rather than with the mythologically correct, scissors-bearing Fate, Atropos.

Even earlier, when the swain entertains the possibility of willingly abandoning his poetic vocation, Milton uses hair to describe the swain's ersatz erotic pastime: instead of contending for a crown of laurel, myrtle, or ivy, he would take pleasure in "the tangles of Neaera's hair" (line 69). Weaving this hair motif into his elegy, Milton emphasizes how much is at stake for Lycidas and the speaker; the Fury's snaky wreaths and the mistress's tangles can supersede the immortality that the evergreen crowns symbolize.

Milton continues to pursue this latter idea in heady terms as he describes the poem's procession of oracular mourners. The reference to Orpheus emphasizes

how his severed head floated down the Hebrus (lines 62–63), the description
of Camus's sedge-lined banks as a "mantle hairy" associates the sire's authority
with his tresses (line 104), and even the appearance of Triton, whom Milton calls
"the herald of the sea" (line 89), may conjure up an image of hairiness. Triton
was known to have had thick hair that resembled marsh frogs and, according to
one myth, he was decapitated like Orpheus.[16]

Phoebus Apollo's subsequent appearance in the poem may call up the traditional
image of his laurel crown and life-giving locks, but the next direct reference to
hair occurs as Saint Peter shakes his "mitred locks" to express his contempt for
the corrupted clergy (line 112). The saint's Episcopal headdress transcends the
earth-bound futility embodied by Neaera's tangles but also suggests the inadequacy
of the classical, natural garlands that the swain aspires to win.

The final image of Lycidas completes the poem's hair motif. When in the
penultimate verse the shepherd "with nectar pure his oozy locks he laves"
(line 175), Milton casts Lycidas's rebirth as both a pagan cleansing ritual and a
Christian baptism; the line's alliteration and internal rhyme demonstrate how he
has at last harmoniously reconciled nature and antiquity with Christian belief.
Once again, hair unites these competing registers:

> So sinks the day-star in the ocean bed,
> And yet anon repairs his drooping head,
> And tricks his beams, and with new spangled ore,
> Flames in the forehead of the morning sky.   (lines 168–71)

In this culminating image, the sun's "head" and "beams" not only recall Apollo's
locks and the poem's other well-tressed speakers but also evoke the description
of Lycidas's submerged hair and the glorious effulgence of the resurrected Son.
That the larger motif and this final, inclusive image hang by a hair signifies how
fragile yet strong remains the promise of everlasting life to which Lycidas and the
speaker aspire. As the swain at last rises and turns "to fresh woods, and pastures
new" (line 194), he takes comfort in Lycidas's poetic apotheosis and Christian
redemption, and in the continuity he finds in nature's cycles, his monody's
echoing repetition, the pastoral tradition, and the powerful mythic symbols such
as hair that help him to connect all these things.

In the fifth verse, the speaker begins by chastising a group of nymphs,
beautiful maiden deities who often served a superior god. Echoing the ancient
Greek poet Theocritus in his *First Idyl*, the speaker angrily questions why the
nymphs did not intervene and prevent Lycidas from drowning. But he soon
realizes his foolishness – "Ay me, I fondly dream!" (line 56) – as he recollects
that even the Muse of heroic poetry, Calliope, could not save her son, Orpheus,
when he was attacked and dismembered by Dionysus' followers.

The realization that the Muses have limited power leads the speaker in the
next verse to question more generally the value of pursuing a poetic career.
Why should he work so hard if, like Lycidas, he too could suddenly die?

> Alas! What boots it with uncessant care
> To tend the homely slighted shepherd's trade,
> And strictly meditate the thankless muse?
> Were it not better done as others use,
> To sport with Amaryllis in the shade,
> Or with the tangles of Neaera's hair?   (lines 64–69)

Both "Amaryllis" and "Neaera" are not necessarily specific mythological allusions; instead, they represent traditional pastoral names for nymphs or shepherdesses in works by writers such as Theocritus and Virgil. The speaker is wondering whether it would be better simply to have fun instead of continuing to pursue the "thankless muse" and the "homely slighted shepherd's trade," a description that suggests both his clerical and poetic aspirations. He momentarily concludes that he makes so many sacrifices for his work because he wants to be famous – the "last infirmity of noble mind," as he derisively calls it (line 71). Then in a dramatic caesura, Phoebus Apollo interrupts the poem to announce that the swain should pursue heavenly, not earthly fame. Phoebus adds that fame in Heaven is determined solely by God, not humankind. Here we glimpse the speaker's growing awareness of mythology's inadequacy. Even as he continues to address classical figures such as Phoebus, the swain has grown disenchanted with ancient poetic conventions. Now he holds out pastoral pleasures as an indulgent distraction in contrast to his higher vocational aspirations, and he emphasizes the disparity between earthly and heavenly values.

In the sixth verse, the speaker continues to question why Lycidas died tragically. He interrogates Triton, the "herald of the sea" (line 89), and Hippotades (also known as Aeolus), the god of the winds. Both gods provide little insight. They claim that the weather and waves were calm on the day that Lycidas drowned; instead, they suggest, Lycidas's accident may have occurred because his boat was cursed.

The seventh verse paragraph marks the arrival of two more mourners: Camus, whose name is a Latinized version of the river Cam and who thus appears to stand for King's community of friends and tutors at Cambridge University; and St. Peter, whom Milton identifies periphrastically as "pilot of the Galilean lake," a phrase that once again develops the poem's water motif (line 109). In this verse, as we saw in Chapter 2, Milton criticizes England's incompetent Episcopal clergy and prophetically challenges the poem's readers to continue the reformation and cure the "contagion" that the corrupt clergy is spreading through the church (line 127). Lycidas's death is especially unjust because he would have been an excellent spiritual leader, in contrast to the current crop of self-serving shepherds (ministers), who are poorly trained and ignore the well-being of their flocks (congregations).[17]

In the eighth verse, the speaker turns away from organized religion and calls on rivers and flowers to decorate Lycidas's hearse, and he temporarily seems to take some satisfaction in cataloguing the various plants that he might use. He then recognizes his foolishness: because Lycidas's body has been lost at sea, this type of memorial gesture is impossible. Again, as when the swain rejected the idea that the nymphs could have saved Lycidas, he uses the short interjection "Ay me!" to dramatize the realization of his folly (line 154).

But even as pastoral imagery once again fails the swain, he arrives at a sense of consolation in the penultimate verse by embracing a Christian epistemology. In contrast to the pagan symbols and beliefs that dominate the opening verse paragraphs – such as the laurel, the Muses, the nymphs, and Triton – the swain now emphasizes that Lycidas has been saved by Christ's sacrifice and will one day be resurrected. The swain does not entirely abandon nature and mythology in comprehending Lycidas's death, but he now more fully infuses them with Christian meaning. Thus the setting and rising sun represents not only a natural image of renewal but also the death and resurrection of God's Son. The imagery of Revelation also seeps into the swain's final comments: Lycidas, for example, "hears the unexpressive nuptial song, / In the blest kingdoms meek of joy and love" (lines 176–77; cf. Rev. 19:5 and 21:4).

Then, in a surprising shift, the last verse of *Lycidas* abruptly separates readers from the preceding meditation on loss and vocation. As if tracking back cinematically from the "uncouth swain" (line 186), the poem now focuses on a new, unidentified speaker, who begins to comment on the swain as a figure within the landscape. In the final lines, this new voice offers another of the poem's powerful vignettes:

> And now the sun had stretched out all the hills,
> And now was dropped into the western bay;
> At last he rose, and twitched his mantle blue:
> Tomorrow to fresh woods, and pastures new.   (lines 190–93)

In the headnote that Milton added in 1645 he called *Lycidas* a "monody," that is, a Greek ode for one singer who laments a person's death. This choice points to the poetic traditions that directly inform Milton's work, but "monody" also seems a bit of a misnomer, given that the poem contains multiple speakers, including the swain, Phoebus, and Camus. In the above passage, the final, unidentified speaker concludes the poem with an image of a new beginning and a sense of hopeful continuity as the swain rises and turns his thoughts to the future. In the preceding verse, the swain took comfort that the sun sets in the ocean but rises again; he compared the sun's orbit to Lycidas, who also disappeared in the ocean but will be resurrected by Christ. So in the poem's final image, Milton emphasizes the idea of continual renewal: the sun only temporarily sets, as figured in the swain's own rising, and the swain will go on, despite the loss of his dear friend, and he will continue to pursue his poetic and religious aspirations.

Sonnets (1629–1658)

Milton wrote twenty-four sonnets, five in Italian and the rest in English; ten of these poems were included in his 1645 collection, and another ten were added in 1673 in the second edition, *Poems, &c. upon Several Occasions.* (In Chapter 1, I discuss why the remaining four sonnets were not included in either volume.) A sonnet is a fourteen-line lyric poem written in iambic pentameter, a form probably invented in the thirteenth century by a poet at the court of Emperor Frederick II of Sicily and later perfected in Italy by Francesco Petrarch (1304–74). Almost two hundred years later, Thomas Wyatt (1503–42) and Henry Howard, the Earl of Surrey (1517–47), imported the form into England, and it was Surrey who invented the English sonnet's rhyme scheme (also called Shakespearean or Elizabethan), three quatrains followed by a couplet, rhyming *abba cddc effe gg.*

The power and beauty of a sonnet stems from the way a poet negotiates the form's rigid structure and still expresses something unique and meaningful. A sonneteer not only works on a small canvass – fourteen lines of ten syllables each – but also must write in alternating unstressed and stressed syllables within a predetermined rhymed pattern. In Milton's case, he preferred the original structure of the Italian sonnet (also called Petrarchan) instead of the English form. Italian sonnets contain an octave, rhyming *abba abba,* followed by a sestet, rhyming in some combination *cd* or *cde.*[18]

But if Milton was a traditionalist in his preference for the Italian over the English structure, he also challenged poetic conventions in his sonnets. Only his first six sonnets, probably composed in 1629 or the early 1630s, deal with romantic love, the typical subject of the verse form during the height of its popularity in the late sixteenth century. Instead, Milton used the sonnet in a new way – to write about political events, friends, people he admired, and himself. He also deviated from tradition by eschewing a formal sonnet sequence. Whereas Sidney, Shakespeare, and Spenser, for example, seem to have envisioned their sonnets in a rough narrative order, Milton chose a more diverse group of subjects; the only common denominator across all twenty-four of his sonnets appears to be himself.

Milton's decision to address some of his sonnets to political leaders – he wrote sonnets to Fairfax, Cromwell, and Vane (sonnets 15, 16, and 17, respectively) – was not, however, without precedent. He may have been specifically emulating Torquato Tasso's *Heroic Sonnets*, although, as various commentators have noted, Milton was probably more directly indebted to Horace's style of address and his theme of conviviality, as expressed in particular in Horace's *Odes*. While the addressee of Milton's Sonnet 9, "Lady that in the prime of earliest youth," remains unknown, the subjects of his other dedicatory sonnets are easily identified. Collectively, they suggest Milton's social nature. He wrote sonnets to Margaret Ley, the daughter of the statesman James Ley (Sonnet 10); to Henry Lawes, the court musician, who, we have seen, collaborated with Milton on *Arcades* and *A Mask* (Sonnet 13); to Catherine Thomason, the wife of the bookseller and collector George Thomason (Sonnet 14); to Edward Lawrence, a possible former student and a member of Parliament (Sonnet 20); and to Cyriack Skinner, a former student and one of Milton's earliest biographers (sonnets 21 and 22).

Five of Milton's remaining sonnets are occasional: he wrote about an expected Royalist assault on London (Sonnet 8); on the unfavorable reception of his divorce tracts (sonnets 11 and 12); and on the 1655 massacre of the Vaudois, a Christian sect in the Italian Alps deemed heretical by the Catholic Church (Sonnet 18). He also composed a sonnet about Presbyterian opposition to toleration within the Westminster Assembly (see Chapter 2). This final poem, "On the New Forcers of Conscience under the Long Parliament," is a special type of sonnet called tailed or caudated, meaning that it follows the fourteen-line structure of a standard Italian sonnet but contains a few extra lines. In the particular case of "On the New Forcers of Conscience," Milton added two half lines (lines 15 and 18) and two couplets (lines 16–17 and 19–20).

Milton's other three sonnets are among his most personal works. In Sonnet 7, probably composed around 1632, the speaker, who seems to be Milton himself, meditates on his lack of achievement and his confidence in God's guidance as he waits to discover his vocation.[19] In Sonnet 19, the speaker grapples with his loss of sight and questions its implications for both his career and God's expectations for him. And in Sonnet 23, the speaker movingly imagines that his late wife, full of "Love, sweetness, goodness," returns to him in a vision (line 11). All of Milton's sonnets deserve repeated reading; in general, the compressed expression that the form requires creates provocative ambiguities and multiple layers of meaning. But Milton's three

most personal sonnets are especially powerful explorations of poetic structure. Milton incorporates hard enjambments, dramatic caesurae, and other
deliberate prosodic effects to adapt the form to his individual subjects.

In Sonnet 19, to take one example, Milton manipulates the traditional distinction between the octave and the sestet by springing the turn in thought
(called the *volta*) earlier than expected. That the speaker's anxious question
about God's expectations is suddenly answered – not, according to convention,
at the start of the sestet but even earlier, in the first part of line 8 – suggests the
potency of Patience's intervention: "Patience to prevent / That murmur soon
replies" (lines 8–9), with "murmur" implying that being patient can diminish
the speaker's doubt to mere grumbling. The poem's syntax also conveys the
contrast between the speaker's anxiety and the reassurance that comes with
Patience. The octave's cumbersome structure – it comprises one long sentence
dominated by a pair of embedded conditional clauses – underscores the speaker's agitation and sense of contingency. By comparison, the series of enjambments in the sestet give Patience's reply the plain, confident sound of prose.
Patience not only resolves the speaker's anxiety about divine expectation but
also, through enjambment, redefines the sonnet's expected form:

> God doth not need
> Either man's work or his own gifts; who best
> Bear his mild yoke, they serve him best; his state
> Is kingly. Thousands at his bidding speed
> And post o'er land and ocean without rest:
> They also serve who only stand and wait.   (lines 9–14)

In the midst of this sestet, the abrupt pair of caesurae ("best; his" and, more
violently, "kingly. Thousands"), combined with the jarring spondee ("Is'
king' -ly"), help to set off and dramatize God's absolute power. The new
way of measuring the speaker's achievement that Patience proposes finds
expression in the sestet's new poetic measure, which in turn enhances the
epigrammatic authority of the poem's final line. In sharp contrast to the
complex syntax of the speaker's opening question, the sonnet resolves itself
with a single reassuring idea neatly contained within a single verse.

Milton's Sonnet 23 similarly derives much of its force from the way that it
works within and exploits the sonnet's form. Milton concludes the speaker's
vision of his beloved with an image of romantic frustration: "But O as to embrace
me she inclined / I waked, she fled, and day brought back my night" (lines
13–14). The elongated syntax to describe the couple's attempted embrace – the
subject and verb are held back until the end of line 13 – dramatizes the speaker's anticipation and the beloved's straining reach. In contrast, the action in the

Figure 3 Frontispiece and title page from *Poems of Mr. John Milton, Both English and Latin, Compos'd at Several Times* (1645)

final line – Milton crams in three subjects and three verbs – emphasizes how quickly the speaker's beloved disappears. And that the final line contains only monosyllables amplifies this rush of events and the suddenness of the speaker's disappointment.

Poems **(1645)**

As we saw in Chapter 1, most of Milton's early poetry was printed in 1645 in a collection entitled *Poems of Mr. John Milton, both English and Latin*, published by the bookseller Humphrey Moseley. Beginning with Milton's portrait on the frontispiece, the volume foregrounds the poet's identity; the title page, for example, announces Milton's full name and emphasizes the poems' authenticity, adding between two horizontal rules, that the collection has been "*Printed by his true Copies*" (see Figure 3).

Readers, however, should not confuse the authorial persona that the *Poems* conjures with Milton's practical participation in creating the volume.[20] In 1645, Moseley had only begun to earn his reputation as a seller and publisher of fine literature. Flushed with the favorable response that he had received earlier that year for publishing a collection of Edmund Waller's poetry, Moseley was eager to produce a follow-up volume. In his dedicatory epistle to Milton's book, Moseley suggests that the 1645 *Poems* was his idea, not Milton's. Moseley writes that he had encountered so much "*incouragement … from the most ingenious men in their clear and courteous entertainment of Mr.* Wallers *late choice Peeces*" that he decided once again to "*adventure into the World, presenting it with these evergreen, and not to be blasted Laurels.*"[21]

Moseley was taking a chance with a man relatively unknown as a poet. Up to this point in Milton's career, none of his poems had been published with his name except for *Lycidas*, which had appeared with his initials in *Justa Eduardo King Naufrago*. We can detect Moseley's anxiety about the profitability of Milton's works throughout the bookseller's introductory epistle. He admits that "*the slightest Pamphlet is now adayes more vendible then the Works of learnedest men,*" and he attempts to reassure himself, "*Let the event guide it self which way it will, I shall deserve of the age.*"

Those elements of the 1645 text that are often attributed to Milton may thus reflect Moseley's influence; the careful Stationer would not have "*set forth*" the collection of Milton's *Poems* without taking some precautions. Although Moseley claims that "*it's the worth of these both English and Latin* Poems, *not the flourish of any prefixed* encomions *that can invite thee to buy them,*" he nevertheless prefixes several "encomions" to the collection. Moseley hoped to entice readers who were unfamiliar with Milton and to win over those who only knew the author as a sectarian and divorcer.

To market his new poet Moseley also took the unusual step of including biographical tags that precede some of the poems. The tags demonstrate Milton's precocious talent by noting the young age at which he composed the texts (as with "Psalm 114" and "Psalm 136"), and they emphasize the poet's prestigious connections (as in the case of *A Mask* and *Arcades*). Some state only the year of composition (as with "On the Morning of Christ's Nativity") but others offer more detailed information (as with *Lycidas*). The explanatory tags occur with the following poems: "On the Morning of Christ's Nativity," "Psalm 114" and "Psalm 136," "The Passion," *Arcades, Lycidas, A Mask, Elegia secunda* (Elegy 2), *Elegia tertia* (Elegy 3), *Elegia quarta* (Elegy 4), *Elegia quinta* (Elegy 5), *Elegia sexta* (Elegy 6), *Elegia septima* (Elegy 7), *In obitum Procancellarii medici* ("On the Death of the Vice-Chancellor, a Doctor"), *In quintum Novembris* ("On the Fifth of November"), *In obitum Praesulis Eliensis*

("On the Death of the Bishop of Ely"), and *Epitaphium Damonis* ("Epitaph for Damon"). In addition, a biographical tag precedes a group of complimentary notices by Milton's Italian acquaintances, and non-biographical tags explain the occasion behind both "On the University Carrier" and "Another on the Same" and provide a context for *Philosophus ad regem* ("A Philosopher to a King").

Publishing a collection of poems after the start of the civil wars, Moseley responded to the country's recent political upheaval with a text that reasserted traditional values and avoided explicit reference to the conflict. As we saw in Chapter 1, the volume evokes an overriding sense of the author as a learned gentleman. In places, the book reflects Milton's early radicalism – most noticeably in the critique of the clergy in *Lycidas* – but most of the collection tends to drown out such discordant notes with conservative intonations. The book includes four poems celebrating the failure of Guy Fawkes's plot to assassinate James I as well as two elegies composed in honor of the clergy, *In obitum Praesulis Wintoniensis* ("On the Death of the Bishop of Winchester") and *In obitum Praesulis Eliensis*.

Milton, of course, may have influenced the book's layout and thus helped to shape its largely conservative emphasis. As the autobiographical digressions in his prose tracts suggest, Milton was fiercely concerned with his self-presentation, and he at least must have provided the information included in the *Poems*'s biographical tags. Milton's other publications also suggest that he understood the ideological weight that a book's design carried: in *An Apology against a Pamphlet*, for example, he begins his attack on *A Modest Confutation* with its title page (*CPW* I: 875–77), and to refute *Eikon Basilike*, Milton criticizes the book's "conceited portraiture … sett there to catch fools and silly gazers" (*CPW* III: 342). While Moseley was surely trying to produce a lucrative book that would help him establish his reputation as a bookseller of fine literature, Milton was just as likely trying to use the *Poems* to dispel his reputation as a polemicist and divorcer.

But if the depiction of the author in the 1645 *Poems* would have been mutually beneficial to Milton and Moseley, Milton in his only account of the *Poems*'s creation suggests that Moseley determined the design of the 1645 edition. Responding in *Pro Se Defensio* to the accusation that attaching a self-portrait to the book was narcissistic, Milton claims that Moseley insisted on including the frontispiece by William Marshall: "But if, at the suggestion and solicitation of a bookseller, I suffered myself to be crudely engraved by an unskillful engraver because there was no other in the city at that time, that fact argues me rather more unwilling to trouble myself with matters of that kind than too fastidious, as you object" (*CPW* IV: 750–51). Although we risk separating

Milton's comments from their specific rhetorical context – writing in 1655, he might have wished to distance himself politically from Moseley and Marshall, both of whom were Royalists[22] – Milton's rebuttal nevertheless indicates that he did not preside over the book's production. Doing so, Milton implies, would have been too much trouble.

Already in 1645, though, Milton had taken the trouble to assert himself and comment on the collection's design. While Marshall's unflattering portrait seems to undermine Milton's authority at the start of *Poems*, Milton used the Greek epigraph below the portrait to overcome his limited participation in the book's production. Milton evidently asked the unsuspecting Marshall to engrave his own condemnation: "That an unskillful hand had carved this print / You'd say at once, seeing the living face; / But, finding here no jot of me, my friends, / Laugh at the botching artist's mis-attempt."[23] If we begin *Poems* with a caricature of a young Milton commissioned and created by someone else, we also hear the author's voice speaking to us directly, asking us to laugh with him at Marshall's expense.

And regardless of how little practical authority Milton may have had over the design of the 1645 *Poems*, his Latin ode *Ad Joannem Rousium* ("To John Rouse") suggests that he cared deeply about the volume. Looking back on the book's publication, Milton affectionately addresses *Poems* as "parve liber" (line 13) and "libelle" (line 37), as if it were a dear child of his. John Rouse, the librarian at Oxford University, had requested a copy of Milton's *Poems* along with his other publications (which Milton calls the little book's "fratrum," i.e., "brothers," line 39). When the initial copy of *Poems* was lost or pilfered, Rouse asked Milton to provide a replacement. In the verses to Rouse that Milton wrote out and tucked between the English and Latin halves of the substitute copy, the poet imagines his book housed among the librarian's other treasures and passed on to posterity with the works of great, ancient authors. Celebrating his potency as an author, Milton casts himself as a father of immortal children who have exceeded his expectations for them.

But in attempting to take credit for his dear "libelle," Milton in his ode to Rouse also indicates his lack of control and expands the circle of the book's collaborators. For the *Poems* to survive, Milton needs Rouse's alert assistance and institutions such as the Bodleian Library. His fear that the book will fall into the hands of vulgar, unappreciative readers ("lingua procax vulgi," line 79) suggests still another level of dependence: Milton can only hope for sensitive, future readers who will approach his works without prejudice and cherish the treasures that they contain.

Paradise Lost **(1667, 1674)**

Consider Milton's audacity: in rewriting Genesis 1–3 as *Paradise Lost*, he was not just attempting to "soar / Above th' Aonian mount" and surpass his classical poetic predecessors (I.14–15); he was also aspiring to outdo the prophet Moses, the original story's presumptive author. And Milton would do so in an epic (a long narrative poem about a heroic subject written in an elevated style), which, as we saw in Chapter 2, was generally considered the most accomplished and most difficult genre of writing.

Milton announces his specific ambition near the poem's start. In *Paradise Lost*, he wants to "assert eternal providence, / And justify the ways of God to men" (I.25–26). He was boldly presuming, in other words, to defend Christianity. Why do people feel hate, pride, and envy if the God who created humankind is wholly good and all-powerful? Why does such a God allow people to suffer and inflict harm? This type of writing, whether in poetry or prose, has come to be known as a theodicy, a term coined in the eighteenth century by the German philosopher Gottfried Leibniz. A theodicy is an attempt to vindicate divine justice given the existence of evil. From Milton's surviving notes in the Trinity Manuscript, we know that he considered other biblical and national subjects and entertained the possibility of instead writing a tragedy. In settling on the fall of humankind and the epic form, he could not have undertaken a more ambitious project.

Satan

In attempting to "assert eternal providence," Milton did not, however, limit himself to the events in Genesis, and an important strategy for reading *Paradise Lost* is identifying how – and speculating why – Milton in places deviates from his biblical source material. Episodes such as Adam and Eve's argument whether they should work separately (IX.205–384) or Eve's dream as Satan whispers at her ear, "Assaying by his devilish art to reach / The organs of her fancy" (IV.801–02), especially deserve scrutiny because in these passages Milton radically reimagines the narrative in Genesis. He fleshes out the barebones biblical account, anticipating the cause-and-effect plotting and psychological complexity that would come to characterize the novel beginning in the eighteenth century.

Probably Milton's most memorable invention in *Paradise Lost* remains Satan's complex character. Following the conventions of epic, Milton begins his poem *in medias res* ("in the middle of things") as Satan and his followers wake up in Hell.[24] The rebel angels fall from Heaven for nine days (VI.871), lie in a stupor for another nine (I.50–52), and finally awaken in Hell, confused and in pain. But while Satan finds himself lying face down, chained on a burning lake, he valiantly – and absurdly – refuses to admit defeat:

> What though the field be lost?
> All is not lost; the unconquerable will,
> And study of revenge, immortal hate,
> And courage never to submit or yield:
> And what is else not to be overcome?
> That glory never shall his wrath or might
> Extort from me. To bow and sue for grace
> With suppliant knee, and deify his power,
> Who from the terror of this arm so late
> Doubted his empire, that were low indeed,
> That were an ignominy and shame beneath
> This downfall.   (I.105–16)

Readers can appreciate Satan's resolve even as Milton underscores the devil's perversity. We first hear Satan's rousing, Achilles-like rhetoric before Milton fully reveals the fallen angel's humiliating posture, "With head uplift," "Chained on the burning lake" (I.193, 210). And whereas Achilles in the *Iliad* opposes his commander Agamemnon, then heroically battles the Trojan Hector, Satan foolhardily has taken as his adversary an omnipotent, omniscient God.

Milton also gradually exposes the despair and pain behind Satan's bluster, first as the devil cries when addressing his troops (I.604–20) and more fully as he soliloquizes about his conflicted impulses, first to the sun (Book IV), then to the earth (Book IX). In Satan's soliloquy to the sun, he tries to assess honestly the injustice of defying God's authority even as he subtly displaces responsibility for his fall on "pride" and "ambition" instead of directly blaming himself:

> … pride and worse ambition threw me down
> Warring in Heav'n against Heav'n's matchless King:
> Ah wherefore! He deserved no such return
> From me, whom he created what I was
> In that bright eminence, and with his good
> Upbraided none; nor was his service hard.   (IV.40–45)

Like an addict who wants to quit but keeps giving in to the drug, Satan regrets his rebellion but cannot overcome his pride and bring himself to stop and ask for God's help. Thus when Satan famously boasts, "The mind is its own place, and in itself / Can make a Heav'n of Hell, a Hell of Heav'n " (I.254–55), he is right, but not in the way he intends. The irony of Satan's pronouncement is that he makes a Hell of wherever he goes. Hell in *Paradise Lost*, in other words, is an actual place but it also represents a frame of mind. Full of remorse but refusing to repent, Satan feels as unhappy in Hell as he did in Heaven, and when he first alights in Paradise and spies Adam and Eve, he again responds in pain, "Oh Hell!" (IV.358).[25] Only in his soliloquies does he express an understanding of his plight: "Which way I fly is Hell; myself am Hell; / And in the lowest deep a lower deep / Still threat'ning to devour me opens wide" (IV.75–77).

Yet, given the religious and cultural significance that Satan has gained in the centuries since Milton wrote *Paradise Lost*, readers of Milton's epic may be surprised to discover how little of the archfiend's character and story comes directly from scriptures. Although early biblical commentators identified Satan as the serpent that seduces Eve in Paradise, the text of Genesis refers only to a "serpent," not the devil (Genesis 3:1). In like manner, Milton's account of a war in Heaven and God's casting down Satan and his followers – which occupies books V–VI of *Paradise Lost* – comes from a Judeo-Christian tradition, not directly from the Bible.

In a few places, the scriptures do refer to Satan or a fallen angel. Most important, in Luke 10:18, Jesus tells his apostles that he "beheld Satan as lightning fall from heaven"; in Isaiah 14:12, a Babylonian ruler is compared to a "morning star" (in Latin, *Lucifer*) that fell from Heaven and was felled like a tree; and in 2 Peter 1:19, another reference to a "morning star" occurs but with no mention of Satan. The Book of Job contains one of the longest biblical accounts of Satan but without referring to his rebellion or fall; here Satan remains a shadowy, celestial figure who has been "going to and fro in the earth" and challenges God to test Job's faith (Job 1:7). Satan also tempts Jesus in the wilderness (Matthew 4:1–11, Mark 1:12–13, and Luke 4:1–13), but we again learn nothing about the devil's history and character in this episode, which Milton later used as the basis for *Paradise Regained*.

The specific possibility that Satan took on the serpent's form in Genesis so as to tempt Eve is based primarily on a passage in Revelation: "And I saw an angel come down from heaven, having the key of the bottomless pit and a great chain in his hand. And he laid hold on the dragon, that old serpent, which is the Devil, and Satan, and bound him a thousand years" (20:1–2). Similarly, some commentators have inferred from Revelation's prophecy of angelic conflict that an earlier war in Heaven led to Satan's banishment:

> And there was war in heaven: Michael and his angels fought against the
> dragon; and the dragon fought and his angels, and prevailed not; neither
> was their place found any more in heaven. And the great dragon was
> cast out, that old serpent, called the Devil, and Satan, which deceiveth

> the whole world: he was cast out into the earth, and his angels were cast out with him.   (Revelation 12:7–9)

But if Milton in his depiction of Satan was working from such apocalyptic imagery, he also revised his sources to suit his ends. In contrast to the above passage, for example, the Son in *Paradise Lost*, not Michael, drives out the rebel angels. And while various literary works certainly influenced parts of Satan's story in Milton's poem – such as the description of Sin and Death (Book II), or the archfiend's dramatic return to Hell (Book X) – much of Milton's presentation of Satan remains wholly original.

Raphael in *Paradise Lost* gives the fullest account of Satan's name and origin. The angel recalls that Satan (literally, "the adversary") had a different name before he opposed God, but "his former name / Is heard no more in Heav'n" (V.658–59). Raphael goes on to suggest that Adam and Eve should use "Lucifer" to refer to Satan not because that was formerly Satan's name but because before his fall he, like the morning star, once shone more brightly than the other angels and was, "If not the first Archangel, great in power, / In favor and in pre-eminence" (VII.131; V.660–61). When accordingly the poem's narrator also describes Satan before his rebellion as "Lucifer," Milton in a nod to Isaiah 14:12 emphasizes that this name is only metaphorical: "Lucifer, so by allusion called, / Of that bright star to Satan paragoned" (X.425–26).

Satan originally rebelled, we also learn from Raphael, because God exalted the Son "At my right hand" as the angels' "head" (V.606). Satan feels "envy against the Son of God, that day / … proclaimed / Messiah King anointed" and "could not bear / Through pride that sight, and thought himself impaired" (V.662–65). As we saw in Chapter 2, a central doctrine of Milton's mature theology was his opposition to the Trinity and his insistence that the Son, even after the exaltation, was subordinate to God. Thus Milton describes the Son in *Paradise Lost* as "of all creation first" (III.383), whereas God is "omnipotent, / Immutable, immortal, infinite" (III.372–73) and "alone / From all eternity," as he tells Adam, "for none I know / Second to me or like, equal much less" (VIII.405–07). The anti-Trinitarian cast of these lines provides psychological support – but not theological justification – for Satan's reaction to the Son's new status. Given that the Son and God do not have the same being and that the Son did not exist eternally, Satan could reasonably be surprised at the Son's promotion.

But instead of sympathizing with Satan's hostile reaction to the Son's exaltation, Milton seems to use the story of the devil's origin to dramatize and demonize early Gnostic responses to the advent of Christianity. As early church

Attention to detail: the example of Mulciber

Even as *Paradise Lost* tells a grand narrative about Satan's rebellion and the Fall of humankind, Milton takes pains to incorporate short, richly detailed passages which enhance the epic's main action and broader themes. One such moment is the description of Pandemonium's architect, Mulciber (also known as the Roman god Vulcan, or, in Greek mythology, Hephaestos). Milton tells how Mulciber's father, Jupiter, grew angry with him and cast him from Mount Olympus. Mulciber eventually came to live on Lemnos, an island in the northern Aegean Sea:

> his hand was known
> In Heav'n by many a towered structure high,
> Where sceptered angels held their residence,
> And sat as princes, whom the supreme King
> Exalted to such power, and gave to rule,
> Each in his hierarchy, the orders bright.
> Nor was his name unheard or unadored
> In ancient Greece; and in Ausonian land
> Men called him Mulciber; and how he fell
> From Heav'n, they fabled, thrown by angry Jove
> Sheer o'er the crystal battlements: from morn
> To noon he fell, from noon to dewy eve,
> A summer's day; and with the setting sun
> Dropped from the zenith like a falling star,
> On Lemnos th' Aegean isle: thus they relate,
> Erring; for he with this rebellious rout
> Fell long before; nor aught availed him now
> To have built in Heav'n high tow'rs; nor did he scape
> By all his engines, but was headlong sent
> With his industrious crew to build in Hell.   (I.732–51)

In this passage, Milton uses enjambment to dramatize the gradual descent of Mulciber's body – "how he fell / From Heav'n," "thrown by angry Jove / Sheer," "from morn / To noon," and "with the setting sun / Dropped." The repetition of "from … / To" and "from … to" also seems to extend Mulciber's fall, while the specific details that Jove cast him out in the morning and Mulciber fell for the length of a summer's day lend poignancy to his plight.

The impact of Mulciber's body then finds its prosodic complement in the jarring sound of the trochaic "Erring." Although Milton prepares readers near the start of the passage that Mulciber is merely a "fabled" character, the lyric description of his fall may temporarily distract us from the story's falseness, which Milton then drives home by abruptly ending the digression and deviating from the poem's iambic rhythm. Milton thus emphasizes that Mulciber fell long before Greek and Roman culture when he fled Heaven with the rest of Satan's crew. In this way, Milton repudiates classical myth even as he appropriates it. He might be writing centuries after his ancient forebears, but in this brief, virtuoso maneuver, the fall of Mulciber becomes a retelling of Milton's own epic narrative.

leaders began to assert that Jesus was not just a prophet but the Son of God whose coming had been predicted in the Old Testament, some people questioned the Son's new authority and the church's new way of reading Hebrew Scriptures. Thus when Abdiel tells Satan that it was in fact God's "begotten Son, by whom / As by his Word the mighty Father made / All things, ev'n thee" (V.835–37), Satan's shock and indignation anticipate the earliest historical objections to Christianity. Satan responds, "Strange point and new!" (V.855), emphasizing his perception that the Son's achievements are a recent innovation.

God

Milton's portrayal of the Deity in *Paradise Lost* has sometimes disappointed modern readers. Compared with Satan's inner turmoil, Milton's God – constant, all-knowing, and supreme – can seem aloof, even a little boring. In the context of Milton's theology (see Chapter 2), we can appreciate the impossible task that Milton had set for himself. Of course God in *Paradise Lost* seems impersonal because he is largely a theological and metaphysical construct, almost always glimpsed though the perspective of a different character – Satan, Adam, Eve, Raphael, or Michael.[26]

The passages in which God appears accordingly contain some of the poem's most abstract and least sensuous language. Milton strips away the rich imagery of Hell, Chaos, and Paradise (see box, page 169) in an attempt to evoke a divine presence mostly through dialogue and a few metonymic details – a voice, an ear, an eye, or a throne. Addressing the angels about the Son's exaltation, for example, God appears only "in orbs / Or circuit inexpressible" and "Amidst as from a flaming mount, whose top / Brightness had made invisible" (V.594–95, 598–99). Or, when God congratulates the angel Abdiel for refusing to follow Satan, Raphael describes how the other angels acclaim God's servant, but God himself remains unseen. The angels present Abdiel "Before the seat supreme; from whence a voice / From midst a golden cloud thus mild was heard" (VI.27–28).

Perhaps influenced by the impersonality of these images, some readers have complained that God in *Paradise Lost* also seems abrasively dispassionate. God, for example, sees Satan winging his way

> Directly towards the new-created world,
> And man there placed, with purpose to assay
> If him by force he can destroy, or worse,
> By some false guile pervert; and shall pervert;
> For man will hearken to his glozing lies.   (III.89–93)

The abrupt shift in these lines from subjunctive present tense ("If … he can destroy, or … pervert") to indicative future tense ("and shall pervert") – highlighted by a strong caesura – dramatizes God's omniscience and sets him off from the epic's other characters. But this shift in the verb's tense and mood might simultaneously cast God as cruel and indifferent; he confidently pronounces what will happen but refuses to prevent it. God continues by explaining that because "man" disobeyed the "Sole pledge of his obedience," he "will fall" along with "his faithless progeny: whose fault? / Whose but his own? Ingrate, he had of me / All he could have" (III.95–98). Here again God refuses to take responsibility for his creations' mistakes. He sounds angry, like a parent disappointed in his children whom he tried his best to please.

Later, when news of Adam and Eve's Fall reaches Heaven, God again emphasizes humankind's culpability: he recalls that "these tidings from the Earth" were "Foretold so lately" and reminds the assembled angels that "I told ye … [Satan] should prevail and speed / On his bad errand, man should be seduced / And flattered out of all, believing lies / Against his Maker" (X.36, 38, 40–43). God follows this eloquent I-told-you-so by stating what should also be obvious to the angels, that humanity's sin was not God's fault: "no decree of mine / Concurring to necessitate his fall, / Or touch with lightest moment of impulse / His free will, to her own inclining left / In even scale" (X.43–47).

Yet, all these passages, while they might reflect poorly on Christian authority for some readers, occur within a dramatic context. Milton does not simply present the poem's theology as a series of pronouncements from on high but instead repeatedly portrays a dynamic give-and-take between God and the Son, as the Son grapples with and seeks to temper the Father's sometimes defensive claims.

God's stark expressions of blame for Adam and Eve also convey a crucial tenet of Milton's theodicy: Adam and Eve have free will, and they alone shoulder the responsibility for their disobedience.[27] God knows Adam and Eve will disobey his one rule and eat the forbidden fruit as confidently as a human being could predict, say, that an ice cube feels cold or a flame gives off heat. But just as a person does not control the temperatures of ice and fire, so God does not control Adam and Eve's choices. As God succinctly puts it, Adam and Eve "themselves decreed / Their own revolt, not I: if I foreknew, / Foreknowledge had no influence on their fault, / Which had no less proved certain unforeknown" (III.116–19). Existing outside of time, God in *Paradise Lost* knows everything about what Adam and Eve experience as their past, present, and future, but God does not dictate what his creations will choose any more than he interferes with what they have previously chosen.

Adam and Eve

When in Book IV Milton introduces Adam and Eve, he focuses on the couple's appearance:

> His fair large front and eye sublime declared
> Absolute rule; and hyacinthine locks
> Round from his parted forelock manly hung
> Clust'ring, but not beneath his shoulders broad:
> She as a veil down to the slender waist
> Her unadornèd golden tresses wore
> Disheveled, but in wanton ringlets waved
> As the vine curls her tendrils, which implied
> Subjection, but required with gentle sway,
> And by her yielded, by him best received,
> Yielded with coy submission, modest pride,
> And sweet reluctant amorous delay.   (IV.300–11)

In these lines, Milton imaginatively expands on the brief account of the couple from Genesis. He conveys gender difference by combining traditional biological markers (such as "shoulders broad" and "slender waist") with culturally constructed notions of a man and woman's appropriate hair length.[28] In Adam's case, the specific detail of his "hyacinthine locks" suggests that he resembles – and presumably surpasses – Odysseus after Athena curls his hair "like petals of wild hyacinth."[29] Adam's "parted forelock" also distinguishes him from most historical and mythical portraits painted in the seventeenth century. The only two historical figures who have been identified wearing their hair in this way are Milton himself and Oliver Cromwell.[30]

In Eve's case, the significance of her appearance stems in part from what Milton does not say about it. In contrast to early modern sonnet sequences that emphasize the threatening, traplike qualities of a woman's tresses – see, for example, Henry Constable's *Diana* (1594) and Edmund Spenser's *Amoretti* (1595) – Eve's curly locks contain no fetters. On the contrary, the description of her waving ringlets as "wanton" suggests that they are not only "robust" and "amorous" but also "free, unrestrained."[31] While some critics have objected that "wanton" and "Disheveled" indicate that Eve from the start is somehow already fallen, any hints of corruption in the above passage more likely reflect Satan's contaminating influence. The details of Adam's and Eve's appearance occur within a larger survey of Paradise that Milton clearly frames as conveying what Satan views. Thus, immediately before introducing Adam and Eve, the poet announces that "the fiend / Saw undelighted all delight" (IV.285–86), and the scene concludes with a reminder of Satan's abiding presence: "Satan still in gaze, as first he stood" (IV.356).

Satan's voyeurism in this scene may also qualify the epic's staunchest declaration of Eve's inferiority to Adam. In the lines preceding the above passage, the narrator enforces a hierarchical relationship: "For contemplation he and valor formed, / For softness she and sweet attractive grace, / He for God only, she for God in him" (IV.297–99). But the description of Adam and Eve's appearance, occurring immediately afterwards, subtly begins to complicate the difference in their statuses. The mutuality of Adam and Eve's relationship finds expression, for example, in the parallel constructions that describe their physical selves. While Adam's "forelock manly hung / Clust'ring, but not beneath his shoulders," Eve "her unadornèd golden tresses wore / Disheveled, but in wanton ringlets". This echoing gesture fits with other grammatical parallels as the couple first enter the epic – including "He for God only, she for God in him" and "by her yielded, by him best received" – lines that indicate a hierarchy while still suggesting reciprocity. And although the Pauline tenor of "He for God only, she for God in him" clearly subordinates Eve to Adam, the "Subjection" at the end of the passage has been sublimated to the couple's hair and remains a mere implication.

Throughout *Paradise Lost*, Milton continues to develop the tension between the hierarchical and the egalitarian aspects of Adam and Eve's marriage. Sometimes a character will interpret or describe Eve as Adam's inferior, so that, for example, Satan in the form of the serpent is pleased to discover Eve alone, an "unsupported flow'r, / From her best prop so far" (IX.432–33), and Eve herself self-deprecatingly describes Adam as "my guide / And head" and "My author and disposer" (IV.442–43, 635). Milton also may symbolically suggest the spouses' different stations by depicting Adam gazing heavenward at his creation, whereas Eve in her first waking moments stares at a reflection of herself.

Yet other passages in the epic, as we have seen in the description of Adam's and Eve's appearance, instead suggest reciprocity if not equality. When, for example, Adam tells God that Eve and he share an intimate bond, Adam describes their union as "one flesh, one heart, one soul" (VIII.499), a dramatic expansion of the simple reference in Genesis to "one flesh" (2:24) and an apparent attempt to stress the companionate nature of the couple's marriage. Requesting a human consort from God, Adam also emphasizes his desire for an equal partner: "Among unequals what society/ Can sort, what harmony or true delight? / Which must be mutual, in proportion due / Giv'n and received" (VIII.383–86).

Milton also provides ample evidence of Eve's mutual authority. Telling the story of first meeting Adam, Eve recalls that she initially turned away because she found him "less fair, / Less winning soft, less amiably mild" than her own reflection (IV.478–79). Here she may simply be teasing her husband that she is more attractive than he is, and certainly she later concedes that "beauty is excelled by manly grace / And wisdom, which alone is truly fair" (IV.490–91). But Eve in her account of first meeting Adam also sounds more independent and stronger willed, and even in her concession she uses "manly" to modify "grace," not necessarily "wisdom," which both she and Adam possess. Thus, Eve gently corrects Adam that they need not store food because they live in Paradise (V.321–30), and the narrator insists that Eve has the same ability as Adam to comprehend Raphael's astronomical discourse (VIII.48–57). Eve after the Fall also plays a crucial role in subduing Adam's anger and rescuing him from despair, thereby saving their marriage: she is the first to acknowledge her fault and selflessly asks that God punish her alone – "Me me only just object of his ire" (X.936) – an apparently sincere plea that "in Adam wrought / Commiseration" (X.939–40). Nor should we completely dismiss the power of Eve's superior beauty. When, for example, Satan first spies Eve gardening alone, her appearance so overwhelms him that it momentarily renders him good: "her every air / Of gesture or least action overawed / His malice, and with rapine sweet bereaved / His fierceness of the fierce intent it brought" (IX.459–62).

Any doubts readers might have about the paradoxically hierarchical but egalitarian nature of the marriage of Adam and Eve are answered by looking at their punishment for eating the forbidden fruit. As a consequence of the Fall, the Son tells Eve that not only will she now suffer in childbirth but also "to thy husband's will / Thine shall submit, he over thee shall rule" (X.195–96). If this submission is part of the couple's postlapsarian existence, then Adam and Eve must have enjoyed a more mutual marriage before they disobeyed God and were punished.

The difference between pre- and postlapsarian experience in *Paradise Lost* represents the other principal tension that informs Milton's depiction of Adam and Eve. But instead of a straightforward contrast of the characters' lives before and after the Fall, Milton treats the couple's fallen condition as a debased form of their previous lives in Paradise. Before the Fall, Adam and Eve, while not perfect, live happily and harmoniously as they together pray, garden, and make love. In particular, the couple begin and end their days bowing lowly "to praise / Their Maker, in fit strains pronounced or sung / Unmeditated" (V.147–49). Their prayer is a spontaneous, unanimous expression of their gratitude, unaccompanied by any formal ceremonies – a detail that Milton apparently adds as a critique of Catholic and Laudian rituals (see Chapter 2) (IV.736–38). After the Fall, Adam and Eve also pray, but now they plaintively ask for God's forgiveness, "with tears / Watering the ground, and with … sighs the air / Frequenting" (X.1089–91).

In like manner, Adam and Eve work both before and after the Fall, but Milton explains that originally tending Eden's flowers and pruning its "growing plants" is a "delightful task" (IV.438, 437). The pair's gardening only becomes toilsome after the Fall. As the Son pronounces, doling out the couple's punishment,

> Cursed is the ground for thy sake, thou in sorrow
> Shalt eat thereof all the days of thy life;
> Thorns also and thistles it shall bring thee forth
> Unbid, and thou shalt eat th' herb of th' field,
> In the sweat of thy face shalt thou eat bread.   (X.201–5)

Before the Fall, Adam and Eve apparently gardened without worrying about bad soil, weeds, or even perspiration.

And if Adam and Eve's prelapsarian gardening helps to prevent their becoming bored in Paradise, so does the "sweet reluctant amorous delay" of their ongoing flirtatious romance (IV.311). Milton emphasizes that before the Fall Adam and Eve enjoy an innocent sexual relationship, free of lust and "Founded in reason, loyal, just, and pure, / Relations dear" (IV.755–56). Milton also interjects a scornful critique of "hypocrites" who might find fault with the possibility of sinless sex in Paradise: these critics, he says, merely "talk / Of purity and place and innocence, / Defaming as impure what God declares / Pure, and commands to some, leaves free to all" (IV.744–47). Only after the Fall do Adam and Eve become tainted by "Carnal desire" and burn "in lust" (IX.1013, 1015). Adam and Eve now look at each other with "lascivious eyes" (IX.1014), and instead of finding their "amorous play" refreshing, they feel guilty and tired afterwards (IX.1045).

As all these changes that come with the Fall suggest, readers trying to analyze Adam or Eve must not conflate the couple's post- and prelapsarian selves and experiences. While the various connections between their lives before and after they have sinned echo, on one level, the complex interrelationship between *L'Allegro* and *Il Penseroso*, Adam and Eve before and after the Fall are, on another level, as radically different from each other as mirth and melancholy. Thus, an instance of Eve deceiving Adam after she sins does not prove that before the Fall she also lied, and Adam's surliness after the Fall should not be read backwards as evidence of marital discord before the couple sinned. Part of the challenge – and pleasure – of reading Milton's depiction of the couple lies in gradually discovering how their prelapsarian experience finds new, degraded expression once they eat the fruit and disobey God.

To take one more, specific example: when Eve first meets Adam, she turns away. As Adam later recounts the scene to Raphael, "seeing me, she turned; / I followed her," until "with obsequious majesty" she "approved / My pleaded reason," and "To the nuptial bow'r / I led her blushing like the morn" (VIII.507–11). Eve in her version adds a few salient details: she recalls that Adam "following criedst aloud, 'Return fair Eve,'" and his "gentle hand / Seized mine" before finally "I yielded" (IV.481, 488–89). The gesture of Adam's hand touching Eve's forms part of a broader motif of hand-holding in Milton's epic. In fact, we first spy Adam and Eve, "hand in hand … the loveliest pair / That ever since in love's embraces met" (IV.321–22), and our final glimpse of the couple has them once again joined by a handclasp: "They hand in hand with wand'ring steps and slow, / Through Eden took their solitary way" (XII.648–49).

But Adam's seizing Eve's hand at their first meeting is especially significant because, evoking the Renaissance marriage ceremony, it suggests that the couple freely take each other as husband and wife. Here Milton may have been in part responding to Luther, who had argued, on the contrary, that "Adam does not snatch Eve of his own will after she has been created, but he waits for God to bring her to him."[32] While Milton, in keeping with Genesis 2:22, has both Eve and Adam recollect that Eve was "invisibly … led" to Adam by "her Heav'nly Maker" (IV.476, VIII.485), Milton also emphasizes the couple's free will by staging a second part to their initial meeting. After Eve decides to turn away, Adam freely chooses her, and Eve freely acquiesces.

Milton highlights the contrast between pre- and postlapsarian experience by then repeating "seize" after Adam and Eve eat from the Tree of Knowledge and are overcome by carnal desire: "Her hand he seized, and to a shady bank, / Thick overhead with verdant roof embow'red / He led her nothing loath"

The settings of *Paradise Lost*

Milton's epic encompasses multiple locations, and understanding the relation between its settings can be confusing. On the largest scale, the cosmos of *Paradise Lost* contains three separate spaces: Heaven, Hell, and chaos (see Figure 4). Heaven, as we might expect, sits at the top, and God sits at the highest point in Heaven, "High throned above all highth" (III.58). Far below sits Hell, "a dungeon horrible" that is "As far removed from God and light of Heav'n / As from the center [of earth] thrice to th' utmost pole" (I.61, 73–74). The dark and vast abyss of chaos separates and fills the space between Heaven and Hell, and it is chaos that God uses to create Hell and the "world" in which Adam and Eve live (II.347). Milton also suggests that God might eventually create "new worlds" out of chaos's primal matter (I.650). As the narrator explains, the warring elements of chaos "must ever fight, / Unless th' Almighty Maker them ordain / His dark materials to create more worlds" (II.914–16).

"World" in *Paradise Lost*, then, most often refers to our universe or galaxy, which Milton imagines as spherical, encased in a "firm opacous globe" (III.418).

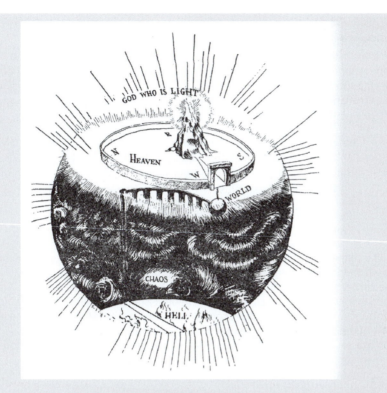

Figure 4 Diagram of the cosmos in *Paradise Lost*, by David A. Ruffin

Satan initially spies it from afar, "hanging in a golden chain" from Heaven on the side where he and the rebel angels fell (II.1051; and see 1004–6). First, Satan asks the personified Chaos for directions to our universe; then the fiend asks the unsuspecting archangel Uriel for directions to Earth. Arriving "into the world's first region" (III.562) and alighting on the sun (III.591), Satan specifically requests that Uriel tell him on "which of all these shining orbs hath man / His fixèd seat, or fixèd seat hath none, / But all these shining orbs his choice to dwell" (III.668–70). Satan's question subtly suggests that Milton did not accept a geocentric universe: traveling through our galaxy, Satan evidently cannot ascertain which orb is Earth because it is not unique in its size or location.

Elsewhere in the epic, though, Milton seems deliberately to obfuscate the structure of our universe. Readers may wonder whether he believed in a sun-centered or earth-centered model because, for example, Satan travels uncertainly, "Through the calm firmament; but up or down / By center, or eccentric, hard to tell" (III.574–75). And later, when Adam asks Raphael whether the sun or Earth sits at the center of the universe, Raphael resolutely refuses to answer: "whether heav'n move or Earth, / Imports not" (VIII.70–71). (In such passages, we should also note, "heav'n" refers to the stars and sky in our universe, as distinct from Heaven, often capitalized by modern editors, where God and the angels reside.)

Nevertheless, other details in the poem confirm that Milton accepted the findings of Galileo, whose telescopic discoveries supported Copernicus's theory of a sun-centered universe. In particular, Uriel in his response to Satan's request for directions sounds unambiguously Galilean.[33] The angel points to Earth and relegates it to the status of a satellite, reflecting the sun's light:

> Look downward on that globe whose hither side
> With light from hence, though but reflected, shines;
> That place is Earth the seat of man, that light
> His day, which else as th' other hemisphere
> Night would invade, but there the neighboring moon
> (So call that opposite fair star) her aid
> Timely interposes.   (III.722–28)

In like manner, following close upon Raphael's noncommittal reply to Adam about the universe's configuration, Satan's pronouncement that the Earth is the center seems especially wrongheaded (IX.103–9). Raphael says that Adam need not know about such astronomical details, and then Satan, sitting alone, announces (incorrectly) that he knows that the Earth is the center. Raphael's ambiguous description of the universe may be Milton's coy attempt not to commit to a specific astronomical model for his epic's universe, but it more immediately highlights Satan's ignorance and directionlessness.

Comparatively straightforward are the poem's remaining, terrestrial settings. Once Satan arrives on Earth, Milton distinguishes – in order from largest to smallest – between Earth, Eden, Paradise, and Adam and Eve's bower. Perhaps most important, Paradise is not the same as Eden; instead, Paradise is the part of Eden where Adam and Eve reside: "blissful Paradise / Of God the Garden was, by him in the east / Of Eden planted" (IV.208–10). And Adam and Eve dwell in Paradise in a bower, the epic's most intimate space, a "shady lodge" where they retire hand in hand and together enjoy "the rites / Mysterious of connubial love" (IV.720, 742–43).

(IX.1037–39). Gone in this postlapsarian scene is both the qualifying "gentle hand" from Eve's account of their earlier meeting and the description of Eve "blushing like the morn" from Adam's version (VIII.511). *Seize* now seems to signify to take possession "by force," or "to take hold of suddenly or eagerly" with the "hands, claws, teeth."[34] The repetition of this one word to depict both pre- and postlapsarian desire complicates a simple dichotomy of innocence versus lust; Milton encourages us to see the similarity as well as the difference between the two gestures. "Seized" fits with other ambivalent signifiers in Book IV, words such as "Luxuriant" (260) and "wanton" (306), which measure Eden's integrity before the Fall by anticipating its ultimate ruin.[35]

Spirit and matter

To understand fully the implications of Milton's portrayal of Adam and Eve as well as of Satan also requires some knowledge of the author's philosophy of matter. Milton was not, strictly speaking, a philosopher, and he never composed a systematic metaphysics to complement his theological treatise. But he did become close friends with men who were deeply engaged with philosophical issues, and Milton himself took an active interest in the debate over free will and substance that flourished in the 1650s, the period in which he began writing *De Doctrina Christiana* and *Paradise Lost*.[36]

As both these works demonstrate, Milton came to espouse a heretical concept of the body and soul. Rejecting the centuries of Christian tradition that supported a dichotomy of flesh and spirit, he instead adopted a monistic theory of matter, that is, he believed that God created everything from the same material – "one first matter all," as Raphael succinctly states in *Paradise Lost*, "Endued with various forms, various degrees / Of substance, and in things that live, of life" (V.472–74). Thus, for Milton, humankind "is not double or separable: not, as is commonly thought, produced from and composed of two different and distinct elements, soul and body. On the contrary, the whole man is the soul, and the soul the man: a body, in other words, or individual substance, animated, sensitive, and rational" (*CPW* VI: 318).

But, as this quotation from *De Doctrina Christiana* also suggests, Milton still distinguished between body and soul. In contrast to, say, the mechanistic materialist philosophy of Thomas Hobbes (1588–1679) which denied the existence of incorporeal spirits, Milton believed that spirit was a more rarified version of the substance from which God creates everything. One way of explaining this theory, sometimes called "animist materialism," is to compare Milton's concept of eternal matter to water, which can take the form of ice, liquid, or steam but remains the same chemical compound. In like manner, the matter that God uses to create can take on more or less spirituous forms but remains essentially the same substance.

In *Paradise Lost*, Raphael explains Milton's theory of matter with a plant metaphor. Like the parts of a flower, God's creations, Raphael observes, are "more refined, more spirituous, and pure, / As nearer to him placed" (V.475–76): the least refined creations resemble a plant's roots, while more spirituous creations correspond to the green stalk, even more spirituous creations correspond to the leaves, and so on. This continuum of nature helps to clarify the relationship between angels and humans: angels resemble humans in some material ways – both, for example, have bodies, eat, and blush – but angels are "more spirituous, and pure" than their earthly counterparts. Whereas humans rely on discursive knowledge, angels more often use intuition; and whereas Adam and Eve enjoy a loving physical relationship, angels have a more spiritual sex life. As Raphael shyly explains, "Whatever pure thou in the body enjoy'st / … we enjoy / In eminence, and obstacle find none / Of membrane, joint, or limb, exclusive bars: / Easier than air with air, if spirits embrace, / Total they mix, union of pure with pure / Desiring; nor restrained conveyance need / As flesh to mix with flesh, or soul with soul" (VIII.622–29).

Most immediately, Raphael offers his plant comparison in an attempt to explain how he can "convert … / To proper substance" Adam and Eve's "earthly fruits" (V.492–93, 464) and how the couple can similarly transform their own material "nourishment" into "vital spirits" that enable motion and thought (V.483, 484). But the dynamic nature of Raphael's metaphor also applies more generally to all of God's creations, who can rise or descend on the "scale of nature" based on their moral choices (V.509). Just as human beings or angels can turn their physical food into sustenance, so in the hierarchy of existence, God's creations can, within limits, improve (or decline) in their material form, "Till body up to spirit work, in bounds / Proportioned to each kind" (V.478–79). Raphael also raises the possibility that Adam and Eve will eventually ascend to Heaven if they remain faithful to God: "from these corporal nutriments perhaps / Your bodies may at last turn all to spirit, / Improved by tract of time, and winged ascend / Ethereal" (V.496–99).

Conversely, when Satan rebels and turns away from God, he becomes less spirituous and pure – "now gross by sinning grown," as Raphael explains (VI.661). That is, Satan's fall is not only moral but also material (and spatial and temporal): Satan's spirit becomes less rarified, and he literally hardens (I.572).[37] Thus, during the War in Heaven, Satan "first knew pain" (VI.327) because with his sin his body calcifies, whereas the good, more spirituous angels – except for their material arms – could "Have easily as spirits evaded swift / By quick contraction or remove" the rebel angels' gunfire (VI.596–97).

Satan's corporeal decline also expresses itself in his attraction to things like himself that are more matter than spirit. Instead of returning to God and seeking forgiveness, he repeatedly puts his faith in things – whether a sword, a cannon, or an apple. Satan's material armament in particular illustrates the folly of his rebellion. Unlike the spiritual armor that Paul described in his letter to the Ephesians (Eph. 6:11–17), Satan's shield actually exists but it fails to protect him, first from Abdiel (VI.192–93), then from Michael (VI.323–28), until finally the rebels drop their shields while fleeing the Son:

> … they astonished all resistance lost,
> All courage; down their idle weapons dropped;
> O'er shields and helms, and helmèd heads he rode
> Of Thrones and mighty Seraphim prostrate.   (VI.838–41)

While this image of discarded armament is hardly original to Milton, the specific term "astonished" punningly suggests the link between the rebels' material arms and their own material debasement: the rebels may drop their weapons, but their forms, like their hearts, are already becoming "stony."[38]

Later, Milton repeats the image of discarded weaponry when Satan, returning to Hell, expects to hear his cohorts' "high applause" but is instead confronted with "A dismal universal hiss" as God changes the rebels into serpents (X.505, 508). Once again, the devils' moral and material fall is figured in their hardening forms and falling weapons: "down their arms, / Down fell both spear and shield, down they as fast" (X.541–42). Milton thus invokes Dante's concept of *contrapasso* as Satan and the rebels are "punished in the shape he sinned" (X.516). They not only take the shape of snakes, but also, having taken up material arms in a war against God, they fittingly come to resemble their own lost shields, fallen and hardened.

Paradise Regained (1671)

Although the title suggests a sequel, *Paradise Regained* complements rather than competes with Milton's earlier epic. According to Milton's nephew Edward Phillips, the author "could not hear with patience" when *Paradise Regained* was deemed "inferiour" to *Paradise Lost* (*EL* 76) – a recollection that likely indicates, not Milton's preference for the later poem, but his awareness that each should be read on its own terms. Near the end of his life, Milton had scaled back his epic ambitions. Instead of undertaking a second long, heroic poem, he chose a much narrower subject – the Son's temptation in the wilderness – and a much plainer style, suitable to the sublime simplicity of the Son's life.

Probably most surprising to first-time readers of *Paradise Regained* is the fact that the poem does not depict Christ's sacrifice on the cross. Given also that Milton never finished his earlier attempt to write about the Crucifixion in "The Passion," some critics have concluded that his theology somehow distanced him from the Eucharist. But Milton may have had a didactic reason in *Paradise Regained* for choosing to depict the Son's moral and intellectual trials. In contrast to a poem about the Crucifixion, *Paradise Regained* dramatizes the type of divine obedience and resistance to temptation that readers could aspire to emulate in their daily lives.

Paradise Regained is sometimes described as a brief epic, a genre of biblical poetry written in either Latin or a vernacular language and usually three or four books in length. Brief epics include many of the same conventions as epic poetry but focus more narrowly on an individual Christian hero engaged in an intellectual struggle against temptation.[39] The classic example is the Book of Job, which Milton had singled out decades earlier in *The Reason of Church-Government Urg'd against Prelaty*: "that Epick form whereof … the book of *Job* [is] a brief model" (*CPW* I: 813). Some commentators, however, have challenged this classification, arguing, for example, that *Paradise Regained's* lack of epic devices and the exalted debates between Satan and the Son distinguish the poem from sixteenth- and seventeenth-century biblical brief epics. Certainly Milton seems to have drawn on a wide range of sources, including Giles Fletcher's biblical poem *Christ's Victorie and Triumph* as well as John's gospel, Plato's dialogues, Virgil's *Georgics*, Malory's *Morte d'Arthur*, Joseph Beaumont's *Psyche*, and Book II of *The Faerie Queene*.

Yet, even with so many notable influences, *Paradise Regained* is intensely original in its content and form. Poetically, it has no clear descendants and no direct precursors. Working from the copious biblical commentary that had grown up around the temptation of Jesus in Matthew (4:1–11), Mark (1:12–13), and Luke (4:1–13), Milton greatly expands the few details included in the gospels. He most closely follows Luke's version of the Son's temptation, beginning with the trial of bread and concluding with the scene on the pinnacle. But while *Paradise Regained's* three-day structure may allude to the three original temptations in Luke (as well as in Matthew), Milton's poem instead depicts Satan tempting Jesus nine separate times.

Part of the poem's drama stems from Milton's Arianism and the subordinate role that he assigned the Son.[40] Readers can confidently predict that the Son will not succumb to Satan, but because the Son is not God, the devil's temptations seem a more genuine test of the virtue and wisdom of Jesus. Milton also underscores the Son's limitations by having him not fully comprehend his role on earth. Near the start, he is still "Musing and much revolving in his breast, / How best the mighty work he might begin / Of savior to mankind, and which way first / Publish his Godlike office now mature" (I.185–88). Jesus has read the Hebrew scriptures (I.207–11), and his mother tells him that he is God's Son (I.230–41), but he appears to have no recollection of his existence before the incarnation, and not until successfully completing the devil's trials does he seem prepared to fulfill his earthly purpose.

How much Satan knows about the Son is less clear. The devil acknowledges that Jesus is "Declared the Son of God" (I.385), but he does not recognize the Son from the War in Heaven and does not seem to understand fully what the title "Son" means. Thus, late in the poem, Satan uncertainly explains to Jesus, "The Son of God I also am, or was, / And if I was, I am; relation stands; / All men are Sons of God; yet thee I thought / In some respect far higher so declared" (IV.518–21). Is Satan genuinely confused, feigning ignorance, or deluding himself? He realizes that he might "now be overmatched" after first meeting Jesus (II.146), and he senses that seducing Jesus will require "Far other labor to be undergone / Than when I dealt with Adam" (II.132–3). But at the end of the poem Satan is still unprepared for the Son's steadfast posture, and he falls from the pinnacle with amazement as he finally seems to recognize that Jesus is the divine Son.

A brief summary of Satan's temptations and the Son's responses demonstrates how Milton develops the theme of identity while building on his biblical source-texts. In the opening three trials, the devil wants the Son to distrust God's providence. As in Matthew's and Luke's accounts, Satan first tempts Jesus to end his fast by turning stones into bread. Milton, though, pushes this idea further, adding a second trial in which Satan again tempts Jesus with intemperance but this time in the form of an elaborate banquet – "A table richly spread, in regal mode" (II.340) – attended by seductive nymphs and "Tall stripling youths rich-clad" (II.352). And in a third trial, Satan also tempts the Son's faith in God by offering him money to build up his authority and buy "honor, friends, conquest, and realms" (II.422).

Jesus rejects all of these offers. Comparing himself to Moses and Elijah, he first affirms his faith in his Father: "Man lives not by bread alone, but each word / Proceeding from the mouth of God" (I.349–50). He disdains what he calls Satan's "pompous delicacies" (II.390), explains that as Lord he already possesses all of nature, and discounts wealth as less important than virtue, valor, and wisdom. In what may be an allusion to Milton's Commonwealth prose, Jesus also seems to challenge the legitimacy of earthly monarchies in general: "he who reigns within himself, and rules / Passions, desires, and fears, is more a king" (II.466–67).

Milton at the same time pursues the theme of identity by having the devil disguise himself in his first encounters with Jesus. Whereas Satan's knowledge of the Son seems incomplete, the Son immediately discerns that the devil is other than he seems. In the first temptation, Satan conceals himself as "an aged man in rural weeds" (I.314), a parody of the Son's pastoral role as the good shepherd, while in the second temptation, Satan appears, "seemlier clad, / As one in city, or court, or palace bred" (II.299–300), perhaps another glancing nod at Milton's Commonwealth prose and a subtle critique of the Stuart court.

Satan then emphasizes the Son's inexperience as he offers the Son authority over worldly kingdoms (cf. Luke 4:5, Matthew 4:8). He suggests that Jesus should seek fame and glory instead of hiding his talents in the wilderness. Jesus explains that by daring to "be singularly good" he wants to achieve God's glory, not his own (III.57). His caustic dismissal of popularity both echoes the importance of heavenly renown over earthly fame from *Lycidas* (lines 76–84) and may reflect Milton's own disillusionment with his fellow citizens for allowing England to return to monarchy: "For what is glory but the blaze of fame, / The people's praise, if always praise unmixed? / And what the people but a herd confused, / A miscellaneous rabble, who extol / Things vulgar, and well weighed, scarce worth the praise?" (III.47–51).

Satan again challenges the Son's motive with the fifth trial. Even if the Son is not interested in worldly power, Satan reasons, he should still act swiftly out of a sense of zeal and duty, "Zeal of thy Father's house, duty to free / Thy country from her heathen servitude" (III.175–76). Jesus explains that he is in no hurry and accepts that God must test his merit: "Who best / Can suffer, best can do; best reign, who first / Well hath obeyed; just trial ere I merit / My exaltation without change or end" (III.194–97).

Satan, although "inly racked," continues to stress the Son's lack of worldly experience and offers to teach him about the earth's monarchies so that he "may'st know / How best their opposition to withstand" (III.203, 249–50). Bringing Jesus to the top of a mountain, Satan proposes that the Son regain the throne of his ancestor King David by wielding military might, as symbolized by the Parthian empire (the sixth temptation), or by embracing secular luxury, as symbolized by Rome (the seventh temptation).

The Son of course rejects both offers. He dismisses the "cumbersome / Luggage of war" (III.400–1) and is equally uninterested in "Civility of manners, arts, and arms" (IV.83). Instead of replacing Tiberius as emperor of Rome, he leaves the ruler to his conscience and adds that the Romans deserve to be vassals to such a bad ruler because they have become corrupted. Emphasizing his spiritual kingship, the Son announces that he will ultimately supersede all other monarchies, a pledge that could be read once again in the context of Milton's political prose and his opposition to Charles I:

> … to guide nations in the way of truth
> By saving doctrine, and from error lead
> To know, and knowing worship God aright,
> Is yet more kingly; this attracts the soul,
> Governs the inner man, the nobler part,
> That other o'er the body only reigns,
> And oft by force, which to a generous mind
> So reigning can be no sincere delight.   (II.473–80)

Satan's subsequent rhetorical maneuver seems desperate and a little foolish. Even though the Son has rejected the devil's proposal to rule Rome, Satan chooses this moment to make explicit the stipulation behind all his offers. He will give the Son power over worldly kingdoms "On this condition, if thou wilt fall down, / And worship me as thy superior lord" (IV.166–67). The Son responds sharply, "I never liked thy talk, thy offers less, / Now both abhor" (IV.171–72).

So far, Milton's depiction of Satan's temptations derives loosely from the trials that Jesus endures in the Bible. But the devil's eighth offer does not appear in any surviving commentary and seems to be wholly original to Milton. Satan presents Jesus with the sum of ancient Greek literature, art, and philosophy – and the Son rejects this knowledge absolutely. As Jesus explains, classical writers lack the true wisdom of the Christian God: "he who receives / Light from above, from the fountain of light, / No other doctrine needs, though granted true; / But these are false, or little else but dreams, / Conjectures, fancies, built on nothing firm" (IV.288–92). Such a thorough rebuke of ancient Greek culture is surprising, given Milton's own indebtedness to his classical forebears. How could an author who so effectively borrowed from classical literature and learning treat antiquity as "little else but dreams" near the end of his life? And how could he do so in a poem that he based at least in part on the structure of Plato's dialogues?

One way of understanding the Son's position here is that the devil corrupts anything he proposes. Just as when Milton in *Areopagitica* insisted that people must arrive at the truth through their own efforts – or otherwise become a "heretick in the truth" (*CPW* II: 543) – so Satan's easy presentation of ancient learning as a means to power may undermine the value of the knowledge that he presents to the Son. Alternatively, in rejecting classical learning outright, the Son may be vehemently overstating his position, the way that Milton in *The Doctrine and Discipline of Divorce* claimed that the Son's "rigid sentence against divorce" is not to be taken literally but instead represents, as discussed in Chapter 3, a rhetorical exaggeration to counteract the Pharisees' extravagance (*CPW* II: 283). In the particular case of *Paradise Regained*, the Son seems to be expressing more emphatically an idea that Milton himself espoused in, for example, *De Doctrina Christiana*: a minister's knowledge should be founded exclusively on his inner conscience and the study of scriptures.[41] The Son's disavowal could thus be read in the context of Milton's own dismissive remarks about the ancient authorities that his prelatical opponents repeatedly cited instead of relying on the plain meaning of the Scripture.

Still another possible way of understanding the Son's rejection of ancient learning is that Milton was subtly acknowledging his own weakness. Whereas Jesus demonstrates his perfection as the Son of God by overcoming all of the devil's temptations, Milton throughout his career gave in to the lure of classical literature and learning. As William Riley Parker first observed, Milton paradoxically continues to yield to this temptation even in the act of portraying how the perfect man would repudiate it.[42]

The final and ninth temptation in *Paradise Regained* occurs on the Temple's pinnacle, as Satan taunts Jesus either to "stand upright" or

> "Cast thyself down; safely if Son of God:
> For it is written, 'He will give command
> Concerning thee to his angels, in their hands
> They shall uplift thee, lest at any time
> Thou chance to dash thy foot against a stone.'"
>   To whom thus Jesus, "Also it is written,
> 'Tempt not the Lord thy God,'" he said and stood.
> But Satan smitten with amazement fell.   (IV.555–62)

Here Milton provides the dramatic pay-off for the preceding series of temptations and refusals. The debate between the devil and the Son that dominates the poem abruptly breaks off as the Son at last comprehends his identity. He no longer opposes Satan only intellectually but defeats him utterly, as Milton puns on the devil's literal and figurative fall. In like manner, the Son literally stands on the pinnacle but also takes a figuratively strong stand against worldly temptation. His steadfast position represents the type of heroic action that Adam and Eve failed to achieve in *Paradise Lost* when they gave in to temptation and disobeyed God.

Critics disagree on whether Jesus uses supernatural powers to defeat Satan on the pinnacle or maintains his balance on the tower through only human effort. Yet, more important may be that God and the angels do not immediately intercede. In keeping with Milton's Arminian theology, Jesus must save himself instead of relying on divine intervention, just as Satan in the final scene causes his own fall instead of being shoved. God had originally sent his Son into the wilderness and exposed him to Satan's temptations because "I mean / To exercise him" (I.155–56) and "show him worthy of his birth divine" (I.141). Similarly, in *Samson Agonistes*, as we will see in the next section, God wishes to test Samson's fortitude: "debased / Lower than bondslave" (lines 37–38), Samson must first own up to his past errors, then overcome them by applying the "gifts and graces" with which he has been "eminently adorned" (line 679). For God suddenly to interfere in *Paradise Regained* – or *Samson Agonistes* – would deny his ministers the opportunity to prove their allegiance; a *deus ex machina* resolution to either poem would liberate both protagonists but paradoxically limit their free will.

The ending of *Paradise Regained* recalls the sense of quiet anticipation that Milton also conveyed in the final stanza of "On the Morning of Christ's

Nativity." Following the angels' jubilant celebration of the Son's victory, Jesus returns privately and "unobserved" to his mother's house (IV.638). He waits to fulfill the role that he now understands and to defeat the devil on the last day as his trials in the wilderness have foretold.

Samson Agonistes (1671)

Published in a double volume with *Paradise Regained*, *Samson Agonistes* (literally, "Samson the Grappler" or "Samson the Player") is a classical, Hebraic tragedy – that is, Milton follows the form of an ancient Greek play but borrows Samson's story from the Book of Judges. Although we cannot determine when exactly Milton began writing this poem, he probably composed most of *Samson* shortly before its publication. A few critics in the early twentieth century tried to use biographical evidence and stylistic analyses to support an earlier date of composition in the 1640s.[43] But more recently the traditional dates of 1667–70 have become widely accepted based largely on the poem's engagement with other late seventeenth-century publications and the religious-political milieu of post-Restoration England.

Certainly placing the poem in a post-Restoration context draws attention to its political implications. Most obviously, the blind and defeated figure of Samson whom Milton presents at the start has been compared to Milton himself, forced into hiding and briefly imprisoned after the Interregnum. But the character of Samson may also have had a broader political significance. In radical print culture, Samson had become a symbol of the revolution, especially the revolutionary army.[44]

Individual passages in Milton's poem also recall England's political circumstances after 1660. When, for example, the Chorus bemoans how God suddenly changes his countenance toward his solemnly elected ministers, the Chorus could be describing what happened to supporters of regicide after the restoration of monarchy. God does not just remit his former champions to obscurity,

> But throw'st them lower than thou didst exalt them high,
> Unseemly falls in human eye,
> Too grievous for the trespass or omission,
> Oft leav'st them to the hostile sword
> Of heathen and profane, their carcasses
> To dogs and fowls a prey, or else captíved:
> Or to th' unjust tribunals, under change of times,
> And condemnation of the ingrateful multitude.   (lines 689–96)

After the civil war period, Milton's republican friends and collaborators faced similar consequences for having supported the execution of Charles I. Regicides were tried, condemned, and hanged, drawn, and quartered.

But beyond the poem's possible political significance, *Samson Agonistes* remains one of Milton's most discussed works because it raises – and then beguilingly refuses to answer – a series of provocative questions about Samson's violent final act and the motives of the drama's other characters. Following the rules of classical drama (as interpreted by Italian commentators), Milton compresses Samson's story from Judges 13–16 into a single day, an adaptive strategy that requires him to leave out much of the detail from scriptures. Thus Milton artfully includes some earlier episodes from Samson's life only in passing, such as his birth being foretold twice by an angel (lines 23–24; cf. Judges 13:3–5, 10–20), his disastrous first marriage to an unnamed woman from Timnath (lines 219–27; cf. Judges 14:1–15:7), and his slaying of a thousand Philistines with an ass's jawbone (lines 263–64; cf. Judges 15:15–16).

Milton constructs a simple plot. As *Samson Agonistes* opens, Samson is already blind and in prison, but his strength has returned, and the Philistines have put him to work as a slave. Because the Philistines are celebrating the feast of their god Dagon, Samson is granted a one-day reprieve to rest and receive visitors. Following the arrival of the Chorus, made up of Samson's hometown friends and neighbors, he meets with his father Manoa, his wife Dalila, and the Philistine giant Harapha. An Officer then arrives, requesting that Samson perform feats of strength to honor the Philistine assembly on their feast-day. Samson eventually agrees to do so, but during the performance he pulls down the pillars holding up the roof and kills everyone inside the theater, including himself.

While this narrative seems relatively straightforward, much of what Milton portrays nevertheless remains ambiguous. Each of the principal characters, for example, has a separate view of who is responsible for Samson's blindness and imprisonment. The Chorus accuses Dalila as part of a long, misogynistic rant (lines 1010–60), Dalila admits she was weak for cooperating with the Philistines but also blames Samson for revealing his secret (lines 773–84), Manoa sounds angry with God for treating his son so poorly (lines 368–72), and Samson is furious with Dalila but states emphatically, "Sole author I, sole cause" (line 376).

One of the poem's liveliest controversies concerns Milton's complex depiction of Dalila (most likely to be read as *Da' -li-la*, based on Hebrew pronunciation and metrical scansion; see, for example, line 229). The account in Judges reveals relatively little about her character. We learn that Samson "loved a woman in the valley of Sorek, whose name was Delilah" (16:4), and we witness her persistently demanding that Samson reveal the source of his strength. When at last he relents, Delilah has him sleep on her knees and has a man shave off his seven locks: "and she began to afflict him, and his strength went from him. And she said, The Philistines *be* upon thee, Samson" (Judges 16:19–20). With this pronouncement, Delilah disappears from both Samson's life and biblical history.

In *Samson Agonistes*, Milton's first innovation is to depict Dalila not as a prostitute, as some biblical commentators recommended, but as Samson's wife. Milton's Samson seems to have loved Dalila – he tells her, for example, that love should have guided her actions (lines 836–40) – but he also had political reasons for marrying her. Because God had previously inspired him to marry the woman from Timnath, he thought marrying Dalila would be "lawful from my former act" and would help him effect Israel's deliverance (line 231). Milton does not confirm or deny this supposition, and readers must decide on their own whether Samson's marriage to Dalila was woefully misguided, morally neutral, or divinely sanctioned.

Milton deviates more radically from his biblical source by then imagining Dalila visiting Samson in prison. She has come back, she says, to seek Samson's forgiveness and to ease her husband's suffering (lines 739–47). That she arrives perfumed and "bedecked, ornate, and gay" (line 712) and then expresses no shock at Samson's tragic condition may undermine her claims of innocence. But, in contrast to the simple motive for betraying Samson attributed to Delilah in scriptures – the Philistine lords offer her 1,100 pieces of silver (Judges 16:5) – Milton provides a psychologically compelling account of why Dalila agreed to turn over her husband to his enemies. She says she was afraid that he would one day leave her, that she wanted him to spend more time with her, and that the Philistines assured her he would not be hurt. Perhaps most striking, she also claims that the Philistines coerced her into betraying her husband:

> … the magistrates
> And princes of my country came in person,
> Solicited, commanded, threatened, urged,
> Adjured by all the bonds of civil duty
> And of religion, pressed how just it was,
> How honorable, how glorious to entrap
> A common enemy, who had destroyed
> Such numbers of our nation: and the priest
> Was not behind, but ever at my ear,
> Preaching how meritorious with the gods
> It would be to ensnare an irreligious
> Dishonorer of Dagon.   (lines 850–61)

Readers must decide whether Dalila is here telling the truth – and, if so, whether these extenuating circumstances should affect how we evaluate her actions. Does Milton portray Dalila sympathetically? While her loyalty to the fish-god Dagon would have no doubt made her suspicious for Milton and the poem's contemporary audience, does Dalila nevertheless justify successfully her reasons for turning over Samson?

At the end of Dalila's visit, after Samson has refused her offer to take care of him, Dalila makes one final plea, "Let me approach at least, and touch thy hand" (line 951). This hardly sounds like the request of an evil temptress, but Samson responds ferociously, "Not for thy life, lest fierce remembrance wake / My sudden rage to tear thee joint by joint" (lines 952–53). Surely the simplicity of Dalia's final appeal – especially in contrast to Samson's brutal reaction – sounds sympathetic. She must genuinely love her husband and want to reunite with him. The gesture of hands touching in love would presumably reawaken Samson's physical desire and, as a re-enactment of the early modern marriage ceremony, could remind Samson of his matrimonial bond.

But is Dalila's final request sincere? After Samson rejects it utterly, Dalila replies with an angry outburst of her own, in which she takes satisfaction that in her country she will receive honor and rewards for having helped capture Samson. Milton once again prompts readers to reach their own conclusions. We must decide whether Dalila's final angry statement reveals what she was thinking all along and thus undermines her previous defense. Or is she merely lashing out defensively because of Samson's gruff repulse?

Milton similarly complicates the depiction of Samson's final act and challenges readers to determine whether the destruction of the Philistines in the theater is an act of heroism, terrorism, or something else. When Samson first

The missing ten lines in *Samson Agonistes*

Milton further challenges readers in 1671 by omitting ten lines from *Samson Agonistes* as Manoa and the Chorus react to the noise of Samson, offstage, performing for the Philistines. Manoa worries that the Philistines "have slain my son" and wonders if he "should stay here or run and see" (lines 1516, 1520). The Chorus tries to reassure him:

> *Chor.* Best keep together here, lest running thither
> We unawares run into dangers mouth.
> This evil on the *Philistines* is fall'n,
> From whom could else a general cry be heard?
> The sufferers then will scarce molest us here,
> From other hands we need not much to fear.
> A little stay will bring some notice hither,

> For evil news rides post, while good news baits.
> And to our wish I see one hither speeding,
> An *Ebrew*, as I guess, and of our Tribe.   (lines 1521–40)[45]

Readers turning to the back of the volume would then discover that the above scene is missing ten lines. On the book's penultimate leaf appears the following text and instructions:

> *Omissa.*
> Page 89 [O5r] after verse 537. which ends,
> *Not much to fear*, insert these.

> What if his eye-sight (for to *Israels* God
> Nothing is hard) by miracle restor'd,
> He now be dealing dole among his foes,
> And over heaps of slaughter'd walk his way?
>   *Man.* That were a joy presumptuous to be thought.
>   *Chor.* Yet God hath wrought things as incredible
> For his people of old; what hinders now?
>   *Man.* He can I know, but doubt to think he will;
> Yet Hope would fain subscribe, and tempts Belief.

> After the next verse which begins, *A little stay*,
>   insert this.

>   *Chor.* Of good or bad so great, of bad the sooner;

>   Then follows in order, *For evil news*, &c.

Although we may be tempted to dismiss the missing text as just a mistake made at the printing house, the *Omissa* represents a unique kind of oversight. Through each step of the publication process, no member of the printing house could have easily ignored ten nonconsecutive lines of text.[46] If the *Omissa* had been a printing error, the compositor would also need to have altered the final punctuation mark in the line, "A little stay will bring some notice hither" (line 1536). In the original edition, a comma follows "hither" in the Chorus's speech, but with the insertion of the *Omissa*, Manoa would now say "A little stay will bring some notice hither", and the Chorus would now reply, "Of good or bad so great, of bad the sooner" (line 1537). The word "hither" (line 1536) thus becomes Manoa's last word, and a full stop is now needed to separate the characters' speeches.

But if the *Omissa* does not suggest a mistake made in the printing house and instead represents an authorial addendum, why would Milton have bothered to make such a seemingly minor revision? On the simplest level, inserting the *Omissa* modifies *Samson*'s dramatic structure by delaying the revelation of what has occurred off-stage. Like the Messenger's long-winded explanation that follows, the added exchange between Manoa and the Chorus heightens the suspense. Raising the possibility that Samson has regained his sight, the Chorus's teasing comments conclude with the Messenger's abrupt revelation, "Then take the worst in brief, *Samson* is dead" (line 1570).

More important, though, the *Omissa* momentarily introduces a different, potentially more satisfying outcome for Milton's poem. The difference between the *Omissa* and the conclusion that Milton writes for *Samson Agonistes* is the difference between divine intervention and tragedy, and between revenge fantasy and real-world violence. Like Satan's quick-fix solutions for the Son in *Paradise Regained*, the *Omissa*'s miraculous image of revenge and regeneration is tempting – Samson regains his sight, conquers the Philistines, and walks away. As the Chorus and Manoa emphasize, God could perform such a miracle, "for to *Israels* God / Nothing is hard" (lines 1527–28). But, in contrast to the satisfying vision of Samson's restitution in the *Omissa*, the poem concludes more somberly. Milton offers instead a problematic image of Samson's final act – suicidal, large-scale, "dearly-bought …, yet glorious!" (line 1660) – which, we know from the Book of Judges, ironically failed to effect a lasting political change for Israel.

agrees to perform for the Philistines, he tells the Chorus that he has begun to "feel / Some rousing motions in me which dispose / To something extraordinary my thoughts" (lines 1381–83). But Milton does not fully explain Samson's "rousing motions," and we do not know whether Samson's feeling is divinely inspired. That in the same speech Samson wrongly predicts "This day will be remarkable in my life / By some great act, or of my days the last" (lines 1388–89) raises doubts about his reliability. He creates a false either/or and will in fact both perform a great act and die at the feast. As Samson departs, he announces, "The last of me or no I cannot warrant" (line 1426), which again indicates his limited knowledge: he evidently does not yet know what he plans to accomplish at the theater.

Milton enhances the ambiguity of Samson's final act by denying readers a firsthand account of the scene at the theater. A Messenger reports that Samson put his arms on the two massive pillars holding up the theater's arched roof; then, "with head a while inclined, / And eyes fast fixed he stood, as one who prayed, / Or some great matter in his mind revolved" (lines 1636–38). But we cannot know whether Samson is praying in this moment or merely standing in a prayerful posture. When the Messenger then recalls Samson's final words, Milton again refuses to confirm whether God inspires Samson's action:

> Hitherto, lords, what your commands imposed
> I have performed, as reason was, obeying,
> Not without wonder or delight beheld.
> Now of my own accord such other trial
> I mean to show you of my strength, yet greater.   (lines 1640–44)

Clearly the phrase "of my own accord" distinguishes Samson's personal choice in killing his enemies from the feats of strength that he has just finished performing at the Philistines' request. But less certain is whether the phrase carries the added implication that Samson now acts alone, without divine guidance.

As all these examples suggest, Milton repeatedly presents readers of *Samson Agonistes* with what Samson himself refers to as "strenuous liberty" (line 271). Having slain hundreds of Philistines with the jawbone of an ass, he recalls that the Israelites refused to support him and failed to free themselves from Philistine bondage. The Israelites, he complains, had grown corrupt in their servitude and began to "love bondage more than liberty, / Bondage with ease than strenuous liberty" (lines 270–71). Readers of *Samson Agonistes* – and Milton's poetry more generally – must again and again confront a strenuous interpretive liberty. Milton sometimes in his poems presents readers with varying degrees of freedom, sometimes offering an interpretive choice and guiding us in a specific direction, as at the beginning of *Paradise Lost* as Milton considers various inspirational sites before concluding that his muse "dost prefer / Before all temples th' upright heart and pure" (I.17–18).

But at other times Milton encourages readers to think for themselves and apparently withholds definitive answers, as in his depiction of Dalila and the conclusion of *Samson Agonistes*. If "the knowledge and survay of vice is in this world so necessary to the constituting of human vertue," Milton reasons in *Areopagitica*, then readers need above all to cultivate good reading habits: "how can we more safely, and with lesse danger scout into the regions of sin and falsity then by reading all manner of tractats, and hearing all manner of reason?" (*CPW* II: 516–17). For readers of Milton's poetry, the challenge remains to rise to his high standards and to recognize that in Milton's view our active, critical engagement with his texts may relate directly to our salvation.

After *Paradise Regained … Samson Agonistes*, Milton's final poetic publication was a new edition of his collected shorter poetry, *Poems, &c. upon Several Occasions* (1673), which reprinted all the shorter poems discussed in this chapter – "On the Morning of Christ's Nativity," *L'Allegro, Il Penseroso, Lycidas, A Mask*, and the sonnets that appeared in the 1645 *Poems*. The new volume also included for the first time sonnets 11–14, 18–21, and 23; Milton's translation of psalms 1–8 and 80–88; and such early works as "On the Death of a Fair Infant Dying of a Cough" and "At a Vacation Exercise."[47] As we saw in Chapter 2, it is in these last verses, composed for delivery at Cambridge's summer vacation festivities in 1628, that Milton first meditated publicly on his poetic future and anticipated using his "native language" to write heroic poetry that would express divine truths (line 1). Stepping out of his assigned role, he momentarily paused in the humorous performance and announced that he aspired to write about "some graver subject" and travel "where the deep transported mind may soar / Above the wheeling poles, and at Heav'n's door / Look in" (lines 30, 33–35).

Choosing to include "At a Vacation Exercise" for the first time in his 1673 collection, Milton must have appreciated his youthful foresight. We can imagine the elderly author, blind and in ill health, having these lines read to him as the new collection was being prepared for the press. Perhaps he was pleased to rediscover the merits of a half-forgotten youthful work; perhaps he felt nostalgia for the unvarnished ambition of his university days. But for all of Milton's uncanny prescience as a nineteen-year-old Cambridge student, he could never have predicted that he would ultimately compose three long poems – *Paradise Lost*, *Paradise Regained*, and *Samson Agonistes* – that would look so memorably through "Heav'n's door" and surpass even his most audacious early aspirations. For the music of their verse, the richness of their language, the complexity of their characters, and the depth of their engagement with theological, philosophical, and political issues – Milton's three late poems rank among the greatest poetic achievements not just in his "native language" but in all literatures.

Chapter 5

Afterlife

When toward the end of the eighteenth century the parish church of St. Giles, Cripplegate, was undergoing a general repair, parishioners requested that John Milton's coffin be disinterred so that the exact location could be established and a monument erected to honor the parish's most famous son. On the afternoon of Tuesday, 3 August 1790, after about five days of digging, workers unearthed a leaden coffin on the north side of the chancel beneath the common-councilmen's pew. Based on the coffin's position and apparent age, church officials concluded that the grave probably belonged to Milton, and the churchwarden John Coles ordered the ground to be closed.

Coles, however, must have had some nagging doubts or a morbid curiosity because the next morning he changed his mind. After reportedly keeping a "merry-meeting" at the home of a nearby tavern owner, Coles led a group of men back to the grave site, where one parishioner used a mallet and chisel to break the coffin's lid.[1] Reading Philip Neve's contemporary account of what happened next, we may be reminded of "the rout," as Milton describes it in *Lycidas*, "that made the hideous roar" and dismembered Orpheus (line 61). Neve himself calls it a "most sacrilegious scene."[2] Parishioners began rifling through the coffin's remains and snatching up the corpse's relics – teeth, a rib, and clumps of hair.

While Milton's biographers have traditionally ignored this grisly account of his body's disinterment (no doubt in part because it is so grisly), Neve's narrative nevertheless testifies to the poet's fame near the end of the eighteenth century. The desire to build a monument to Milton and to confirm his grave's location – even the avid grabbing of Milton's relics – suggests his status as a literary celebrity. In the same year, according to one newspaper report, street vendors in London began selling strands of hair that purportedly belonged to Milton, the type of enterprise that would presumably be undertaken for only the most admired entertainers or artists.[3]

In Milton's case, the desecration of his grave and Neve's subsequent effort to collect Milton's relics – "in hope," as Neve writes, "of bearing part in a pious and honorable restitution of all that has been taken"[4] – also provide an apt metaphor for Milton's critical legacy. Centuries of commentators have eagerly rummaged through his literary corpus, trying to grasp the meaning of his individual works and to re-member Milton's writings within his specific historical and cultural circumstances. In addition to the countless real and poetic monuments that Milton has inspired, an industry of Milton criticism sprang up shortly after his death as readers pored over and commented on his prose and poetry.

And these critical efforts are ongoing. Students may be surprised that an international community of scholars continues to research, analyze, and write about Milton's life and works. As attested by the number of books, articles, and dissertations on Milton published annually – almost 200 in 2008, for example[5] – literary critics are still discovering new information and arriving at new insights about his writings. Recent debates about Milton's heterodox theology and his depiction of religious violence demonstrate that, although the author passed away centuries ago, his works remain very much alive.

Milton himself began early on to anticipate how future readers might receive his works. Already in his early thirties, as we saw in Chapter 1, he was wondering whether he "might perhaps leave something so written to aftertimes, as they should not willingly let it die" (*CPW* I: 810), and in his Latin ode *Ad Joannem Rousium* ("To John Rouse"), he calls on the librarian of Oxford University to preserve his 1645 *Poems* among the library's "eternal works" and "famous monuments of men" ("*Aeternorum operum,*" "*virum monumenta,*" lines 54, 51). In contrast to the "unruly tongue of the mob" and "degenerate crowd of readers" ("*lingua procax vulgi … longe / Turba legentum,*" lines 79–80), Milton holds out hope that "future descendants and a more sensible age will perhaps make fairer judgments with an unprejudiced heart" ("*At ultimi nepotes, / Et cordatior aetas / Iudicia rebus aequiora forsitan / Adhibebit integro sinu,*" lines 81–84).

In the years after the Restoration, however, Milton's readers were hardly without prejudice. The controversial positions that he took in his prose continued to affect his poetry's reception. Milton may have played a limited role in the Commonwealth government, but his publications on behalf of Cromwell and the Council of State left him susceptible to virulent political attacks. Most often Milton was depicted as an unprincipled pen-for-hire who in his critique of Charles I had libeled a misunderstood saint. The jotting by one anonymous early reader on a copy of *The History of Britain* neatly summarizes a prevailing attitude: "A good Author though an ill subject to his Prince."[6] Thus William Winstanley begrudgingly includes Milton in a 1687 overview of English poetry but condemns him as a "notorious Traytor" who "most impiously and villanously bely'd that blessed Martyr *King Charles* the First."

Winstanley concludes that Milton's "Fame is gone out like a Candle in a Snuff, and his Memory will always stink, which might have ever lived in honourable Repute."[7] Similarly, in 1700, the anonymous editor of *Oliver Cromwell's Letters to Foreign Princes and States* shows only a little more circumspection. He concedes that Milton's poetry and Latin prose "were the glory of the Man" but condemns Milton as unethical, "a Man, if of any Religion, of the *Romish* stamp."[8] The editor faults in particular Milton's "unhappy Talent of Raillery" and sums up his religious and political tracts as "Fictitious, Wild, Seditious, Heretical and Antimonarchical ... only fitted to pervert and seduce those who are of youthful and unstable minds."[9]

Yet, despite such harsh assessments of Milton's polemical prose, his poetry remained continuously in print during the first twenty-five years after his death, both in expensive, larger formats and in more affordable, smaller editions.[10] Arguably Patrick Hume's copious annotations on *Paradise Lost*, published in 1695, established Milton as England's national poet.[11] Hume's detailed critical notes represent the most thorough commentary on any English author published before the modern period.

The elaborate folio edition of *Paradise Lost* published in 1688 also helped to secure Milton's reputation for a broad audience. The volume contains twelve full-page engraved illustrations, one for each of the poem's books, and begins with a flattering frontispiece portrait of Milton by the artist Robert White, based on William Faithorne's 1670 engraving. Below the portrait is printed an epigraph by John Dryden, then England's Poet Laureate:

> Three Poets, in three distant Ages born,
> Greece, Italy, and England did adorn.
> The First in loftiness of thought Surpass'd;
> The Next in Majesty; in both the Last.
> The force of Nature cou'd no farther goe:
> To make a Third, she joynd the former two.[12]

Here Dryden confirms Milton's epic as a work of genius. He announces not just that Milton bears comparison with Homer and Virgil but that Milton surpassed his classical forebears. And that this volume was published by subscription – the names of the more than five hundred "Nobility and Gentry" who helped to finance its printing are listed at the end – further suggests that by the turn of the century a large group of readers appreciated the significance of Milton's accomplishments.[13]

Many early readers of Milton, though, continued to evaluate his work in terms of his life. Surely the eight biographies published within sixty years of his death would have encouraged such an approach, and Milton himself in

An Apology against a Pamphlet had invited this type of reading. As we saw in Chapter 1, he specifically proposed "that he who would not be frustrate of his hope to write well hereafter in laudable things, ought him selfe to bee a true Poem, that is, a composition, and patterne of the best and honourablest things" (*CPW* I: 890). Eighteenth-century readers apparently accepted this biographical premise: those who liked Milton the man and were sympathetic to his political positions came to view him nostalgically as a champion of reform and liberty, while readers who felt antipathy for Milton and opposed his radical politics more likely found fault with his poetry. Even Samuel Johnson, one of Milton's most astute early readers, could not completely separate Milton's biography from his poetic achievements. Johnson dismissed Milton's "political notions" as "those of an acrimonious and surly republican" and tried to explain away the poet's support of a non-hereditary government as merely "an envious hatred of greatness, and a sullen desire of independence; in petulance impatient of controul, and pride disdainful of superiority … [H]e felt not so much the love of liberty as repugnance to authority."[14]

But if Johnson despised Milton the man, Johnson's keen eye for detail and persistent pursuit of truth enabled him to compose one of the most perceptive critical commentaries on Milton's works produced during any period. Some of Johnson's critical assessments are most memorable for their impertinence: about *Paradise Lost*, he wrote, "None ever wished it longer than it is," and about *Lycidas* he commented, "Its form is that of a pastoral, easy, vulgar, and therefore disgusting."[15] Yet even when Johnson held too firmly to eighteenth-century literary conventions and opinions, he helpfully identified key aspects of Milton's poetry, so that, for example, Johnson recognized that *L'Allegro* and *Il Penseroso* overlap in various ways. For Johnson, these commonalities were a flaw, but, as we saw in Chapter 4, the poems' interconnections may instead reveal the companionate nature of the two dispositions that Milton describes. Similarly, while Johnson could not see beyond his dislike for pastoral and appreciate the merits of *Lycidas*, his complaint that the poem's "diction is harsh, the rhymes uncertain, and the numbers unpleasing" aptly suggests some of the ways that Milton conveys the uncouth swain's shifting emotions and sense of unpreparedness.[16]

Johnson's most penetrating observations concern *Paradise Lost*. Following Joseph Addison, who among the eighteen pieces on Milton's epic that he published in 1712 had lauded the poem's "Sublimity," Johnson also emphasized the ambition and majesty of Milton's style.[17] Milton, Johnson explains, "sometimes descends to the elegant, but his element is the great. He can occasionally invest himself with grace; but his natural port is gigantick loftiness. He can please when pleasure is required; but it is his peculiar power to astonish."[18]

Johnson goes on to offer a measured blend of sharp critique and lavish praise for Milton's epic. He objects, for example, to the "confusion of spirit and matter" in the depiction of the War in Heaven but commends Milton's imagination and the poem's broad structure. Johnson concludes that *Paradise Lost* "is not the greatest of heroick poems, only because it is not the first," and he ranks it "among the productions of the human mind" as first in design and second (presumably behind only the *Aeneid*) in execution.[19]

In the following century, the biographical approach favored by critics such as Johnson continued to dominate discussions of Milton. Perhaps because of Milton's manifest self-concern in so much of his poetry and prose, commentators tended to view his works as much more personal than, say, the writings of Spenser or Shakespeare. Nineteenth-century responses often echo Ralph Waldo Emerson's belief that "one may see, under a thin veil, the opinions, the feelings, even the incidents of the poet's life, still reappearing … It was plainly needful that his poetry should be a version of his own life."[20] This sentiment grew in part from the work of Romantic poets and critics, who beginning in the late 1700s revered Milton's individuality and read *Paradise Lost* as a personal epic. Samuel Taylor Coleridge, for example, praised Milton's "intense egotism" as "a revelation of spirit" and the source of the "greatest pleasure" in reading Milton's works: "in every one of his poems … it is Milton himself whom you see; his Satan, his Adam, his Raphael, almost his Eve – are all John Milton."[21] William Blake similarly proposed that Milton himself was the subject of *Paradise Lost*. Blake saw Milton in his epic engaging in an internal debate between, on the one hand, a staunch commitment to Christian theology, and, on the other, an exploration of his own subjective ideas about religion. Blake concluded that, in depicting this struggle, Milton used imaginative poetry to express his unconscious attraction to Satan's rebelliousness and heroism – or, as Blake succinctly put it, Milton "was a true Poet and of the Devil's party without knowing it."[22]

In contrast to Johnson, who had faulted Milton for seeming aloof, Romantic writers tended to glorify Milton as a revolutionary and poet-prophet. Conflating the author's personality with his poetry, they equated the greatness of his verse with the greatness of his character. Percy Bysshe Shelley, for example, praised Milton for having "stood alone illuminating an age unworthy of him," and William Wordsworth in *The Prelude* similarly imagined a lone, undaunted champion of virtue, "uttering odious truth, / Darkness before and danger's voice behind."[23] In the sonnet "London, 1802," Wordsworth again depicts Milton as a solitary moral hero, whose "soul was like a Star, and dwelt apart."[24] The poem's speaker beseeches Milton directly, "Milton! thou should'st be living at this hour: / England hath need of thee: she is a fen / Of stagnant waters" (lines 1–3). The speaker hopes that the author of *Paradise Lost* can rid England of its vanity "And give us manners, virtue, freedom, power" (line 8).

Wordsworth apparently undertook his own epic *The Prelude* in part as a response to Milton's long poem, and other Romantic writers seem to have been similarly inspired by Milton's writings.[25] Thus Mary Shelley in *Frankenstein* re-imagines Adam's divine creation through the characters of Victor and the Creature – Shelley even takes her novel's epigraph from *Paradise Lost* (X.743–45) – while Blake in his works reveals a lifelong fascination with Milton's imagination and intellect. Not only did Blake paint two complete sets of watercolor illustrations for *Paradise Lost* but he also composed his own highly personal epic entitled *Milton* in which he envisions Milton's spirit returning to earth and communing personally with Blake's mind. In these works, Blake developed a nuanced and influential reading of Milton: while persisting in treating the God of *Paradise Lost* as a stern, moralistic patriarch, Blake recognized Satan's narcissism and came to view the Son as the epic's true hero.

In the later nineteenth century, interest in Milton's personality and life continued, but the author lost some of his heroic luster. Among the most significant Victorian responses to Milton remains David Masson's monumental six-volume biography, published between 1859 and 1880, *The Life of Milton: Narrated in Connexion with the Political, Ecclesiastical, and Literary History of His Time*. Approaching Milton as a representative of his age, Masson wrote what is still considered the most comprehensive account of the poet's character, experience, and circumstances. Although later biographers and scholars have added important new information about Milton, Masson's keen insights and extensive research continue to undergird much recent commentary on Milton's life and writings.

More immediately during the nineteenth century, Masson's expansive biography countered two popular misrepresentations of Milton as, alternatively, a passionate young lover and a patriarchal tyrant. The former, perhaps surprising tradition grew in part from speculations about Milton's Latin poems to the Italian singer Leonora Baroni, while the more enduring portrait of the artist as a troubled husband and father was based largely on fictionalized accounts of his first marriage and secondhand anecdotes about his relationship with his daughters.[26] Thus, the Victorian writer Edward Bulwer-Lytton begins his poem *Milton* by imagining a Tuscan maiden coming upon a young Milton, who lies dreaming on "violet banks." As she leans over him, her breath or hair startles him awake: "And their eyes met – one moment and no more; / Moment in time that center'd years in feeling."[27] In contrast, a series of paintings and engravings from the same period depict a detached, older Milton dictating to

Figure 5 George Romney, "Milton and His Two Daughters," from *The Poetical Works of John Milton*, 3 vols., ed. William Hayley (London, 1794)

his laboring daughters, who are frequently rendered as timid or cowed.[28] Most well known is probably George Romney's "Milton and His Daughters," published in William Hayley's 1794 edition of Milton's poetry (see Figure 5).

Yet even as these opposing biographical traditions continued to appear in nineteenth-century novels, plays, and art works, other Victorian writers, like Masson, began to reassess Milton's personality and re-evaluate in particular his relationship to women. The novelist Anne Manning, for example, wrote a fictional diary by Milton's first wife in which Manning sympathetically examined why Milton and Mary Powell might have become estranged, and in another novel Manning portrays Milton's daughter Deborah not as an unthinking drudge but as an intelligent and insightful reader and writer who actively assisted her father.[29] Perhaps more notably for literary historians, the novelist George Eliot (Mary Ann Evans) also defended Milton's character by endorsing his decision to publish his defense of divorce and risk public scorn and scrutiny.[30] Eliot throughout her career engaged intensely with Milton's works, in some novels criticizing the excesses of his popular reputation as a domestic tyrant and in other places entering into direct conversation with his poetry and prose by, for example, questioning his ideas about heroism and human relationships.[31]

Victorian poets, by comparison, tended to focus less on Milton's character and beliefs, and concentrated on the author's classicism and what Alfred, Lord Tennyson called Milton's "grand style."[32] Tennyson told his son that he thought Milton's poetry "even finer than that of Virgil, 'the lord of language,'" and in the poem "Milton (Alcaics)" Tennyson praises the author of *Paradise Lost* as a "mighty-mouth'd inventor of harmonies" and the "God-gifted organ-voice of England."[33] Tennyson's deep-seated admiration for Milton's verse finds expression in various of his other poems, most notably his personal lament, *In Memoriam*, which directly echoes the themes of *Lycidas*, in particular its marriage of pastoral and Christian elements; and *Idylls of the King*, a cycle of twelve poems about King Arthur that contains a rich series of allusions, both philosophical and formal, to Milton's epic.

Other Victorian poets such as Gerard Manley Hopkins also emphasized Milton's formal achievement. A devout Roman Catholic, Hopkins apparently disapproved of Milton's religious and political beliefs – Hopkins called Milton "a very bad man" – but he could still appreciate Milton's complex, sometimes experimental versification.[34] Milton, Hopkins thought, was "ahead of his own time as well as all after-times in verse-structure," and Hopkins singled out the "rhythm and metrical system" of the Chorus's speeches in *Samson Agonistes* as Milton's "own highwater mark."[35] Like Tennyson, Hopkins especially admired the classical grandeur of Milton's poetry: in one letter, Hopkins writes that Milton's "art is incomparable, not only in English literature but … almost in any; equal, if not more than equal, to the finest of Greek or Roman." [36]

But if Victorian writers on the whole praised Milton's style – Matthew Arnold, to take one last example, believed that Milton's heterodox religious beliefs impaired his poetry but Arnold still lauded the "power" and "charm" of Milton's "diction and rhythm"[37] – a group of New Critics emerged in the twentieth century who emphasized what they perceived as deficiencies in Milton's writing. New Criticism is an interpretive method foregrounding the relationship between a work's structure and its meaning that dominated literary studies in America and Britain from the 1920s to the early 1960s. During this period, a small group of New Critics, led by F. R. Leavis and T. S. Eliot, became known as anti-Miltonists for their sometimes blunt condemnation of Milton's poetry. The anti-Miltonists objected in particular to Milton's lofty, Latinized diction and syntax, and his "heavy, inflexible, and unnatural formalism of speech and rhythm."[38] Leavis, for example, detected "a certain sensuous poverty" in

Milton's poetry and faulted *Paradise Lost* for exhibiting "a feeling *for* words rather than a capacity for feeling *through* words."[39] Similarly, Eliot, building on Samuel Johnson's critique of the epic's imagery, complained about Milton's lack of "visual imagination."[40] Eliot described Milton's poetry as "purely auditory," adding that even before Milton went blind he "may be said never to have seen anything." "Indeed," Eliot writes, "I find, in reading *Paradise Lost*, that I am happiest where there is least to visualize."[41]

Among Milton's most influential modern defenders was Christopher Ricks, who accepted the anti-Miltonists' premise that Milton's style is grand, but argued that its grandeur does not preclude subtle and delicate effects.[42] Ricks showed, for example, that the poet mingles sight and sound, and enriches his depictions through a suggestive, fluid syntax. Robert Adams also squarely answered Milton's detractors by arguing that the author of *Paradise Lost* used Latinate elements to create "a language more rich, complex, extended, and resourceful than English traditionally is."[43] The anti-Miltonists, Adams added, should more properly judge Milton's style in terms of other heroic poems instead of according to the "taste of one's time" and within the "narrow bounds" of modern conventions.[44]

Other twentieth-century critics also ably defended Milton's language and imagery, sometimes directly, as when Roland Frye challenged the New Critics by demonstrating that Milton in *Paradise Lost* was responding to and borrowing from a wide array of traditional visual images in order to render more vividly the epic's scenes and characters.[45] More often, though, modern critics indirectly defended the nuanced style of Milton's works. Instead of explicitly refuting the anti-Miltonists' claims, these commentators reinforced the literary merits of Milton's poetry by taking Milton seriously and analyzing his works in sometimes painstaking detail.

The other debate that dominated the study of Milton in the first half of the twentieth century focused less on Milton's poetic style and more on the depiction of God and Satan in *Paradise Lost*. Critics were divided about the sincerity of Milton's theodicy. According to one group, for which C. S. Lewis became the most eloquent spokesperson, the success of Milton's poem stemmed from its successful defense of divine justice. Lewis deemed the epic "overwhelmingly Christian" and asserted that, aside from "a few isolated passages," *Paradise Lost* does not reflect a particular set of beliefs but rather "gives the great central tradition."[46] Thus, readers who object to Milton's God, Lewis concluded, "only mean that they dislike God."[47]

Another group of critics instead detected in *Paradise Lost* evidence of Milton's attraction to Satan and the author's own uncertainty about the Christian Deity. This tradition found probably its most influential voice in

William Empson. Building on, as we have seen, Blake's Romantic suggestion that Milton was "of the Devil's party without knowing it," Empson argued that Milton in *Paradise Lost* was genuinely "searching" and "struggling to make his God appear less wicked," an attempt that Empson considered "the chief source" of the poem's "fascination and poignancy."[48] To support Milton's sympathy for the devil, these critics could once again turn to the author's life, in particular his strident opposition to absolute kingship. Surely a poet who devoted so much time and energy to defending rebellion must have sympathized with Satan's passionate opposition to the monarchy of Heaven.

In 1967 Stanley Fish deftly reconciled the two traditions by deploying the then burgeoning theoretical approach known as reader response criticism.[49] He argued, in short, that both groups of critics – the Satanists and the orthodox Christians – were right. Placing the drama of the epic within the reader, Fish suggested that Milton didactically ensnares his audience with passages that make Satan look heroic and God seem wicked (Empson's perspective) so that Milton can then correct such a response by insisting on God's justice (Lewis's position). Readers thus repeatedly rediscover their own sinfulness as they are tempted to admire Satan's heroism – and then are admonished for not unquestioningly accepting divine obedience.

But if Fish's reading of Satan's eloquence as a temptation for the reader continues to influence the teaching of Milton (and indeed grew out of Fish's own teaching at the University of Berkeley in the 1960s), the historical accuracy of Fish's theory has been effectively challenged and his representation of a punitive, Calvinist God in *Paradise Lost* has been dislodged.[50] In describing the poem's effect, Fish, like many early practitioners of reader response criticism, posited an idealized, imaginary reader and overlooked the diversity of possible reactions that Milton's epic can prompt. Flattening *Paradise Lost* into a single didactic maneuver, Fish's theory required readers who behaved as simpletons, repeatedly falling for the same trick, while it correspondingly distorted Milton into a finger-wagging pedant who takes almost sadistic glee in successively trapping and punishing the poem's fit audience.

On the contrary, as John Rumrich has shown, Milton in his poetry and prose accepts doubt and indeterminacy as fundamental to human experience.[51] And, as we have seen throughout this book, Milton in such diverse works as *Areopagitica*, *Paradise Lost*, and *De Doctrina Christiana* emphasizes the importance of interpretive freedom. Certainly Milton held strong religious and political convictions, but he understood the search for truth as a rational process and in his own works expected a "fit audience ... though few" (*Paradise Lost* VII.31). Milton, in other words, believed firmly in his own positions but wanted an audience that would think independently and not accept any author's ideas without judging on their own those ideas thoroughly.

Yet, perhaps in part because of the appealing consensus that Fish's reading finessed – it effectively eliminated the possibility of genuine readerly opposition – the biographical tradition of Milton as an overbearing despot that became popular during the Victorian period continued to influence some late twentieth-century readings of Milton's epic. Writing in 1978 as part of the so-called second wave of feminism, Sandra Gilbert, for example, criticized Milton and his writings as the "misogynistic essence of what Gertrude Stein called 'patriarchal poetry'"; Gilbert found evidence of Milton's god complex in his decision to write a theodicy, his portrayal of Eve and Sin, and in his epic's Latinate syntax.[52] Other feminist critics – in particular, Marcia Landy (1972) and Christine Froula (1983) – also interpreted Milton's depiction of Eve in *Paradise Lost* as reflecting and endorsing predominant patriarchal attitudes that deemed women to be inferior and/or dangerous.[53]

Complaints about the depiction of women in Milton's works were not entirely new. Samuel Johnson (in language that reveals his own cultural prejudice) sharply rebuked Milton for evincing "in his books something like a Turkish contempt of females," and earlier in the eighteenth century Thomas Newton proposed that the Chorus's virulent attack on women in *Samson Agonistes* reflected Milton's own "uneasiness" about women.[54] Newton speculated that Milton in *Samson* "indulges his spleen a little" and gives such sentiments "the greatest weight" by having the Chorus speak them.[55]

But for the first time in the 1970s essays such as Gilbert's began to open up Milton studies by challenging the resolutely male perspective that had dominated previous scholarship. Subsequent discussions of Milton's epic have necessarily become more sensitive to issues of gender and power as critics debate the implications of Milton's portrayal of Eve, Dalila, and (in *A Mask Presented at Ludlow Castle*) the Lady. Essays such as Gilbert's have also led to an investigation of the difference between patriarchal misconstructions of Milton's works and Milton's own ideas about women, a distinction that Gilbert herself had failed to make. Thus, whereas Gilbert used Virginia Woolf's remark in *A Room of One's Own* that women should "look past Milton's bogey" as a judgment of how reading Milton inhibited female readers, later critics discovered that such claims about the debilitating effect of reading Milton are historically unfounded.[56] Joseph Wittreich demonstrated, on the contrary, that female readers from the eighteenth and early nineteenth century detected in Milton's works the authority for opposing prejudice and bigotry.[57] If Milton did not explicitly challenge traditional gender roles, he still provoked enlightened thinking about the role of women; in particular, Wittreich argued, the complex portrayal of the characters in *Paradise Lost* inspired radical thinking and disturbed conventional assumptions.

Diane McColley in a seminal defense of Milton's Eve showed, moreover, that Milton's vision of humankind's first mother reversed a misogynistic tradition, both in literature and art, depicting Eve as subordinate and inherently corrupt. McColley acknowledged the hierarchy between Adam and Eve in *Paradise Lost* but argued that Eve through her intelligence and linguistic ability transcends gender difference and the poem's broader historical circumstances. Milton's Eve, McColley concluded, represents both a "pattern and composition of active goodness" and a "speaking picture of the recreative power of poetry itself."[58]

Other, more recent studies have built on Wittreich's and McColley's conclusions in an attempt to show more fully that Milton was not antifeminist. In the early 2000s, for example, Catherine Gimelli Martin assembled a cogent collection of essays that, as a whole, illustrates the poet's strikingly modern ideas about gender and marriage.[59] While some critics continue to defend the early antifeminist charges leveled against Milton, most readers now explore the tension between egalitarian and hierarchical impulses in his works, especially in his divorce tracts and, as we saw in Chapter 4, *Paradise Lost* and *Samson Agonistes*. How one defines Milton's attitude toward women, as J. Martin Evans has observed, may ultimately depend on whether his works are read in the context of seventeenth-century attitudes about gender, the typical preference of Milton's defenders, or whether his works are read in relation to our own period's values and beliefs, the approach typically favored by Milton's detractors.[60]

Although few other recent debates about Milton have reached the breadth or intensity of early twentieth-century controversies, one additional subject, the author's heterodox theology, briefly dominated discussions of Milton beginning in the 1990s. More specifically, at a symposium in 1991, William B. Hunter raised the possibility that Milton did not write *De Doctrina Christiana*.[61] The treatise was first discovered in 1823 in the State Papers Office in London and was published two years later. Perhaps, Hunter suggested, Milton's name was added to this text posthumously but Milton himself was not actually the author. The implication of Hunter's argument was that the heretical views in *De Doctrina Christiana* should thus not be used to corroborate ideas in other works for which Milton's authorship is certain.

Two papers delivered at the same conference in 1991 answered Hunter's proposal, and the subsequent outpouring of counterarguments by some of the most respected scholars in early modern studies confirmed the treatise's Miltonic provenance.[62] As Maurice Kelley had decisively demonstrated decades earlier, the textual and historical evidence of Milton's authorship of *De Doctrina Christiana* is virtually indisputable, and the treatise and *Paradise Lost* are "synchronous," engaging in a direct dialogue and evincing a consistent heterodox theology.[63] Although a committee that formed to investigate the treatise's origin initially equivocated on whether Milton wrote all of *De Doctrina Christiana*, a final report published in 2007 reiterated the critical consensus that the theology properly belongs to the Milton canon. As the committee concluded, the treatise's "powerful argumentation, its undeferential perspective on key issues in Christian belief, and its robust yet flexible expression are worthy of their author."[64]

While the controversy over the authorship of Milton's theological treatise proved less important than it may have initially seemed, it had the beneficial effect of reminding readers of Milton's specific heterodox beliefs and prompting both new research on seventeenth-century religion and a new English translation of *De Doctrina Christiana* forthcoming from Oxford University Press. The controversy over the treatise also underscores a broader trend in Milton studies. No doubt influenced by the publication of *The Complete Prose Works of John Milton*, edited by Don Wolfe (1953–82), modern commentators have become increasingly more engaged with Milton's prose than were early twentieth-century critics. Distinguished collections of essays have appeared focusing on Milton's polemical works – Michael Lieb and John T. Shawcross's *Achievements of the Left Hand: Essays on the Prose of John Milton* (1974); David Loewenstein and James Grantham Turner's *Politics, Poetics, and Hermeneutics in Milton's Prose* (1990); Sharon Achinstein and Elizabeth Sauer's *Milton and Toleration* (2007); and David Loewenstein and Paul Stevens's *Early Modern Nationalism and Milton's England* (2008). The emphasis on historicism within early modern studies since the late 1980s has also likely encouraged this ongoing interest. Piecing together the cultural and historical milieu that helped to shape Milton and his works, critics now regularly attempt to explore the sometimes complex interrelation between his prose and poetry.

But while historicism informs much recent criticism on Milton, one of the most remarkable characteristics of Milton studies in the modern era is the diversity of the analyses that critics undertake. Milton remains a vibrant figure in English literary history in part because his works accommodate a wide range of critical approaches. Thus, postcolonial scholars can examine the author in the context of English imperialism and try to ascertain whether his works explicitly or implicitly approve of the English colonial enterprise,[65] while eco-critics, influenced by current concerns about the planet's sustainability, can analyze Milton's depiction of the natural world to determine whether he was responding to contemporary environmental problems and expressing a presciently "green" sensibility.[66] Late twentieth- and early twenty-first-century studies of Milton include almost every conceivable methodology and theoretical orientation – bibliographical, eco-critical, feminist, formalist, Freudian, historicist, Jungian, Marxist, materialist, postcolonial, postmodern, poststructural, and queer.

The heterogeneity of these critical approaches is matched by the geographical diversity of scholars and students studying Milton's works. Milton's poetry and prose have been translated into more than twenty-five languages, beginning with a French edition of *Eikonoklastes* while Milton was still living.[67] Since Milton's death, translations of his works have appeared in almost every national language, including Arabic, Chinese, Farsi, Hebrew, Portuguese, Serbo-Croatian, and Urdu. Scholars currently researching and teaching Milton reside in Australia, Bulgaria, Canada, China, England, France, Ireland, Italy, Japan, New Zealand, Norway, Scotland, Singapore, South Korea, Switzerland, the United States, and Wales.

Nor is Milton's ongoing relevance limited to the classroom and research library. Often influenced by the Romantics' views, modern writers and artists continue to find new uses for Milton's works.[68] Allusions and direct references to Milton appear in a wide array of literary and popular texts, from an X-Men comic book entitled "Colossus Agonistes" that casts the Russian member of Charles Xavier's team as a Samson figure; to *Deconstructing Harry*, a film by Woody Allen that includes a trip to the underworld in which Allen's character paraphrases Satan, "Better to rule down here than serve in heaven, right?"; to a greeting card that quotes *Paradise Lost* on the front, "See golden days, fruitful of golden deeds, with Joy and Love triumphing" (III.337–38) and inside reads "Warm Wishes for a Happy Birthday."[69]

Other recent texts such as Philip Pullman's trilogy of young adult novels, *His Dark Materials*, engage more fully with Milton's works. Pullman, who also annotated a popular, illustrated edition of *Paradise Lost*, has described his series as "*Paradise Lost* for teenagers in three volumes."[70] The title of Pullman's books comes from a passage in Milton's epic (quoted on page 176) referring to the unformed matter that God uses to create (II.916), but *His Dark Materials* appropriates more than Milton's philosophy of substance.[71] The trilogy also explores many of the themes that interested Milton, in particular the idea of individual choice and responsibility.

And if the film version of the first volume in Pullman's series, *The Golden Compass* (2007), increased the allusive reach of Milton's ideas – the title also comes from a passage in *Paradise Lost* describing divine creation (VII.224–31)[72] – surely the movie version of *Paradise Lost* in production at Legendary Pictures at the time of this book's publication should grant Milton an even larger claim in the popular consciousness. Admittedly, though, readers of Milton's epic may feel some anxiety about the fidelity of this cinematic adaptation. The production company's chairman and chief executive has concluded about *Paradise Lost*, "if you get past the Milton of it all, … the story itself is pretty compelling."[73]

But as all these examples and the ongoing advances made in Milton studies suggest, there is no getting past Milton. We can only speculate where Milton criticism will go in future decades and what new lines of inquiry scholars will devise and discover. And we can only guess what new inspiration writers and artists working today will find by turning yet once more to Milton's writings. Some readers today may object to the difficulty of reading Milton, but on the strength of his poetic achievement and the power of his engagement with fundamental, modern concepts – personal liberty, free expression, religious violence – no one can doubt Milton's undying relevance.

Notes

1 Life

1 Milton also refers to Galileo in *Paradise Lost*, I.287–91 and III.588–90.
2 See BL Add MS 32,310.
3 Ian Archer, "London," in *Milton in Context*, ed. Stephen B. Dobranski (Cambridge University Press, 2010), pp. 361–71.
4 See *Oxford Dictionary of National Biography*, 60 vols. (Oxford University Press, 2004), s.v. "Stock, Richard."
5 Similarly, in *The Reason of Church-Government Urg'd against Prelaty*, Milton goes out of his way to credit the "ceaselesse diligence and care of my father" as the basis for his learning and later accomplishments (*CPW* I: 808).
6 John Aubrey, "Minutes of the Life of Mr. John Milton," in *EL* 2. On the likelihood that this schoolmaster was Thomas Young, William Riley Parker notes that Milton's mother had relatives in Essex, so another schoolmaster may have been responsible for Milton's haircut, since Young was evidently not from Essex. See Parker, *Milton: A Biography*, 2nd edn., ed. Gordon Campbell, 2 vols. (Oxford: Clarendon, 1996), pp. 701–2. In *Reason of Church-Government*, Milton writes that he had "sundry masters and teachers both at home and at the schools" (*CPW* I: 809). For the meaning of "Puritan" during the seventeenth century, see the section on "The civil wars" in Chapter 2.
7 Harris Francis Fletcher, *The Intellectual Development of John Milton*, 2 vols. (Urbana: University of Illinois Press, 1956–61), II: 17–18.
8 Barbara K. Lewalski, *The Life of John Milton: A Critical Biography* (Oxford: Blackwell, 2000), p. 20.
9 Bromley Smith offers a more decorous translation than mine: "because my hand has not become calloused by holding the plow-handle; or because I never lay down on my back under the sun at mid-day, like a seven-year ox-driver" (*WJM* XII: 240–41).
10 David Masson, *The Life of John Milton*, 7 vols. (London: Macmillan, 1859–80), IV: 351.
11 See Wotton's letter to Milton in *Poems of Mr. John Milton, both English and Latin, Compos'd at Several Times* (London, 1645), henceforth 1645 *Poems*, E4r–E5r.
12 A Gaudy Day is a holiday or festival day. Masson, *The Life of John Milton*, identifies the two friends as Thomas Alfray and John Miller, both of whom were members

of Gray's Inn, one of London's legal professional associations (II: 209). For a fuller description of Milton's temperament, see *LR* V: 103–4.

13 See Christopher Hill, *Milton and the English Revolution* (London: Faber and Faber, 1977), p. 455.

14 Lewalski, *The Life of John Milton*, p. 20.

15 Milton also copied the concluding two lines from *A Mask*, "if Vertue feeble were, / Heaven it selfe would stoope to her" (lines 1022–23). See Lewalski, *The Life of John Milton*, p. 108.

16 Milton similarly misrepresents his age in *The Judgement of Martin Bucer*: he claims to have argued for divorce in "his youth" (*CPW* II: 438), but in fact *The Doctrine and Discipline of Divorce* was first published in 1643 when Milton was thirty-five. While we should note that Milton's father lived to be eighty-four, the average life expectancy was considerably shorter in the seventeenth century than it is today.

17 See *A Modest Confutation of a Slanderous, Scurrilous Libell, Entituled, Animadversions* (London, 1642).

18 *An Answer to a Book, Intituled, The Doctrine and Discipline of Divorce* (London, 1644), E2v; and Herbert Palmer, *The Glasse of Gods Providence towards His Faithfull Ones* (London, 1644), I1r.

19 *Journal of the House of Commons: Volume 3: 1643–1644* (London, 1802), p. 606.

20 For the former possibility, see Aubrey, who writes that Mary "was brought up & lived where there was a great deale of company & merriment, and when she came to live with her husband … she found it very solitary: no company came to her, often-times heard his Nephews cry, and beaten. This life was irkesome to her; & so she went to her Parents …" (*EL* 14).

21 1645 *Poems*, a3v.

22 The statistic in the first part of this sentence is based on D. F. McKenzie's study of the items published in 1644 and 1688. See McKenzie, "The London Book Trade in 1644," in *Bibliographia: Lectures 1975–1988 by Recipients of the March Fitch Prize for Bibliography*, ed. John Horden (Oxford: Leopard's Head, 1992), pp. 131–51.

23 1645 *Poems*, a2r.

24 For a fuller discussion of this volume, see Chapter 4.

25 I discuss Milton's reference to left-handedness in Chapter 3 (p. 95).

26 *Calendar of State Papers, Domestic Series: Interregnum*, 13 vols., ed. Mary Anne Everett Green (London, 1874–86), V: 474, II: 179. We find further evidence of Milton's involvement in the regulation of printing among the Council's State Papers on 23 June 1649, 24 Oct. 1649, 21 Nov. 1649, 2 Feb. 1650, 6 May 1650, 15 May 1650, 14 Aug. 1650, and 9 July 1653. Milton's duties in this regard apparently decreased after he became blind in 1652.

27 *A Transcript of the Registers of the Worshipful Company of Stationers, from 1640–1708 A.D.*, 3 vols. (1913–15; Gloucester, MA: Peter Smith, 1967), I: 333, 380.

28 The tract's actual title is *Catechesis Ecclesiarum quae in Regno Poloniae* (London, 1649).

29 *Journal of the House of Commons: Volume 7: 1651–1660* (London, 1802), pp. 113–14.

30 *LR* III: 206. The catechism had been entered in the Stationers' *Register* on 13 November 1651, but we do not know whether this entry named a specific licenser, for the Council had it canceled two days after issuing a warrant for the arrest of the book's printer, William Dugard. See *Transcript of the Registers of the Worshipful Company*, I: 383. Accepting Aitzema's claim that Milton licensed *The Racovian Catechism* also raises some logistical problems. See Dobranski, *Milton, Authorship, and the Book Trade* (Cambridge University Press, 1999), pp. 126–31.

31 Interestingly, *Eikonoklastes* was also translated into French and published with some additional materials in 1652.

32 Gordon Campbell, *A Milton Chronology* (New York: St. Martin's, 1997), p. 113.

33 Parker, *Biography*, p. 870. The "regicides," strictly speaking, were the prosecutors and officers of the court that found Charles I guilty as well as the commissioners that signed his death warrant.

34 *The Diary of Bulstrode Whitelocke, 1605–1675*, ed. Ruth Spalding (Oxford University Press, 1990), pp. 606, 612, 613.

35 Samuel Johnson, *Lives of the Poets*, ed. Robina Napier, 3 vols. (London: George Bell, 1900), I: 155, 157.

36 Dobranski, *Milton, Authorship, and the Book Trade*, pp. 154–78. For this paragraph and the next, I am drawing on this earlier argument.

37 As Michael Fixler has noted, Milton's choice of psalms "had some significance." As a group, they explore "kindred themes: God's displeasure with his chosen people, praise of Zion, prayers for renewal of grace and divine guidance for a nation racked by conspiracies and surrounded by its enemies, assurance that deliverance will follow and the saints triumph, and that the Kingdom of God will be established." See Fixler, *Milton and the Kingdoms of God* (Evanston: Northwestern University Press, 1964), p. 143.

38 See Campbell, *A Milton Chronology*, p. 217.

39 For the copy owned by Charles II, see *LR* IV: 438.

40 R. G. Moyles notes that approximately 37 other comparatively minor changes were also made between the first and second edition – "founded" *versus* "fount out" (I.703), for example, or "where" *versus* "were" (II.282) – which may or may not have been authorial. See Moyles, *The Text of "Paradise Lost": A Study in Editorial Procedure* (University of Toronto Press, 1985), pp. 21–28.

2   Contexts

1 *The Monitor*, vol. 1, no. 17 (6–10 April 1713), p. 1.

2 Thomas Newton, "The Life of Milton," in *Paradise Lost: A Poem, in Twelve Books*, ed. Newton, 2 vols. (London, 1749), I: i–lxi (I: lvii).

3 See Walter J. Ong, Preface, in Sister Joan Marie Lechner, *Renaissance Concepts of the Commonplace* (New York: Pagent, 1962), pp. vii–ix.

4 Jonson, *Discoveries*, lines 2469–75, in *Works of Benjamin Jonson*, ed. C. H. Herford, Percy Simpson, and Evelyn Simpson, 11 vols. (Oxford: Clarendon, 1925–52), VIII: 638.

5 E. M. W. Tillyard, *Milton*, rev. edn. (New York: Barnes and Noble, 1967), pp. 10–11.

6 *EL* 179, 211; and Newton, "The Life of Milton," I: lvii–lviii.

7 John Peter Rumrich, *Matter of Glory: A New Preface to "Paradise Lost"* (University of Pittsburgh Press, 1987), p. 175.

8 Aristotle, *Poetics*, trans. Stephen Halliwell (Cambridge, MA: Harvard University Press, 1986), Chapter XXVI; and Philip Sidney, *An Apology for Poetry, Or, The Defence of Poesy*, ed. Geoffrey Shepherd, rev. R. W. Maslen, 3rd edn. (Manchester University Press, 2002), p. 99.

9 Virgil, *Eclogues, Georgics, Aeneid*, trans. H. Rushton Fairclough, rev. edn., 2 vols., (Cambridge, MA: Harvard University Press, 1986), I: 240–41.

10 Aristotle, *Poetics*, p. 121 (XXIV.20–26).

11 Sidney, *An Apology for Poetry*, p. 97.

12 George Puttenham, *The Art of English Poesy*, ed. Frank Whigham and Wayne A. Rebhorn (Ithaca, NY: Cornell University Press, 2008), p. 128 (Book I, Chapter 18).

13 See the section on "The civil wars" in this chapter for a fuller discussion of Puritans.

14 On Milton senior's management of Burbage's share in Blackfriars for his widow and children, see Herbert Berry, "The Miltons and the Blackfriars Playhouse," *Modern Philology* 89 (1992): 510–14.

15 Nigel Smith, *Literature and Revolution in England 1640–1660* (New Haven and London: Yale University Press, 1994), pp. 73–92.

16 *Coleridge on the Seventeenth Century*, ed. Roberta Florence Brinkley (Durham, NC: Duke University, 1955), p. 606.

17 We know, moreover, that Milton purchased a two-volume edition of Euripides (Geneva, 1602), which is now in the Bodleian Library.

18 See C. S. Lewis, *A Preface to "Paradise Lost"* (London: Oxford University Press, 1961), pp. 13–51.

19 *Select Translations from Scaliger's Poetics*, trans. Frederick Morgan Padelford, ed. Albert S. Cook (New York: Henry Holt, 1905), p. 54.

20 John Dennis, *The Grounds of Criticism in Poetry* (London, 1704), b3r.

21 We detect a similar tension as Milton discusses his poetic aspirations in *Reason of Church-Government*: "if to the instinct of nature and the imboldning of art ought may be trusted, and that there be nothing advers in our climat, or the fate of this age, it haply would be no rashnesse from an equal diligence and inclination to present the like offer in our own ancient stories" (*CPW* I: 814).

22 Newton, "The Life of Milton," I: lvi.

23 Abraham Cowley, "On the Death of Mr William Hervey," in *Seventeenth-Century Poetry: An Annotated Edition*, ed. Robert Cummings (Oxford: Blackwell, 2000), pp. 372–77. Quotations from Cowley's poetry are taken from this edition.

24 Arthur H. Nethercot, "Milton, Jonson, and the Young Cowley," *Modern Language Notes* 49 (1934): 158–62.

25 But if this reading is correct, the line's word order seems anti-climactic: we should expect *bud* to come after *blossom* because it signifies the lesser accomplishment. Perhaps Milton incorporated such an awkward construction to illustrate subtly his lack of poetic readiness, or perhaps he adheres to a natural progression (first a bud, then a blossom) to underscore the passing of time.

26 Abraham Cowley, Preface, *Poems* (London, 1656), a1r–b3v (b3r, b2v–b3r). All subsequent quotations from Cowley's preface are taken from this edition and cited parenthetically within the text.

27 Neil Forsyth, *The Satanic Epic* (Princeton University Press, 2003), pp. 160–61.

28 Another early biographer, Anthony á Wood, adds that Marvell became "very intimate and conversant" with Milton while they were working for the Commonwealth government. See Wood, *Athenae Oxonienses*, 2 vols. (1690–91; London, 1721), II: 818.

29 *The Parliamentary or Constitutional History of England*, ed. William Cobbett et al., 2nd edn., 24 vols. (London, 1761–63), vol. IV, column 162.

30 Andrew Marvell, *The Rehearsall Transpos'd: The Second Part*, 2nd edn. (London, 1673), P2v–P3v.

31 W. Arthur Turner, "Milton, Marvell and 'Dradon' at Cromwell's Funeral," *Philological Quarterly* 28.2 (1949): 320–23.

32 See Blair Worden, *Literature and Politics in Cromwellian England: John Milton, Andrew Marvell, Marchamont Nedham* (Oxford University Press, 2007), p. 11.

33 Marvell, *A Poem upon the Death of His Late Highness the Lord Protector*, in *Andrew Marvell*, ed. Frank Kermode and Keith Walker (Oxford University Press, 1990), pp. 110–18.

34 Barbara K. Lewalski, *The Life of John Milton: A Critical Biography* (Oxford: Blackwell, 2000), p. 449.

35 *The Poems of Andrew Marvell*, ed. Nigel Smith (Harlow and New York: Pearson Longman, 2007), p. 373.

36 I am quoting Marvell's poem as it appears in *CPEP* 287–89.

37 George Watson, ed., *John Dryden: "Of Dramatic Poesy" and Other Critical Essays*, 2 vols. (London: J. M. Dent; New York: Dutton, 1962), I: 89.

38 D. D. Arundell, ed., *Dryden & Howard 1664–1668: The Text of "An Essay of Dramatick Poesy," "The Indian Emperor," and "The Duke of Lerma" with Other Controversial Matter* (Cambridge University Press, 1929), p. 8.

39 For the latter possibility, see Gordon Campbell, "Shakespeare and the Youth of Milton," *Milton Quarterly* 33 (1999): 95–105.

40 Alwin Thaler, "The Shaksperian [*sic*] Element in Milton," *PMLA* 40 (1925): 645–91; and Thaler, "Shakespeare and Milton Once More," in *SAMLA Studies in Milton*, ed. J. Max Patrick (Gainesville: University of Florida Press, 1953), pp. 80–99.

41 *Mr. William Shakespeare's Comedies, Histories, and Tragedies* (London, 1632), A5r. After its initial publication in the second folio, "An Epitaph on … Shakespeare" appeared in another collection, *Poems: Written by Wil. Shakespeare* (1640) and again in Shakespeare's third folio (1663–64).

42 E. M. W. Tillyard, *The Miltonic Setting, Past and Present* (Cambridge University Press, 1938), p. 185.

43 John Dryden, Preface, in *Fables Antient and Modern; Translated into Verse, from Homer, Ovid, Boccace and Chaucer: with Original Poems*, vol. 1 (Glasgow: Robert and Andrew Foulis, 1771), B1r–D4v (B1v).

44 *OED*, s.v. "original," defs. II.5.c and B.I.3.

45 Edmund Spenser, *Amoretti*, in *"Amoretti" and "Epithalamion": A Critical Edition*, ed. Kenneth J. Larsen (Tempe, AZ: Medieval and Renaissance Texts and Studies, 1997), Sonnet 67, lines 6, 9–10, 11.

46 Spenser, "Letter to Raleigh," in *The Faerie Queene*, ed. A. C. Hamilton (Harlow: Longman, 2001), pp. 714–18.

47 I discuss Milton's position as secretary in Chapter 1 (pp. 21–24) and his governmental writings in Chapter 3 (pp. 130–34).

48 In this section, I am drawing on my chapter "The Book Trade" in Stephen B. Dobranski, ed., *Milton in Context* (Cambridge University Press, 2010), pp. 226–36.

49 See *LR* IV: 429–31. The contract survives in the British Library, Add. MS. 18,8661.

50 Samuel Simmons worked mostly as a printer; *Paradise Lost* was the first book entered in the Stationers' *Register* as his own copy. He thus qualified as the epic's printer and publisher, the latter term signifying that he financed its production.

51 *A Transcript of the Registers of the Company of Stationers of London, 1554–1640 A. D.*, ed. Edward Arber, 5 vols. (London, 1875–94), I: xxviii.

52 Joseph Moxon, *Mechanick Exercises of the Whole Art of Printing (1683–4)*, ed. Herbert Davies and Harry Carter, 2nd edn. (London: Oxford University Press, 1962), p. 192.

53 Moxon, *Mechanick Exercises*, p. 193.

54 John T. Shawcross, "Orthography and the Text of *Paradise Lost*," in Ronald David Emma and John T. Shawcross, eds., *Language and Style in Milton* (New York: F. Ungar, 1967), pp. 120–53.

55 These numbers come from Mindele Treip, *Milton's Punctuation and Changing English Usage 1582–1676* (London: Methuen, 1970), pp. 150–52.

56 *Areopagitica* (London, 1644; shelfmark Pforz 707), B3v; and *A Mask Presented at Ludlow Castle* (London, 1637; shelfmark Pforz 714), B1v, B3r, C4r, E2r.

57 On the differences between the first and second editions of *Paradise Lost*, see "Life after the Restoration" in Chapter 1.

58 *Poems of Mr. John Milton, both English and Latin, Compos'd at Several Times* (London, 1645), a2r. See Chapter 4 for a fuller discussion of this volume.

59 In this section I am relying on various accounts of the civil wars: Robert Ashton, *The English Civil War: Conservatism and Revolution 1603–1649*, 2nd edn. (London: Weidenfeld and Nicolson, 1989); Martyn Bennett, *The English Civil War, 1640–1649* (London: Longman, 1995); Michael Braddick, *God's Fury, England's Fire: A New History of the English Civil Wars* (London: Penguin, 2008); Conrad Russell, *The Fall of the British Monarchies 1637–1642* (Oxford: Clarendon, 1991); and David Plant, "British Civil Wars. Commonwealth, and Protectorate, 1638–60," 2001–9 <http://www.british-civil-wars.co.uk>.

60 That the war is sometimes referred to as "The War of the Three Kingdoms" – as opposed to "The War of the Four Kingdoms" – reflects how closely Wales had become integrated with England beginning in the sixteenth century.

61 *The History of the Trouble and Tryal of the Most Reverend Father in God and Blessed Martyr, William Laud* (London, 1695), X3v.

62 See David R. Como, "Predestination and Political Conflict in Laud's London," *The Historical Journal* 46.2 (2003): 263–94.

63 The former phrase comes from Christopher Hill, *Milton and the English Revolution* (London: Faber and Faber, 1977), p. 272; the latter term occurs in Ellen More, "John Goodwin and the Origins of the New Arminianism," *Journal of British Studies* 22.1 (1982): 50–70 (p. 51).

64 For a fuller explanation of Presbyterianism and Episcopacy, see "Anti-prelatical tracts" in Chapter 3.

65 See John Morrill, *Revolt in the Provinces: The People of England and the Tragedies of War, 1630–1648*, 2nd edn. (London: Longman, 1999), esp. pp. 70–72.

66 Morrill, *Revolt in the Provinces*, pp. 89–90.

67 For a discussion of *Eikonoklastes* and Milton's other writings for the government, see "Commonwealth prose" in Chapter 3.

68 Braddick, *God's Fury, England's Fire*, pp. xxii, 389.

69 Gordon Campbell, Thomas N. Corns, John K. Hale, and Fiona J. Tweedie, *Milton and the Manuscript of "De Doctrina Christiana"* (Oxford University Press, 2007), p. 97; and Maurice Kelley, *This Great Argument: A Study of Milton's "De Doctrina Christiana" as a Gloss upon "Paradise Lost"* (Princeton University Press, 1941).

70 Milton's earliest readers apparently did not have difficulty recognizing the epic's heterodox theology: late seventeenth- and early eighteenth-century responses repeatedly refer to *Paradise Lost* as heretical and Arian. See Michael E. Bauman, "Heresy in Paradise and the Ghost of Readers Past," *College Language Association Journal* 30 (1986): 59–68.

71 For a detailed discussion of Arminianism, see Dennis Danielson, *Milton's Good God: A Study in Literary Theodicy* (Cambridge University Press, 1982), pp. 58–91.

72 Maurice Kelley, Introduction, *Christian Doctrine*, in *CPW* II: 3–99 (see p. 82).

73 John P. Rumrich, *Milton Unbound: Controversy and Reinterpretation* (Cambridge University Press, 1996), pp. 118–46. I am indebted in this discussion of chaos to Rumrich's excellent analysis.

74 Campbell et al., *Milton and the Manuscript of "De Doctrina Christiana,"* p. 117.

75 William Poole, "Theology," in *Milton in Context*, pp. 475–86 (pp. 482–83).

3   Prose

1 Thomas Newton, "The Life of Milton," in *Paradise Lost: A Poem, in Twelve Books*, ed. Newton, 2 vols. (London, 1749), I: i–lxi (I: lvi–lvii).

2 Newton, "The Life of Milton," I: lvii.

3 *The Secret History of the Court and Reign of Charles the Second*, 2 vols. (London, 1792), I: b4v; and Thomas Fuller, *The Church History of Britain*, 3 vols. (London, 1837), III: 189.

4 William Laud, *The History of the Trouble and Tryal of the Most Reverend Father in God and Blessed Martyr, William Laud* (London, 1695), Y3v.

5 *The Works of the Most Reverend Father in God, William Laud, Sometime Lord Archbishop of Canterbury*, ed. William Scott and James Bliss, 7 vols. (Oxford: J. H. Parker, 1847–60), IV: 430–33.

6 *The Kings Majesties Declaration to His Subjects, Concerning Lawfull Sports to bee Used* (London, 1633), B2r, B4r.

7 *The Kings Majesties Declaration*, B4r.

8 By the time Milton wrote *De Doctrina Christiana*, he had apparently modified his position on the Sabbath. See *CPW* VI: 704–15.

9 Milton also probably contributed "A Postscript" to Smectymnuus's *An Answere to a Book Entitled An Humble Remonstrance* (1641). He either wrote the postscript outright or compiled the examples from English history that it enumerates.

10 Adding to the confusion of this exchange, Smectymnuus also answered Hall's *Defence* in *A Vindication of the Answer to the Humble Remonstrance* (26 June 1641), to which Hall responded a month later with *A Short Answer to the Tedious Vindication of Smectymnuus* (28 July 1641). When *A Modest Confutation of a Slanderous and Scurrilous Libell, Entituled, Animadversions* (1642) was published early the following year, Milton answered again with *An Apology against a Pamphlet* (April 1642), a tract that I discuss on pp. 101–3.

11 Essays by both of these clerics had appeared in a book defending Episcopacy, *Certain Briefe Treatises, Written by Diverse Learned Men, Concerning the Ancient and Moderne Government of the Church* (Oxford, 1641), which Milton in *Reason* announces that he is trying to refute.

12 *A Modest Confutation of a Slanderous, Scurrilous Libell, Entituled, Animadversions* (London, 1642), A3r. Subsequent references to this text are cited parenthetically by signature. Milton suggested that Joseph Hall most likely wrote the pamphlet, but he also claimed to have been told that Hall's son wrote it. See *CPW* I: 876, 897.

13 For information about the Long Parliament, see "The civil wars" in Chapter 2.

14 R. H. Helmholz, *Marriage Litigation in Medieval England* (Cambridge University Press, 1974), p. 74.

15 James A. Brundage, *Law, Sex, and Christian Society in Medieval Europe* (University of Chicago Press, 1987), pp. 453–55.

16 Merry E. Wiesner-Hanks, *Christianity and Sexuality in the Early Modern World* (London: Routledge, 2000), p. 78.

17 Wiesner-Hanks, *Christianity and Sexuality*, p. 78; and *United Nations Economic Commission for Europe, Trends in Europe and North America 2001* (New York: United Nations, 2001), p. 74.

18 Martin Luther, *On Marriage Matters* (1530), in *Works*, ed. Jaroslav Pelikan, 54 vols. (Saint Louis: Concordia, 1955–58), XLVI: 311.

19 Brundage, *Law, Sex, and Christian Society*, pp. 558–60.

20 Roderick Phillips, *Putting Asunder: A History of Divorce in Western Society* (Cambridge University Press, 1988), pp. 46, 54; and Brundage, *Law, Sex, and Christian Society*, pp. 558–60.

21 Phillips, *Putting Asunder*, p. 45; and Brundage, *Law, Sex, and Christian Society*, p. 559.

22 Phillips, *Putting Asunder*, p. 71.

23 *Tudor Church Reform: The Henrician Canons of 1535 and the "Reformatio Legum Ecclesiasticarum,"* ed. Gerald Bray (Suffolk: Boydell, 2000), p. 271.

24 *English Church Canons*, ed. C. H. Davis (London, 1869), p. 97 (canon 107).

25 Wiesner-Hanks, *Christianity and Sexuality*, p. 79.

26 Shigeo Suzuki, "Marriage and Divorce," in Stephen B. Dobranski, ed., *Milton in Context* (Cambridge University Press, 2010), pp. 382–93 (p. 391).

27 Gilbert Burnet, *The History of the Reformation of the Church of England*, ed. Nicholas Pocock, 7 vols. (Oxford: Clarendon, 1865), II: 275.

28 Thomas More, *Utopia*, trans. Paul Turner (London: Penguin, 2003), pp. 84–85.

29 Phillips, *Putting Asunder*, p. 108.

30 Edmund Bunny, *Of Divorce for Adulterie, and Marrying Againe* (London, 1610), *2v.

31 Phillips, *Putting Asunder*, pp. 108–9.

32 Phillips, *Putting Asunder*, pp. 110–11.

33 Phillips, *Putting Asunder*, pp. 116, 101–2.

34 In this paragraph and the next, I am drawing on John Spurr, *English Puritanism, 1603–1689* (London: Macmillan; New York: St. Martin's, 1998), pp. 104–6; and Ernest Sirluck, Preface, in *CPW* II: 139–41.

35 See Stephen M. Fallon, *Milton's Peculiar Grace: Self-Representation and Authority* (Ithaca, NY: Cornell University Press, 2007), pp. 124–32.

36 Here and in the subsequent discussion of the distinction between primary and secondary laws, I am indebted to Ernest Sirluck's preface in *CPW* II: 153–58.

37 Milton seems to have taken this expression – and concept – from the work by the English scholar and jurist John Selden (1584–1654), *De Jure Naturali et Gentium* (1640). Milton refers favorably to Selden's book in both *The Doctrine and Discipline of Divorce* (*CPW* II: 350) and *Areopagitica* (*CPW* II: 513).

38 In this section, I am borrowing from my essay "Principle and Politics in Milton's *Areopagitica*," in Laura Lunger Knoppers, ed., *The Oxford Handbook of Literature and the English Revolution* (Oxford University Press, in press).

39 For these statistics, see John Barnard, D. F. McKenzie, and Maureen Bell, *The Cambridge History of the Book in Britain: Vol. IV: 1557–1695* (Cambridge University Press, 2002), pp. 779–93.

40 "An Ordinance for the Regulating of Printing [14 June 1643]," in *Acts and Ordinances of the Interregnum, 1642–1660*, ed. C. H. Firth and R. S. Rait, 3 vols. (London, 1911), I: 184.

41 In this paragraph and the next, I am drawing on Dobranski, "The Book Trade," in *Milton in Context*, pp. 226–36.

42 This statistic is taken from D. F. McKenzie, "The London Book Trade in 1644," in his *Making Meaning: "Printers of the Mind" and Other Essays,* ed. Peter D. McDonald and Michael F. Suarez (Amherst: University of Massachusetts Press, 2002), pp. 126–43 (p. 131).

43 David Norbrook, "*Areopagitica,* Censorship, and the Early Modern Public Sphere," in Richard Burt, ed., *The Administration of Aesthetics: Censorship, Political Criticism, and the Public Sphere* (Minneapolis: University of Minnesota Press, 1994), pp. 3–33 (pp. 20–21).

44 Walwyn, *The Compassionate Samaritane* [1644], in *The Writings of William Walwyn,* ed. Jack R. McMichael and Barbara Taft (Athens, GA: University of Georgia Press, 1989), pp. 112–13.

45 See the discussions of "The civil wars" and "Theology" in Chapter 2.

46 Sirluck, Introduction, *Areopagitica,* in *CPW* II: 180–81.

47 Bacon, *The Advancement of Learning,* in *Francis Bacon: The Major Works,* ed. Brian Vickers (Oxford, 1996), pp. 120–299 (pp. 140, 139).

48 Sabrina A. Baron, "Licensing Readers, Licensing Authorities in Seventeenth-Century England," in Jennifer Andersen and Elizabeth Sauer, eds., *Books and Readers in Early Modern England* (Philadelphia: University of Pennsylvania Press, 2002), pp. 217–42 (p. 237).

49 Five years later in *Eikonoklastes,* Milton continues to empower readers over writers. He justifies his own interpretation of Charles I's intention in *Eikon Basilike* by arguing that "in words which admitt of various sense, the libertie is ours to choose that interpretation which may best minde us of what our restless enemies endeavor, and what wee are timely to prevent" (*CPW* III: 342).

50 For Milton's role as a press licenser, see Chapter 1.

51 *Paradise Lost,* "The Verse," in *CPEP* 291; and Sonnet 12, "I did but prompt the age," lines 3–4. See also Sonnet 11, "A Book was writ of late."

52 *Paradise Lost,* "The Printer to the Reader," in *CPEP* 291.

53 Joan Bennett, "'Go': Milton's Antinomianism and the Separation Scene in *Paradise Lost,* Book 9," *PMLA* 98.3 (1983): 388–401 (p. 401).

54 See "The civil wars" in Chapter 2.

55 David Loewenstein, "The Interregnum," in Dobranski, ed., *Milton in Context,* pp. 305–17 (p. 306).

56 Merritt Y. Hughes, Preface, *CPW* II: 68.

57 Mark Rose, *Authors and Owners: the Invention of Copyright* (Cambridge, MA: Harvard University Press, 1993).

58 Stephen B. Dobranski, *Readers and Authorship in Early Modern England* (Cambridge University Press, 2005), pp. 63–96.

59 *Calendar of State Papers Domestic: Interregnum, 1649–50,* ed. Mary Ann Everett Green (London: Her Majesty's Stationery Office, 1875), V: 464–500.

60 Excerpts from *Regii Sanguinis Clamor* are translated in *CPW* IV: 1036–81; these quotations IV: 1048, 1049.

61 *Regii Sanguinis Clamor,* in *CPW* IV: 1078, 1050–51.

62 According to Kester Svendsen, Preface, *Pro Se Defensio*, in *CPW* IV: 687, even before *Defensio Secunda* reached the press, Milton learned from Samuel Hartlib and the Dutch ambassador Lord Nieuport that More had in fact not written *Clamor*. Svendsen explains Milton's insistence as an act of "political expediency."

63 In this paragraph, I am drawing on Stephen B. Dobranski, *Milton, Authorship, and the Book Trade* (Cambridge University Press, 1999), pp. 31–33.

64 *CPMP* 898; *CPW* VII: 388. A similar account of John the Baptist's speech occurs in Luke 3:8.

4 Poetry

1 J. N. Hays, *Epidemics and Pandemics: Their Impacts on Human History* (Santa Barbara: ABC-CLIO, 2005), p. 120.

2 Thomas Ellwood, *The History of the Life of Thomas Ellwood*, ed. S. Graveson, with an introduction by W. H. Summers (London: Headley Brothers, 1906), pp. 199–200.

3 Ellwood, *The History of the Life of Thomas Ellwood*, p. 200.

4 *OED*, s.v. "prevent," defs. II.8, II.10; I.1.b, I.3.

5 On the relationship between *Paradise Regained* and *Samson Agonistes*, see Mary Ann Radzinowicz, *Toward "Samson Agonistes": The Growth of Milton's Mind* (Princeton University Press, 1978), pp. 227–60; and Joseph Wittreich, *Interpreting "Samson Agonistes"* (Princeton University Press, 1986), pp. 329–85.

6 For a further discussion of Shakespeare's possible influence on *A Mask*, see "Literary contemporaries" in Chapter 2.

7 I discuss both of these biographical details more fully in Chapter 1.

8 John Rumrich, *Milton Unbound: Controversy and Reinterpretation* (Cambridge University Press, 1996), pp. 70–93.

9 William Kerrigan, *The Sacred Complex* (Cambridge, MA: Harvard University Press, 1983), pp. 22–72.

10 Barbara Breasted, "*Comus* and the Castlehaven Scandal," *Milton Studies* 3 (1971): 201–24.

11 Leah Marcus, "The Milieu of Milton's *Comus*: Judicial Reform at Ludlow and the Problem of Sexual Assault," *Criticism* 25 (1983): 293–327.

12 The didactic reading of *A Mask* in this and the following paragraph is taken largely from Cedric C. Brown, *John Milton: A Literary Life* (New York: St. Martin's, 1995).

13 *OED*, s.v. "bewail" v. 2; and *EL* 54.

14 Stella P. Revard, *Milton and the Tangles of Neaera's Hair: The Making of the 1645 "Poems"* (Columbia: University of Missouri Press, 1997), pp. 199–202.

15 In this section, I am building on my observations about *Lycidas* in Dobranski, "Clustering and Curling Locks: The Matter of Hair in *Paradise Lost*," *PMLA* 125 (2010): 337–53.

16 For the myths surrounding Triton, see Pausanias, *Description of Greece*, trans. and ed. J. G. Frazer, 6 vols. (London: Macmillan, 1898), I: 468–69 (Book IX, chapters 20–21).

17 For a fuller discussion of this verse, see "Literary traditions and predecessors" in Chapter 2.

18 A third rhyming pattern was devised by Edmund Spenser in his *Amoretti* (1595). Spenser revamped the English sonnet, retaining the final couplet but incorporating instead an interlocking rhyme scheme in the first three quatrains, *abab bcbc cdcd*.

19 For a close reading of Milton's theology in Sonnet 7, see the shaded box on page 86.

20 In this section, I am drawing on Dobranski, *Milton, Authorship, and the Book Trade* (Cambridge University Press, 1999), pp. 82–103.

21 This and all subsequent references to Moseley's epistle are taken from *Poems of Mr. John Milton, both English and Latin, Compos'd at Several Times* (London, 1645), a3r–a4v.

22 Having worked as part of the Commonwealth government, Milton would have especially wanted to disassociate himself from Marshall, who designed the frontispiece of *Eikon Basilike* and who was known for his portraits of Charles I and the Duke of Buckingham.

23 David Masson, *The Life of John Milton*, 7 vols. (London: Macmillan, 1859–1894), III: 459.

24 See the more detailed discussion of epic in "Literary traditions and predecessors" in Chapter 2.

25 Michael will echo this idea but in an encouraging way when after the Fall he informs Adam and Eve that they must leave Paradise. The archangel tells the couple not to overvalue place and holds out the possibility that they can achieve a "paradise within ... happier far" (XII.587).

26 See Alastair Fowler, ed., *Paradise Lost*, by John Milton, 2nd edn. (London: Longman, 1998), pp. 39–40.

27 See the discussion of Milton's Arminianism in "Theology" in Chapter 2.

28 In discussing Adam and Eve's hair, I am drawing on Dobranski, "Clustering and Curling Locks."

29 Homer, *Odyssey*, trans. Robert Fitzgerald (New York: Vintage, 1989), VI.243–45.

30 Roland Mushat Frye, *Milton's Imagery and the Visual Arts* (Princeton University Press, 1978), p. 272.

31 *OED*, s.v. "wanton," defs. A.2, 7.b, 3.c.

32 Martin Luther, *Lectures on Genesis, Chapters 1–5*, in vol. 1 of *Luther's Works*, trans. Jaroslav Pelikan (St. Louis: Concordia, 1958), p. 134.

33 Dennis Danielson, "Astronomy," in Stephen B. Dobranski, ed., *Milton in Context* (Cambridge University Press, 2010), pp. 213–25 (p. 216).

34 *OED*, s.v. "seize," defs. II.6.a, 7.a.

35 Christopher Ricks, *Milton's Grand Style* (Oxford University Press, 1963), p. 111.

36 Stephen M. Fallon, *Milton among the Philosophers* (Ithaca, NY: Cornell University Press, 1991), pp. 8–10.

37 As Fallon observes, "Satan's literal hardening is the monist complement of the figurative scriptural trope of the hardened heart." See Fallon, *Milton among the*

Philosophers, p. 208. In this paragraph and the next, I am drawing on Dobranski, "Pondering Satan's Shield in Milton's *Paradise Lost*," *ELR* 35 (2000): 490–506.

38 Classical instances of discarded weapons include Virgil, *Aeneid*, trans. H. Rushton Fairclough, 2 vols. (Cambridge, MA: Harvard University Press, 1999), VIII.538–40.

39 Barbara K. Lewalski, *Milton's Brief Epic: The Genre, Meaning, and Art of "Paradise Regained"* (Providence: Brown University Press, 1966), pp. 3–126. For the genre of *Paradise Regained*, see also the discussion of the poem's opening reference to pastoral in "Literary traditions and predecessors" in Chapter 2 (p. 39).

40 For Milton's Arianism, see "Theology" in Chapter 2. Barbara K. Lewalski makes a similar claim about *Paradise Regained* in *The Life of John Milton: A Critical Biography* (Oxford: Blackwell, 2000), p. 513.

41 See "Theology" in Chapter 2.

42 William Riley Parker, *Milton: A Biography*, 2nd edn., ed. Gordon Campbell, 2 vols. (Oxford: Clarendon, 1996), p. 620.

43 For a cogent overview of the dating controversy, see Laura Lunger Knoppers, ed., *The 1671 Poems: "Paradise Regain'd" and "Samson Agonistes,"* vol. 2 of *The Complete Works of John Milton* (Oxford University Press, 2008), pp. xciii–xcviii.

44 Christopher Hill, *Milton and the English Revolution* (London: Faber and Faber, 1977), p. 435; and Hill, *The Experience of Defeat: Milton and Some Contemporaries* (New York: Viking, 1984), pp. 312, 318.

45 All quotations from the first edition in this section are taken from *Paradise Regain'd. To Which Is Added Samson Agonistes* (London, 1671).

46 For more detailed evidence that the *Omissa* is not a printing error, see Dobranski, *Milton, Authorship, and the Book Trade*, pp. 41–61.

47 On the broader theme of the poems added in 1673, see Chapter 1 (p. 28).

5   Afterlife

1 Philip Neve, *A Narrative of the Disinterment of Milton's Coffin*, 2nd edn. (London, 1790), p. 15. This pamphlet, originally comprising 34 pages, first appeared on 14 August 1790; the second edition appeared on 8 September 1790 with a sixteen-page postscript in which Neve defends Coles's original verdict that the corpse was Milton's.

2 Neve, *A Narrative of the Disinterment of Milton's Coffin*, p. 33.

3 *The English Chronicle and Universal Evening Post* (7–9 Sept. 1790), p. 3 (column 4).

4 Neve, *A Narrative of the Disinterment of Milton's Coffin*, p. 32.

5 I arrived at this number by consulting the *Modern Language Association International Bibliography*, EBSCO, 2010.

6 William Riley Parker, *Milton's Contemporary Reputation* (Columbus: Ohio State University Press, 1940), p. 52.

7 William Winstanley, *The Lives of the Most Famous English Poets* (London, 1687), O2r. See also John Rumrich, "Critical Responses, Early," in Stephen B. Dobranski, ed., *Milton in Context* (Cambridge University Press, 2010), pp. 119–29.

8 *Oliver Cromwell's Letters to Foreign Princes and States* (London, 1700), F4v.

9 *Oliver Cromwell's Letters*, G1r.

10 John T. Shawcross, "Later Publishing History," in Dobranski, ed., *Milton in Context*, pp. 155–68 (p. 159).

11 Patrick Hume, *Annotations on Milton's "Paradise Lost." Wherein the Texts of Sacred Writ, Relating to the Poem, are Quoted, the Parallel Places and Imitations of the Most Excellent Homer and Virgil, Cited and Compared* (London, 1695).

12 Milton, *Paradise Lost*, 4th edn. (London, 1688), π1v.

13 Milton, *Paradise Lost*, Zz2r–²Aa2v.

14 Samuel Johnson, *Lives of the English Poets*, ed. George Birkbeck Hill, 3 vols. (New York: Octagon, 1967), I: 156, 157.

15 Johnson, *Lives of the English Poets*, I: 183, 163.

16 Johnson, *Lives of the English Poets*, I: 163.

17 Joseph Addison, *Criticism on Milton's "Paradise Lost,"* ed. Edward Arber (London, 1869), p. 28.

18 Johnson, *Lives of the English Poets*, I: 177.

19 Johnson, *Lives of the English Poets*, I: 185, 194, 170.

20 Ralph Waldo Emerson, "Milton [1838]," in James Thorpe, ed., *Milton Criticism: Selections from Four Centuries* (New York: Octagon, 1950), p. 367; also quoted in P. J. Klemp, "Critical Responses, 1825–1970," in Dobranski, ed., *Milton in Context*, pp. 130–42 (p. 131).

21 Samuel Taylor Coleridge, *Table Talk*, ed. Carl Woodring, in *The Collected Works of Samuel Taylor Coleridge*, gen. ed. Kathleen Coburn, 16 vols. (London: Routledge; Princeton University Press, 1969–), XIV part 2, p. 253 (18 August 1833).

22 William Blake, "The Marriage of Heaven and Hell," in his *Complete Writings*, ed. Geoffrey Keynes (London: Oxford University Press, 1972), p. 150.

23 Percy Bysshe Shelley, *A Defence of Poetry* in *The Complete Works of Percy Bysshe Shelley*, ed. Roger Ingpen and Walter E. Peck, 10 vols. (New York: Gordian, 1965), VII: 122; and William Wordsworth, *The Fourteen-Book Prelude*, ed. W. J. B. Owen (Ithaca, NY, and London: Cornell University Press, 1985), p. 69 (Book III, lines 287–88).

24 Wordsworth, "London, 1802," in *William Wordsworth*, ed. Stephen Gill (Oxford University Press, 1984), p. 286 (line 9). All subsequent quotations of this poem are taken from this edition and cited parenthetically.

25 Wordsworth, *The Fourteen-Book Prelude*, p. 32 (Book I, lines 179–84).

26 See Anna K. Nardo, *George Eliot's Dialogue with John Milton* (Columbia and London: University of Missouri Press, 2003), pp. 31–65.

27 Edward Bulwer-Lytton, *Milton*, in *The Poetical and Dramatic Works of Sir Edward Bulwer Lytton*, 2 vols. (London, 1852), I: 213–52 (Part I, lines 8, 68–69).

28 Marcia R. Pointon, *Milton and English Art* (University of Toronto Press, 1970), pp. 252–53; and Nardo, *George Eliot's Dialogue with John Milton*, pp. 47–57.

29 Nardo, *George Eliot's Dialogue with John Milton*, pp. 46, 62.

30 Dayton Haskin, "George Eliot as a 'Miltonist': Marriage and Milton in *Middlemarch*," in *Milton and Gender*, ed. Catherine Gimelli Martin (Cambridge University Press, 2004), pp. 207–22.

31 See Nardo, *George Eliot's Dialogue with John Milton*.

32 Hallam Tennyson, *Alfred Lord Tennyson: A Memoir by His Son*, 2 vols. (London: Macmillan, 1897), II: 284.

33 Hallam Tennyson, *Alfred Lord Tennyson: A Memoir*, II: 284; and Alfred Tennyson, "Milton (Alcaics)," in *Alfred Tennyson*, ed. Adam Roberts (Oxford University Press, 2000), p. 375.

34 Gerard Manley Hopkins, *The Letters of Gerard Manley Hopkins to Robert Bridges*, ed. Claude Colleer Abbott (London: Oxford University Press, 1935), p. 39.

35 Gerard Manley Hopkins, *The Correspondence of Gerard Manley Hopkins to Richard Watson Dixon*, ed. Claude Colleer Abbott (London: Oxford University Press, 1935), p. 13.

36 Ibid.

37 Matthew Arnold, "A French Critic on Milton," in his *Essays Religious and Mixed*, ed. R. H. Super (Ann Arbor: University of Michigan Press, 1972), pp. 165–87 (p. 183).

38 James Thorpe, Introduction, *Milton Criticism*, pp. 3–19 (p. 18).

39 F. R. Leavis, "Milton's Verse," *Scrutiny* 2 (1933): 123–36; reprinted in his *Revaluation: Tradition and Development in English Poetry* (London: Chatto and Windus, 1936), pp. 42–67 (pp. 47, 50).

40 T. S. Eliot, "Milton I [1936]," in his *On Poetry and Poets* (New York: Farrar, Straus, and Cudahy, 1957), pp. 156–64 (p. 158); and see Johnson, *Lives of the English Poets*, I: 178, 184.

41 Eliot, "Milton I," p. 162. In a later essay, Eliot amplifies this argument: "Milton's weakness of visual observation … was always present – the effect of his blindness may have been rather to strengthen the compensatory qualities than to increase a fault which was already present." See Eliot, "Milton II [1947]," in his *On Poetry and Poets*, pp. 165–83 (p. 177).

42 Christopher Ricks, *Milton's Grand Style* (Oxford University Press, 1963), p. 22.

43 Robert Martin Adams, *Ikon: John Milton and the Modern Critics* (Westport, CT: Greenwood, 1955), p. 191.

44 Adams, *Ikon: John Milton and the Modern Critics*, p. 209.

45 Roland Mushat Frye, *Milton's Imagery and the Visual Arts* (Princeton University Press, 1978).

46 C. S. Lewis, *A Preface to "Paradise Lost"* (1942; London: Oxford University Press, 1961), p. 92.

47 Lewis, *A Preface to "Paradise Lost,"* p. 130.

48 William Empson, *Milton's God*, rev. edn. (London: Chatto and Windus, 1965), p. 11.

49 See Stanley Fish, *Surprised by Sin: The Reader in "Paradise Lost"* (London: Macmillan, 1967). A second edition of Fish's book with a new preface was published by Harvard University Press in 1997.

50 Instrumental in correcting Fish's reading of *Paradise Lost* was John P. Rumrich, *Milton Unbound: Controversy and Reinterpretation* (Cambridge University Press, 1996). In this paragraph and the preceding one, I am working from Rumrich's narrative of the history of Milton criticism.

51 Rumrich, *Milton Unbound*, p. 22.

52 Sandra M. Gilbert, "Patriarchal Poetry and Women Readers: Reflections on Milton's Bogey," *PMLA* 93.3 (1978): 368–82 (p. 368).

53 Marcia Landy, "Kinship and the Role of Women in *Paradise Lost*," *Milton Studies* 4 (1972): 3–18; and Christine Froula, "When Eve Reads Milton: Undoing the Canonical Economy," *Critical Inquiry* 10 (1983): 321–47.

54 Johnson, *Lives of the English Poets*, I: 157; and Thomas Newton, ed., *"Paradise Regained," "Samson Agonistes," and "Poems upon Several Occasions,"* 2 vols. (1752; London, 1766), Ll3r.

55 Newton, ed., *"Paradise Regained," "Samson Agonistes,"* Ll3r.

56 Virginia Woolf, *A Room of One's Own* (New York: Harcourt Brace, 1957), p. 125.

57 Joseph Wittreich, *Feminist Milton* (Ithaca, NY, and London: University Press, 1987), p. xv.

58 Diane Kelsey McColley, *Milton's Eve* (Urbana: University of Illinois Press, 1983), p. 4.

59 See Catherine Gimelli Martin, ed., *Milton and Gender* (Cambridge University Press, 2004).

60 J. Martin Evans, "Critical Responses, Recent," in *Milton in Context*, pp. 143–54 (p. 148).

61 Hunter's paper later was published in article form as "The Provenance of the *Christian Doctrine*," *SEL* 32 (1992): 129–42. In the nineteenth century, Bishop Thomas Burgess had also tried to deny the treatise's authenticity. See Maurice Kelley, *This Great Argument: A Study of Milton's "De Doctrina Christiana" as a Gloss upon "Paradise Lost"* (Princeton University Press, 1941), p. 4.

62 The papers by the conference's respondents, Barbara K. Lewalski and John T. Shawcross, were printed in "Forum: Milton's *Christian Doctrine*," *SEL* 32 (1992): 143–54 and 155–62. See also Maurice Kelley, "The Provenance of John Milton's *Christian Doctrine*: A Reply to William B. Hunter," *SEL* 34 (1994): 153–63; and Christopher Hill, "Professor William B. Hunter, Bishop Burgess, and John Milton," *SEL* 34 (1994): 165–93.

63 Kelley, *This Great Argument*, p. 192.

64 Gordon Campbell, Thomas N. Corns, John K. Hale, and Fiona J. Tweedie, *Milton and the Manuscript of "De Doctrina Christiana"* (Oxford University Press, 2007), p. 161.

65 See, for example, David Quint, *Epic and Empire: Politics and Generic Form from Virgil to Milton* (Princeton University Press, 1993).

66 See, for example, Diane Kelsey McColley, *Poetry and Ecology in the Age of Milton and Marvell* (Aldershot: Ashgate, 2007).

67 See Christophe Tournu, "Translations," in Dobranski, ed., *Milton in Context*, pp. 169–79.

68 Laura Lunger Knoppers and Gregory M. Colón Semenza, Introduction, in Knoppers and Semenza, ed., *Milton in Popular Culture* (New York: Palgrave, 2006), pp. 1–19 (pp. 6–9).

69 Warren Ellis and Casey Jones, "Colossus Agonistes," *Excalibur* 92 (December 1995); *Deconstructing Harry*, dir. Woody Allen, perf. Woody Allen, Judy Davis,

and Kirstie Alley (1997; New Line, 1998), DVD; and Brenda Walton, Birthday card (Fairfield, CA: Marchel Schurman).

70 Stephen Burt, "'Fighting Since Time Began': Milton and Satan in Philip Pullman's *His Dark Materials*," in Knoppers and Semenza, eds., *Milton in Popular Culture*, pp. 47–57 (p. 48).

71 I discuss Milton's theory of matter in Chapter 2 under "Theology" and in Chapter 4 under "*Paradise Lost.*"

72 As further evidence of Milton's allusive reach, in December 2003 and again in November 2004, the National Theatre in London presented a stage adaptation of Pullman's trilogy in two 3-hour parts.

73 Michael Joseph Gross, "It's God vs. Satan. But What About the Nudity?" *New York Times* (4 March 2007): Arts 18.

Further reading

In addition to the critical essays and books quoted or cited in the preceding chapters, the following works are recommended for continuing research on Milton and his writings.

1 Life

Campbell, Gordon, and Thomas N. Corns. *John Milton: Life, Work, and Thought.* Oxford University Press, 2008. An account of Milton's life and his cultural and historical circumstances.

Darbishire, Helen, ed. *The Early Lives of Milton.* London: Constable, 1932. A collection of five early biographies of Milton published between 1681 and 1734.

Fletcher, Harris F. *The Intellectual Development of John Milton.* 2 vols. Urbana: University of Illinois Press, 1956–61. A historical account of Milton's formal education and intellectual experiences from his boyhood through his years at Cambridge.

French, J. Milton, ed. *The Life Records of John Milton*, 5 vols. New Brunswick: Rutgers University Press, 1949–58. A comprehensive collection of historical documents related to Milton's life.

Lewalski, Barbara K. *The Life of John Milton: A Critical Biography.* Oxford: Blackwell, 2000. A detailed account and analysis of Milton's life and writings.

Masson, David. *The Life of John Milton.* 7 vols. London: Macmillan, 1859–80. A thorough and engaging account of the author's life and times.

Parker, William Riley. *Milton: A Biography.* 2nd edn. Ed. Gordon Campbell. 2 vols. 1968. Oxford: Clarendon Press, 1996. A detailed account of Milton's life and career, supplemented by an updated appendix.

2 Contexts

Bauman, Michael. *A Scripture Index to John Milton's "De Doctrina Christiana."* Binghamton, NY: Medieval and Renaissance Texts and Studies, 1989. A comprehensive list of all the scriptural passages that are quoted, alluded to, or cited in Milton's theological treatise.

Blessington, Francis C. *"Paradise Lost" and the Classical Epic*. Boston, MA: Routledge, l979. A discussion of the various ways that Milton uses the *Iliad, Odyssey*, and *Aeneid* in *Paradise Lost*.

Danielson, Dennis. *Milton's Good God: A Study in Literary Theodicy*. Cambridge University Press, 1982. An examination of how Milton defends divine justice in *Paradise Lost* with discussions of Arminianism, chaos, creation, free will, the Fall, and God's foreknowledge.

Dobranski, Stephen B. *Milton, Authorship, and the Book Trade*. Cambridge University Press, 1999. An examination of Milton's authorial practices and the relation between the material production and the poetic meaning of his works.

ed. *Milton in Context*. Cambridge University Press, 2010. A collection of essays analyzing the social conditions, intellectual currents, and political circumstances that shaped Milton's writings and reputation.

Evans, J. Martin. *"Paradise Lost" and the Genesis Tradition*. Oxford: Clarendon Press, 1968. A survey and analysis of various theological and poetic treatments of the events in Genesis, from the Apocrypha to the early modern play *Adamus Exul*, as a way of understanding Milton's depiction of the Fall in *Paradise Lost*.

Fallon, Stephen M. *Milton among the Philosophers*. Ithaca, NY: Cornell University Press, 1991. An analysis of Milton's engagement with seventeenth-century philosophical debates and an explanation of how his animist materialism informs *Paradise Lost*.

Frye, Roland Mushat. *Milton's Imagery and the Visual Arts: Iconographic Tradition in the Epic Poems*. Princeton University Press, 1978. A comprehensive overview of the Renaissance paintings, mosaics, and sculptures that depict the same subjects as those Milton describes in *Paradise Lost* and *Paradise Regained*.

Helgerson, Richard. *Self-Crowned Laureates: Spenser, Jonson, Milton, and the Literary System*. Berkeley: University of California Press, 1983. A comparative study of the careers of three early modern poets and their different historical circumstances.

Hill, Christopher. *Milton and the English Revolution*. London: Faber and Faber, 1977. A detailed account of Milton's life and intellectual development, emphasizing his engagement with seventeenth-century political and religious radicalism.

Ingram, Martin. *Church Courts, Sex, and Marriage in England, 1570–1640*. Cambridge University Press, 1987. A study of ecclesiastical justice related to sex and marriage.

Kelley, Maurice. *This Great Argument: A Study of Milton's "De Doctrina Christiana" as a Gloss upon "Paradise Lost."* Princeton University Press, 1941. A thorough foundation for understanding Milton's heterodox theology as expressed in *Paradise Lost* and *De Doctrina Christiana*.

Knott, John R. *Milton's Pastoral Vision: An Approach to "Paradise Lost."* University of Chicago Press, 1971. An analysis of the significance of the pastoral mode in *Paradise Lost*.

MacCulloch, Diarmaid. *The Reformation*. New York: Viking, 2003. A broad but richly detailed history of sixteenth-century upheavals in Christianity and a reassessment of the Reformation's effects on the people, culture, and politics of Western Europe.

Martin, Catherine Gimelli, ed. *Milton and Gender*. Cambridge University Press, 2004. A collection of essays that explore the representation of sexuality and gender in Milton's works as well as the responses of individual female readers.

Poole, William. *Milton and the Idea of the Fall*. Cambridge University Press, 2005. An analysis of the debates and depictions that the Fall inspired, from early Christianity through the early modern period.

Quint, David. *Epic and Empire: Politics and Generic Form from Virgil to Milton*. Princeton University Press, 1993. A comprehensive, political analysis of epic poetry beginning with Virgil that situates *Paradise Lost* and *Paradise Regained* within two competing narratives of history: one, linear and goal-driven, and the other, episodic and open-ended.

Smith, Nigel. *Literature and Revolution in England, 1640–1660*. New Haven and London: Yale University Press, 1994. An examination of both the impact that seventeenth-century politics had on English literary works and the effects that English literature had on the period's historical changes.

Spurr, John. *English Puritanism, 1603–1689*. London: Macmillan; New York: St. Martin's, 1998. A detailed account of the history of Puritans in seventeenth-century England.

Tyacke, Nicholas. *Anti-Calvinists: The Rise of English Arminianism, c. 1590–1640*. Oxford: Clarendon Press, 1987. A history of Arminianism from the Elizabethan period through the reign of Charles I that attempts to show how theological disputes about free will and Calvinism contributed to the outbreak of war.

Worden, Blair. *Literature and Politics in Cromwellian England: John Milton, Andrew Marvell, Marchamont Nedham*. Oxford University Press, 2007. A comparative analysis of Milton, Marvell, and the contemporary journalist Marchamont Nedham in the context of the period's political conflicts.

3 Prose

Achinstein, Sharon, and Elizabeth Sauer, eds. *Milton and Toleration*. New York: Oxford University Press, 2007. A wide-ranging collection of essays focusing on the ambiguities and inconsistencies in Milton's commitment to liberty of conscience as expressed in his poetry and prose.

Corns, Thomas N. *The Development of Milton's Prose Style*. Oxford: Clarendon Press, 1982. A lexical, grammatical examination of Milton's style of prose based on a computer analysis of 3,000-word samples.

Fulton, Thomas. *Historicizing Milton: Manuscript, Print, and Popular Culture in Revolutionary England*. Amherst and Boston: University of Massachusetts Press, 2010. An examination of select political publications by Milton in

relation to his private thinking as preserved in his commonplace book
and "The Digression."

Lieb, Michael, and John T. Shawcross, eds. *Achievements of the Left Hand: Essays
on the Prose of John Milton.* Amherst: University of Massachusetts
Press, 1974. A collection of essays about the style, meaning, and context
of Milton's prose with an appendix describing the tracts' publishing
history.

Loewenstein, David, and James Grantham Turner, eds. *Politics, Poetics, and
Hermeneutics in Milton's Prose.* Cambridge University Press, 1990. A
collection of essays that examines Milton's prose in its political and
social context.

Raymond, Joad. *Pamphlets and Pamphleteering in Early Modern Britain.*
Cambridge University Press, 2003. A historical study of the rise and
decline of English pamphlet-writing, including Milton's, from the
Elizabethan period through the Restoration.

4   Poetry

Brown, Cedric C. *John Milton's Aristocratic Entertainments.* Cambridge
University Press, 1985. A thorough examination of Milton's two court
entertainments, *Arcades* and *A Mask*, that especially addresses the
works' genre, textual history, and social and political context.

Burnett, Archie. *Milton's Style: The Shorter Poems, "Paradise Regained" &
"Samson Agonistes."* London: Longman, 1981. A quantitative analysis
of Milton's grammatical style (excluding *Paradise Lost*) that includes
detailed close readings and a thorough engagement with earlier
criticism.

Empson, William. *Milton's God.* Rev. edn. London: Chatto and Windus, 1965. An
examination of mostly *Paradise Lost* that treats Milton's struggle with
traditional Christian faith as the primary source of the epic's power.

Fish, Stanley. *Surprised by Sin: The Reader in "Paradise Lost."* 2nd edn.
Cambridge, MA: Harvard University Press, 1997. An analysis of Milton's
epic that attempts to reconcile readers' attraction to Satan with Milton's
emphasis on the need for divine obedience.

Forsyth, Neil. *The Satanic Epic.* Princeton University Press, 2003. An analysis of
Milton's arch-fiend in the context of other interpretations of Satan from
the ancient world through the early modern period.

Knoppers, Laura Lunger. *Historicizing Milton: Spectacle, Power, and Poetry in
Restoration England.* Athens, GA: University of Georgia Press, 1994. An
examination of Milton's three long poems in relation to political displays
of power and punishment after the Restoration.

Leonard, John. *Naming in Paradise: Milton and the Language of Adam and
Eve.* Oxford: Clarendon Press, 1990. An analysis of how Milton uses
prelapsarian and postlapsarian names – for Eve, the angels, the animals,

and future generations of humans – to enrich the meaning of *Paradise Lost*.

Lewalski, Barbara K. *Milton's Brief Epic: The Genre, Meaning, and Art of "Paradise Regained."* Providence: Brown University Press, 1966. A detailed study of *Paradise Regained* in relation to biblical brief epics, possible sources of Milton's Christology, and traditional interpretations of Christ's temptation in the wilderness.

"Paradise Lost" and the Rhetoric of Literary Forms. Princeton University Press, 1985. An analysis of various literary and rhetorical genres and modes deployed in *Paradise Lost* and the ways that Milton critiqued and/or reinterpreted the values traditionally associated with those forms.

Lewis, C. S. *A Preface to "Paradise Lost."* 1942. London: Oxford University Press, 1961. An introduction to Milton's epic that focuses on questions related to genre, style, theology, and character.

MacCallum, Hugh. *Milton and the Sons of God: The Divine Image in Milton's Epic Poetry.* University of Toronto Press, 1986. An analysis of the theological and moral concept of sonship in *Paradise Lost* and *Paradise Regained*.

McColley, Diane Kelsey. *Milton's Eve.* Urbana: University of Illinois Press, 1983. A thorough analysis of Eve in *Paradise Lost* as a strong, righteous character of active goodness.

Rajan, Balachandra. *"Paradise Lost" and the Seventeenth-Century Reader.* New York: Barnes and Noble, 1947. An analysis of Milton's epic that attempts to reconstruct the response of an early modern reader.

Revard, Stella P. *Milton and the Tangles of Neaera's Hair: The Making of the 1645 "Poems."* Columbia: University of Missouri Press, 1997. A study of Milton's first printed collection of verse in the context of Continental poetic traditions, both neo-Latin and vernacular.

The War in Heaven: "Paradise Lost" and the Tradition of Satan's Rebellion. Ithaca, NY, and London: Cornell University Press, 1980. A analysis of the war in Heaven in *Paradise Lost* and the theological, political, and literary traditions that influenced Milton's depiction.

Ricks, Christopher. *Milton's Grand Style.* Oxford University Press, 1963. A refutation of the anti-Miltonists' criticisms and a close reading of the delicacy and subtlety of Milton's verse.

Rumrich, John P. *Matter of Glory: A New Preface to "Paradise Lost."* University of Pittsburgh Press, 1987. An examination of the philosophical foundation of *Paradise Lost* focusing on the significance of chaos and the meaning of glory.

Milton Unbound: Controversy and Reinterpretation. Cambridge University Press, 1996. A reassessment of the underlying assumptions that shaped twentieth-century misperceptions of Milton and an analysis of Milton's acceptance of doubt and uncertainty as fundamental to human experience.

Wittreich, Joseph. *Interpreting "Samson Agonistes."* Princeton University Press, 1986. A critical reassessment of Milton's dramatic poem that explores

other early modern views of Samson and challenges the once widely
accepted reading that the poem portrays Samson's heroic regeneration.

5   Afterlife

Adams, Robert Martin. *Ikon: John Milton and the Modern Critics*. Ithaca, NY:
Cornell University Press, 1955. A critical re-assessment of modern
scholarship on Milton and a critique of modern editions of his works.

Alpers, Paul. "*Lycidas* and Modern Criticism." *ELH* 49 (1982): 468–96. A close
analysis of Milton's pastoral elegy and a detailed discussion of other
critical approaches to the poem.

Danielson, Dennis, ed., *The Cambridge Companion to Milton*. 2nd edn.
Cambridge University Press, 1999. An introduction to Milton's life
and writings with chapters on his major poems and such topics as his
politics and his readers.

Dobranski, Stephen B. *A Variorum Commentary on the Poems of John Milton:
"Samson Agonistes."* Introduction by Archie Burnett. Ed. P. J. Klemp.
Pittsburgh: Duquesne University Press, 2009. A comprehensive,
historical overview of all significant contributions to understanding
Milton's dramatic poem that were published between 1671 and 1970.

Evans, J. Martin, ed. *John Milton: Twentieth Century Perspectives*. 5 vols.
New York: Routledge, 2003. A collection of influential and
representative Milton scholarship from the twentieth century.

Gray, Erik. *Milton and the Victorians*. Ithaca, NY, and London: Cornell University
Press, 2009. An examination of Milton's influence on major Victorian
poets and prose writers.

Griffin, Dustin H. *Regaining Paradise: Milton and the Eighteenth Century*.
Cambridge University Press, 1968. An examination of Milton's influence
on English poets of the eighteenth century.

Hughes, Merritt Y., gen. ed. *A Variorum Commentary on the Poems of John
Milton*. Vols. 1, 2, and 4 in 5 vols. New York: Columbia University Press,
1970–75. A comprehensive overview of the criticism and commentary
about Milton's shorter poetry and *Paradise Regained*.

Knoppers, Laura Lunger, and Gregory M. Colón Semenza, eds. *Milton in Popular
Culture*. New York: Palgrave, 2006. A collection of essays about the ways
that Milton transforms and is transformed by film, television, and other
forms of popular media.

Parker, William Riley. *Milton's Contemporary Reputation*. Columbus: Ohio State
University Press, 1940. A collection of printed references to Milton
between 1641 and 1674 along with an essay analyzing his fame and
influence during the seventeenth century.

Shawcross, John T. *Milton: The Critical Heritage*. 2 vols. New York: Barnes
and Noble, 1970; London: Routledge and Kegan Paul, 1972.
A comprehensive collection of extracts from early criticism about
Milton between 1628 and 1801.

Stevenson, Kay Gilliland. "Reading Milton, 1674–1800." In Thomas N. Corns, ed., *A Companion to Milton*. Oxford: Blackwell, 2001. 447–62. An examination of how Milton was read in the late seventeenth and the eighteenth century.

Thorpe, James, ed. *Milton Criticism: Selections from Four Centuries*. New York: Octagon, 1950. A collection of influential essays on Milton published between 1712 and 1947 along with excerpts from works by well-known poets and critics responding to Milton's poetry.

Wittreich, Joseph A. *The Romantics on Milton: Formal Essays and Critical Asides*. Cleveland: Press of Case Western Reserve University, 1970. A detailed collection of the commentaries on Milton written by the major Romantic poets and critics.

Index

Cambridge Introductions to …

AUTHORS

Margaret Atwood Heidi Macpherson

Jane Austen Janet Todd

Samuel Beckett Ronan McDonald

Walter Benjamin David Ferris

Chekhov James N. Loehlin

J. M. Coetzee Dominic Head

Samuel Taylor Coleridge John Worthen

Joseph Conrad John Peters

Jacques Derrida Leslie Hill

Charles Dickens Jon Mee

Emily Dickinson Wendy Martin

George Eliot Nancy Henry

T. S. Eliot John Xiros Cooper

William Faulkner Theresa M. Towner

F. Scott Fitzgerald Kirk Curnutt

Michel Foucault Lisa Downing

Robert Frost Robert Faggen

Nathaniel Hawthorne Leland S. Person

Zora Neale Hurston Lovalerie King

James Joyce Eric Bulson

Thomas Mann Todd Kontje

Herman Melville Kevin J. Hayes

Milton Stephen B. Dobranski

Sylvia Plath Jo Gill

Edgar Allan Poe Benjamin F. Fisher

Ezra Pound Ira Nadel

Marcel Proust Adam Watt

Jean Rhys Elaine Savory

Edward Said Conor McCarthy

Shakespeare Emma Smith

Shakespeare's Comedies Penny Gay

Shakespeare's History Plays Warren Chernaik

Shakespeare's Poetry Michael Schoenfeldt

Shakespeare's Tragedies Janette Dillon

Harriet Beecher Stowe Sarah Robbins

Mark Twain Peter Messent

Edith Wharton Pamela Knights

Walt Whitman M. Jimmie Killingsworth

Virginia Woolf Jane Goldman

William Wordsworth Emma Mason

W. B. Yeats David Holdeman

TOPICS

American Literary Realism Phillip Barrish

The American Short Story Martin Scofield

Anglo-Saxon Literature Hugh Magennis

Comedy Eric Weitz

Creative Writing David Morley

Early English Theatre Janette Dillon

English Theatre, 1660–1900 Peter Thomson

Francophone Literature Patrick Corcoran

Literature and the Environment Timothy Clark

Modern British Theatre Simon Shepherd

Modern Irish Poetry Justin Quinn

Modernism Pericles Lewis